Mexican Americans in School:
A History of Educational Neglect

Thomas P. Carter

Professor of Education and Sociology, The University of Texas at El Paso

College Entrance Examination Board, New York : 1970

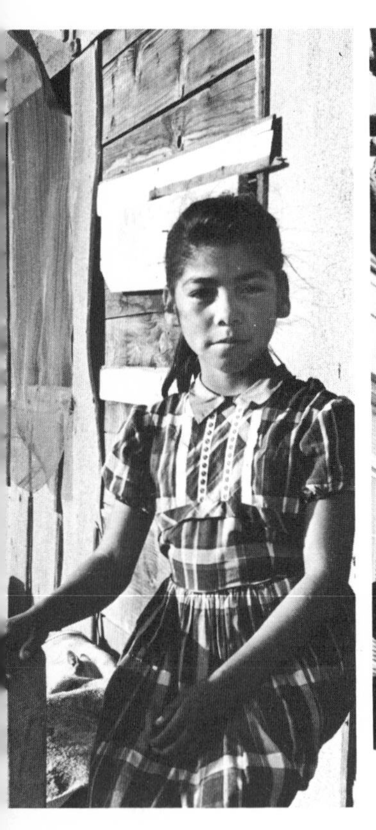

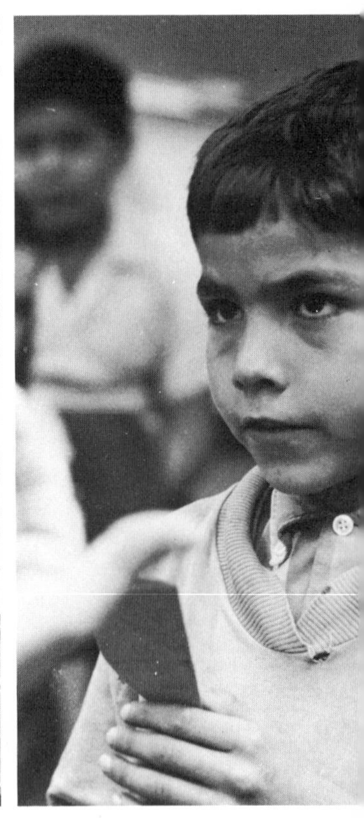

Mexican Americans in School: A History of Educational Neglect

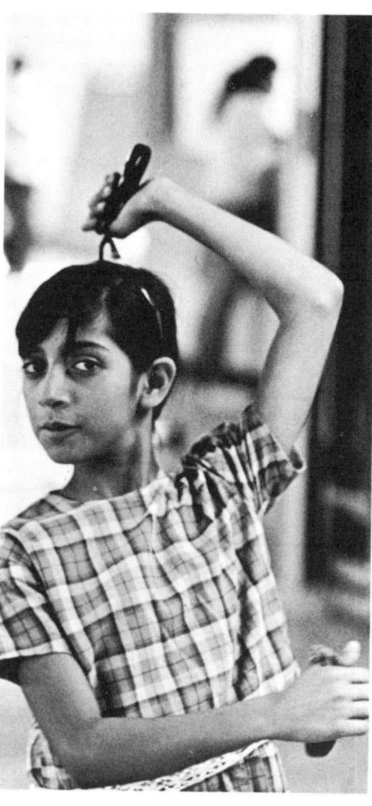

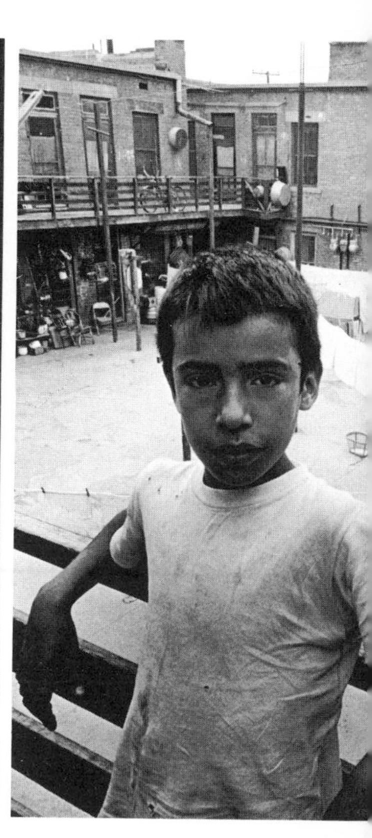

Orders for this book should be sent to the College Entrance Examination Board, Publications Order Office, Box 592, Princeton, New Jersey 08540.

Editorial inquiries concerning this book should be directed to Editorial Office, College Entrance Examination Board, 475 Riverside Drive, New York, New York 10027.

Library of Congress Catalog Card Number: 71-113462

Printed in the United States of America

Contents

Tables

Foreword

The Mexican American of the Southwest United States is referred to by a number of different names: he is designated as Spanish American, Mexican, Latin American, Spanish-speaking, and so on. This confusion is understandable, since none of the above terms is truly adequate or precise, and they all lack authenticity in some degree. The group is not a historically, genetically, or culturally homogeneous one. Some of us in recent years have settled on Mexican American as most closely approximating a suitable term, though it is not acceptable to some sectors of this population group—for example the Spanish Americans of northern New Mexico and southern Colorado.

The Spanish and Indian components of the Mexican American range from 100 percent to zero. Further, the Spanish component in itself is highly heterogeneous. The Spaniard was, and is, a complex of original Iberian man, Greek, Latin, Visigoth, Moroccan, Phoenician, Carthaginian, and others. The degree to which he was, and is, more of one or of some small combination of these varies greatly in the Catalanes, the Gallegos, the Basques, and so on, as evidenced by wide differences in physical features and in languages. The Indian component is no less complex. There were, and still are, numerous major Indian groups—the early Spaniards called them "nations" because they had such distinctly different physical, social, economic, and cultural characteristics. The Mayas of southeastern Mexico are far removed culturally, and in many other ways, from the Yaquis of northwestern Mexico, and from the Tarahumaras, the Otomis, the Mixtecs and Zapotecs, and so on—and all of them are equally far removed from each other. Add to these complications the fact that the Spaniards trickled into New Spain over a period of 300 years and settled in regions that for the most part were isolated from each other.

All these factors combined to result in subcultures with individually distinctive features. When an old New Mexican says *"Con la venia de su merced"* instead of *"Con su permiso"* he is for good reason not understood by the Texas Mexican. The Texas Mexican wonders why the Spanish Americans of northern New Mexico, who began settling there in 1598, have no interest in the Mexican holiday celebrations for the Sixteenth of September or the Fifth of May. The reason is simple: New Mexico was settled long before the Mexican Revolution for Independence, and the New Mexican had no part in it, nor in the Mexican defeat of the French at Puebla in the 1860s. Texas Mexicans did not begin establishing permanent settlements in Texas until after 1700, after they had been thoroughly "Mexicanized." The ease of communication between Texas and Mexico has contributed heavily to this "Mexicanization" of Texas Mexicans. Because New Mexico and Colorado are situated differently, geographically, the Mexican Americans in those states were less "Mexicanized."

It is understandable, therefore, why the emergence of a Southwest-wide Mexican American did not begin to take place until well into the present century—an emergence still in slow process. The Mexican American population, at least in Texas (in spite of the drain of Texas Mexicans to California), is now growing at a faster yearly rate than any other ethnic group. The fact that this group numbers around 4,000,000 in the five southwestern states, and is growing at about the same rate as that of Mexico (suffering from a "population explosion"), should give pause to the educator, the politician, the social worker—to industry and to government planners.

Some of us have pleaded for many years that the immigration of cheap labor from Mexico be curbed, not only for the protection of Mexican Americans but for the protection of Mexican nationals already here. The completely open border before 1925, which was followed by the "wetback" invasion, which was followed by the "bracero" program, which in turn was followed by the "Green Card" system—all these have mitigated grossly against the Mexican Americans.

The wages of political docility and apathy, of unbelievably low income, of incredibly poor education, of virtual serfdom are incalculable—for all citizens, not only for Mexican Americans. Infant mortality, tuberculosis, political bossism, disdain for 'that Mexican,'' disdain for his language and culture—these and many other results of the majority population's presumption of Mexican American inferiority are evidenced wherever one looks in school curriculums, teacher education, appointments to significant political offices. The state of Texas is the worst offender, but it does not by any means stand alone in the default of intelligence and conscience in this field.

Many times I have pointed out that the Mexican American is not an immigrant. As an Indian, the Southwest has been his home from time immemorial. As a Spaniard, borrowing the phrase from Will Rogers, he could have sent a committee to welcome John Smith to Jamestown. The United States took over the Southwest and thereby assumed responsibilities and moral obligations. These are yet to be fully discharged. I would not argue for the return of land grants, nor even for strict compliance with the terms of the Treaty of Guadalupe Hidalgo. But I do argue for a realistic appraisal of the status, and its causes, of the American of Mexican descent.

There can be no doubt that Tom Carter's book offers a valuable part of this appraisal. He is widely experienced in the developments about which he writes. He has an excellent knowledge of the people, of Spanish, and he has a deep understanding of and genuine sympathy for their problems, trials, and tribulations. He is highly appreciative of their past and current achievements, and of their potential for continuing contributions. His book is a most comprehensive work on the role of education in the lives of Mexican Americans. If it contributes, even slightly, to an appreciation of the severity of the educational neglect of this group, and if that appreciation is translated into action, then Dr. Carter will have made a major humanitarian contribution.

George I. Sánchez
Professor of Latin American Education
The University of Texas at Austin

Introduction

The Mexican American minority in the Southwest presents an enigma to laymen as well as to many social scientists. American society has ingested many diverse foreign people, assimilating and acculturating them, but those of Mexican ancestry appear to stand out as a glaring exception. Many Mexican Americans hang onto substantial elements of the Mexican culture and as a group continue to occupy low social status. This situation persists in spite of the fact that a few Mexican Americans can trace their origins in the Southwest to the sixteenth or seventeenth century; others, the majority, are descendants of Mexicans who arrived early in this century. Social scientists concerned with formal educational institutions pose a related question: Why has the school failed to offer Mexican Americans substantial aid toward climbing the social ladder and losing their "foreignness"? It might be argued that the school has played a relatively insignificant role in this regard with other immigrant groups, but it can be stated categorically that both schoolmen and laymen subscribe to the idea that such is a primary function of the American school.

Questions related to the school's obvious failure with Mexican Americans have bothered me for years. How can their low academic achievement be explained? Why do they tend to drop out of school early? During the early period of my interest I found the necessary explanation in the reasoning that the strength or hold of "Mexican culture" was exceptionally great, that it was not only strong enough to resist acculturation but also ingrained and self-sustaining to the point of discouraging individual aspirations for education and social advancement. This position was supported by my stereotypic view of Mexican American or Mexican culture as a monolithic and static folk tradition. A few bits of information that came my way caused me to wonder sometimes if I might be wrong, but I didn't seriously think so. Two events forced me to look much deeper into the matter.

The first of these events was my acquaintance with scholars such as George I. Sánchez of The University of Texas at Austin. Dr. Sánchez led me to look beyond such simplistic arguments and explanations into factors within the dominant socioeconomic system, as well as factors within the schools themselves. His penetrating analysis of a dynamic and diverse Mexican American subculture caused further questioning. Yet few substantial studies described the cultural variation that existed and the rapid changes that were taking place. My questions persisted. A second challenge to my not so firmly held beliefs presented itself in the form of an invitation to cooperate with the Mexican American Study Project, financed by the Ford Foundation, at the University of California at Los Angeles. The project director, Leo Grebler, as well as his colleagues Joan W. Moore and Ralph C. Guzman, shared my questions concerning simplistic explanations. This group had the funds and the investigative skills necessary to make an objective study of Mexican Americans in their Southwestern context. I readily agreed to undertake a substudy of the role of the school in Mexican American life and began my work in January of 1965. This substudy was financed by a grant from the College Entrance Examination Board to the Mexican American Study Project, and the present volume results from it. The parent study is being published by The Free Press under the title *The Mexican American People: The Nation's Second Largest Minority* (Grebler, Moore, Guzman, *et al.*, in press).

To all the individuals and organizations mentioned above and to the Mexican American Study Project's excellent research staff I owe a very real debt of gratitude. The staff's analysis of the data gathered by the project, as well as the pertinent literature, helped me to understand the complexity of the Mexican Americans' situation in the five Southwestern states. The project's findings on the diversity of the culture and the persistently low social status of the group have finally provided the hard data essential to social scientists. It is hoped that this major study will be equally useful to laymen and educators and will help to destroy the widely accepted stereotype of the Mexican American. In so doing it should encourage serious questioning of the use of this stereotype to explain withdrawal from school and low academic achievement.

Planning my study presented many difficulties. A multitude of prior studies, books, and papers exist, but many are of questionable validity. Those relevant to school and education are of five general types: (1) studies of measured achievement and years of schooling (these vary greatly in degree of sophistication); (2) studies relating socioeconomic factors (and occasionally cultural values and orientations) to achievement and years of schooling; (3) explanations for these conditions; (4) papers advocating special programs (some verging on polemics); and (5) curricular materials. Literature in category (3) almost invariably ascribes Mexican American "school failure" (low achievement and early withdrawal) to factors within the home culture. A year-long effort by two very capable graduate students, Elizabeth Ross and Reynaldo Baca, failed to uncover much written material to enlighten a researcher on the interaction of cause and effect among the three important variables—the school, the community social system, and the Mexican American subcultural group. But the literature does clearly demonstrate that Mexican Americans, as a group, tend to: (1) do poorly in school by any measure, (2) drop out early, (3) speak Spanish, and (4) be poor. Relationships among these four factors are usually seen as causal. The circular nature of arguments commonly presented is obvious: Mexican Americans do poorly in school because they are poor, speak Spanish, and are culturally Mexican, or Mexican Americans continue to be poor, speak Spanish, and carry a traditional folk culture because they do poorly in school. Most works slight the influence of the socioeconomic system Mexican Americans live in. Equally slighted was research on the nature and outcomes of school programs, policies, and practices and the more recent concepts of school social climate. Analysis of the influence of school intervention in the apparently self-perpetuating cycle (poverty–school failure–poverty) was generally lacking.

The quandary presented by the lack of a substantial literature had to be resolved. Ideally a large-scale survey of students (Mexican American and other) and schools in the Southwest was called for, but realistically funds for such a large undertaking were not available. The study was finally undertaken in two phases. A search of the relevant literature was discouraging, as described above; however, a few excellent studies were found and are cited in the body of the book. The second phase involved extensive interviewing of educators and visiting schools and special projects throughout the Southwest. For the latter purpose a semistructured interview schedule was developed. Over 250 school people and a few laymen (for example, school-board members) were formally interviewed. In some cases the interviews were tape recorded and later transcribed, but in most cases the interviewer took notes. Special school programs and everyday classes were observed, and teachers were informally questioned about their own perceptions of Mexican American behavior and achievement in school, and the results of schooling. Both urban and rural schools were visited and selected staff interviewed. The field research was concentrated in California and Texas, although the other Southwestern states—Arizona, Colorado, New Mexico—were also visited. There were a number of reasons for devoting most of our attention to the two largest states: (1) the Mexican American population is concentrated there; (2) California has generally the "best" record in regard to schooling for Mexican Americans, and Texas has the worst; and (3) two cities, Los Angeles and San Antonio, were studied intensively by the Mexican American Study Project. Nathaniel Hickerson of the College of Education at the University of Southern California helped greatly by interviewing in selected urban areas of California. Research in the rest of the state and in the other states was conducted by me. All these efforts would have been fruitless without the assistance of a fine secretary. Mrs. Marline Behar's effort, competence, and good spirits were invaluable.

Each formal interview focused on six major areas of concern: (1) the extent and the nature of the experience of the interviewee with Mexican Americans; (2) a description of the ethnic and socioeconomic community served by the school; (3) the nature of the school (organization, finance, degree of segregation, special programs, and so forth); (4) the interviewees' perceptions of Mexican American children, their personalities, families, community; (5) achievement in school and years of schooling of local Mexican Americans contrasted with other groups; (6) reasons for Mexican Americans' success or failure in school. In addition, questions were asked about the influence of specific school practices on Mexican Americans: tracking, segregation, "no-Spanish rules," ethnic cleavage, teachers' personalities, Mexican American teachers, the use of IQ information and its validity, and so forth. This interviewing and observing was extremely informative; a wealth of opinion was elicited. Numerous direct quotations from interviewees are included in the book, but in only a very few cases is the interviewee named.

No doubt certain questions can be asked about how scientific my methods were, but I will stand on my belief that interviewing and observing have allowed me to get beneath the superficial and I hope validly represent the present school situation as well as the perceptions of educators. My eyes have been opened. Some educators' statements and some school conditions truly shook my belief in school people and their works, but I have attempted to discuss such statements and conditions in their proper context. Regardless of sincere attempts to be objective and to develop theories with care, I have to acknowledge that my perceptions and analyses are open to question, coming as they do from one fallible human being, and that in spite of efforts to the contrary, my biases come through. It should be remembered too that much more hard data and analysis are essential before any conclusions can be drawn about the relationships between school and community conditions and Mexican Americans' accomplishments in school. Much more work must be done. My theories must be interpreted as tentative, except in their demand for further research and analysis.

I have reserved the term "Spanish American" to refer only to the group in northern New Mexico and southern Colorado, a group often referred to also as "hispanos." As George I. Sánchez mentions in his Foreword to this book, much confusion exists about the proper way to refer to Mexican Americans. Like him I find "Mexican American" more generally accepted and apparently less objectionable than others. A term that may be unfamiliar to some readers is "Anglo." I dislike this word and find it inaccurate, but it is very common in the Southwest. Anglo refers to the dominant "white" group, those who are not Negro, Mexican American, or members of another minority group. Some people use it to mean White Anglo-Saxon Protestant (WASP), but I restrict it to members of the nonminority population. A term occasionally used in the Southwest to substitute for it is "gringo." No term is perfect.

I have omitted a history of Mexican Americans in the Southwest, as well as a detailed description of the group's present socioeconomic situation, and have included only what I thought was directly pertinent to a discussion of schooling and education. For additional current demographic as well as historical information and analysis I recommend the Mexican American Study Project's book mentioned above. Other relevant works are cited or recommended in the body of the book.

When anyone asks George Sánchez what he prefers to be called (an ever-recurring Anglo question), he always says "I don't care what you call me, just so you call me to dinner." As I hope this book may help to demonstrate, Mexican Americans have not yet been called to dinner, and the schools are failing to prepare them to eat when they are.

T.P.C.
September 1969

Chapter 1: A History of Problems and Influences

Today the poor record in school of Mexican Americans as a group—their low academic achievement, high dropout rate, and so on—is looked on as a social and educational problem in grievous need of solution. Such has not always been the case, for in the past the plight of this group was little known and there was small desire to correct it.

THE EARLY YEARS

In the first three decades of this century, as the Mexican American population in the Southwestern United States began its rapid increase, the concern of "Anglo" society—that is, the dominant white society—for the schooling of Mexican Americans was negligible. Educators shared society's view of the Mexican American as an outsider, one who was never expected to participate fully in American life. Attitudes were tinged with racial prejudice, and literature on the subject emphasized the inadequacies of the child of Mexican descent. The typically low IQ test scores of Mexican American children were considered evidence of innate intellectual inferiority, which in turn was thought to justify segregating the schools. Mexicans were said to be capable only of manual labor, and in fact farmers were afraid that education would make them useless even for farm work. As one Texas Anglo put it: "I am for education and educating my own children, but the Mexicans, like some whites, get some education and then they can't labor.

They think it is a disgrace to work. The illiterates make the best farm labor . . ." (Taylor, 1934, p. 196). Mexican American children shared in the general deficiencies of schooling in rural areas. Many of them labored under the special handicap of moving from place to place, working in the fields with their parents. Attention to their specific educational problems was almost nonexistent.

Very little action to remedy the "Mexican problem" was taken in these early years. Mexican American children rarely attended school past the primary grades. Protestations that were made by educational leaders had a familiar ring, as indicated by this statement made in 1914 (McEwen, 1914, p. 102): "Just so surely as Booker T. Washington is right in saying that Tuskegee and similar institutions are the ultimate solution of the Negro problem, so surely is the same kind of education the necessary basis upon which to build a thorough and complete solution of the Mexican problem. Like the Negro, the Mexicans are a child-race without the generations of civilization and culture back of them which support the people of the United States." (See also Sheldon, 1924; and Garretson, 1928.)

During the Depression, many rural Mexican Americans migrated to cities, bringing their problems to a wider consciousness, as had happened before with other ethnic or racial groups. Some of the educational literature of this period described Mexican Americans as disease-ridden, inclined toward violence and crime, innately inferior, yet simple and artistic (see Carpenter, 1935; Southwest Texas State Teachers College, 1944a; 1944b). The WPA ameliorated the situation somewhat by building schools and establishing a number of vocational and Americanization programs. More important, educators during the 1930s and through the mid-1940s began to consider the school as an agency for the acculturation of the Mexican American. "Appropriate methods" to accomplish Americanization were recommended in the hope that it would change ". . . Mexican children from half-hearted Americans into law-abiding and useful American citizens" (Gould, 1932, p. 1). (For further information about Americanization, see Cornelius, 1941; Hayden, 1934; Kaderli, 1940; Lehman, 1947; Leis, 1931; Mequire, 1938; Murphy, 1939; Treff, 1934.)

School programs for Mexican American children during the 1930s emphasized vocational and manual-arts training, the learning of English, health and cleanliness, and the adoption of such American "core values" as thrift and punctuality. Segregation, especially in the early grades, was regularly recommended and commonly established. Some studies continued to consider Mexican American children to be mentally inferior, although this view gradually changed as IQ began to be seen more as a reflection of social environment. During this period, California and New Mexico showed considerably more concern for the Mexican American minority group than did Texas. In the late 1930s and early 1940s, New Mexico established special programs for Spanish Americans, most notably the Taos County Project and the Nambe Program. (See Chapter 5 of this book as well as Reid, 1946; and Tireman and Watson, 1943.)

World War II brought major changes. It accelerated the movement of Mexican Americans to urban centers, often exacerbating interethnic conflict. It also served to strengthen the "Good Neighbor Policy" between the United States and Latin American countries. The result of these two divergent trends was the development and promulgation of "intercultural education." Usually programs promoting intercultural education were little more than token gestures of appreciation of the distinctive Latin American cultural heritage. Such efforts invariably ignored the very pressing social and economic problems of Mexican Americans in the Southwest.

In Texas, the first significant concern for intercultural education during World War II and the immediate postwar years was probably prompted by economic interest. During the war, when the federal government contracted with Mexico for agricultural labor, the Mexican government refused to permit its nationals to work in some areas of Texas, because of the discrimination rampant. This issue stimulated the creation of the Texas Good Neighbor Commission and encouraged the state's education authorities to consider more thoroughly the problem of schooling for children of Mexican descent. Plans were made for more conferences and programs to improve the education of these children. For the most part, however, this was a token effort by school leaders and effected little change in the attitudes of teachers. The Good Neighbor Commission's limited approach was evidenced by its recommendations of 1949 (Clinchy, 1954, pp. 166–167): "First, to promote adult and youth classes and clubs practicing conversational Spanish. Second, to encourage civic leaders to organize Good Neighbor community committees in every section of the State. Third, to stimulate exchanging of letters so each school child will become his own Good Neighbor and correspond with a child of similar age in Mexico. Fourth, to coordinate our program with other state agencies, businesses, civic and church organizations, Boy Scouts, 4-H, YMCA, etc. Fifth, to urge Latin Americans to become citizens in fact as well as in name by paying their poll tax and voting." (See also Daustin, 1943; Tanner, 1944; Trillingham and Hughes, 1943.)

Clear evidence of increasing public concern for the special educational problems of Mexican Americans is found in the record of teachers' conferences and workshops beginning in the 1930s. Besides efforts to develop special teaching methods and techniques, there were earnest recommendations to instruct teachers in the cultural and socioeconomic background of the pupils and to cope with the problems of instruction in English—including, in more recent years, the teaching of English as a second language. Such conferences proliferated in the years following World War II. A comparison of discussion topics and recommendations of an early postwar conference with one 20 years later reveals little change. The 1946 First Regional Conference on the Education of Spanish-Speaking People in the Southwest held in Austin, Texas, asked for an end to segregation, a relevant curriculum built around the Mexican American community, improved and special teacher training—particularly with respect to teachers' attitudes toward this minority group—increased efficiency in teaching English, and improvement in school physical facilities. It was recognized that Mexican Americans' attendance at school was poor, that their academic achievement was low, and that there was imperative need to improve their minority socioeconomic status. There was also emphasis at the 1946 conference on the importance of education in inter-American relations (Sánchez, 1946, Foreword): "The education of Spanish-speaking people in the United States is a phase . . . a very important phase . . . of inter-American education. Not only is it a significant part of intercultural education in the United States, involving as it does one of the most prominent minorities in the nation, but it is a keystone in the structure of cultural relations between the United States and the other American republics."

The 1964 Orange County Conference on the Education of Spanish-Speaking Children and Youth, held in Garden Grove, California, reiterated the emphasis of the earlier conference on the need for special teacher training, the undemocratic nature of the still continuing de facto segregation, and the need for improving the teaching of English (California State Department of Education, 1964). There was less stress on radical change of the curriculum or intercultural education, but a strong recommendation for the inclusion of "cultural heritage" material such as the celebration of Cinco de Mayo, the Mexican holiday.

In the 1950s and 1960s, the emphasis on socioeconomic problems of minority groups and the civil rights movement contributed to a growing concern for the Mexican American and to the tendency to recognize his problems as characteristic of low socioeconomic status. The increased attention nationally to the defects of urban ghetto schools has contributed to changing attitudes toward educating Mexican Americans. There is now increasing recognition of the necessity for specialized teacher training for teachers of Mexican American children, and a small but significant number of educators are aware that the school and its curriculum may be inadequate. (See Faltis, 1951; Hernandez, 1967; California State Department of Education, 1952.)

Historically, the Southwest school took cognizance of the Mexican American child very belatedly. Considerable time elapsed before it was recognized that people of Mexican descent were here to stay instead of coming and going across the border as migrants. The mass immigration of the 1920s presented the educational apparatus with formidable problems and brought consideration of ethnic groups to the fore. When the school did begin to concern itself with the children of this minority group, it proceeded to fit them into a rigidly conceived system, instead of attempting to adjust the system to the needs of the group. This approach, intentionally or otherwise, served to make the educational system conform to the pressure of Southwest society for perpetuating the low socioeconomic standing of Mexican Americans.

THE ROLE OF THE SCHOOL

All social institutions perform educational functions in the sense that they socialize people—that is, they teach them to operate within the framework of socially set norms. In differing and ever-changing ways, the family, the church, and the school share the prime obligation for socializing each new generation. The school aids society in the enculturation and socialization processes and in the allocation of human resources and thereby of status—the "sorting and sieving" process. Socialization involves bringing the child into membership in society by teaching him certain behavior, expectations, roles, and personality characteristics. Enculturation is the corollary and interrelated activity of teaching the values, knowledge, and skills of the parent culture.

The substance of a school's formal instructional content (knowledge, skills, and values) is derived from the culture of both its local and its national society. The teaching of roles, behavior, and expectations, which might be called a school's informal instructional content, also reflects both societies. The formal content is more likely to follow national models than the informal, on which the local social system and culture exert considerable influence. The formal and informal contents may be in conflict, just as are local mores and national values. For example, school segregation itself intervenes as a significant learning experience for a child. Through segregation, the incongruities between national ideals and local practices become as evident in the school as they are in the community itself. In the Southwest, both Anglo and Mexican American children are expected to internalize the national American culture, including such basic values as equality, at the same time that they are learning the different and unequal roles expected of them by local society.

Superficially, American schools resemble each other a great deal. At first glance, the elements of the school—the formal programs of instruction, the teachers, buildings, organization, finance, and control—are so similar that one might expect to find them administered by a central national agency. Closer examination reveals great differences, however. The local or regional social climate, as reflected in educators' perceptions, beliefs, and expectations, is manifest in school organizational patterns and procedures and, most important, in the treatment of children. The local socioeconomic system affects the sorting and sieving process. Although schooling is idealized as the way to rise in the status system, the local society, if it is to be maintained, requires that children be prepared to occupy the particular slots that the community has available for different categories of its population. The school, reflecting the nature of its local parent society, sorts children into the types necessary to fill the recurring status vacancies. The interrelationship and functional dependence of the American school and its society are well established in this regard. Occupational status, of course, is the most readily understandable and most important of these types, as Clark points out (1965, p. 739): "Whenever formally differentiated agencies of education [schools] exist, their general social function of training the young for adult roles entails also some part of the assignment of status to individuals and groups. This part grows as education connects more closely to the economy. Education's mediation between the demand and supply of workers entails an expanding mediation in the assignment of social position and status. . . ."

If a local society maintains a restricted number of statuses, the school releases children prepared to meet the requirements of the local system, usually in accord with existing status allocations for the various ethnic groups. Thus, one would expect the dropout rate for Mexican American children in a relatively isolated agricultural community with a castelike social system to be high, reflecting the traditional distribution of statuses. Conversely, in an urban-industrial and more open society, one would expect the dropout rate to be lower, reflecting the greater variety of statuses allocated, or open, to the minority group. Where state law demands school attendance to a given age above that required for entrance into available occupations, schools can be expected to evade the law by failing to enforce attendance or by other means.

In regard to "foreign" or culturally different groups, the school is expected to perform an allied role: to be the principal agent of Americanization. According to Brogan (1950, pp. 135, 136), this function of the school ". . . is to teach Americanism, meaning not merely political and patriotic dogma, but the habits necessary to American life . . . the common language, common habits, common tolerances, a common political and national faith. The main . . . achievement of the high schools and grammar schools is to bring together the young of all classes and all origins, to provide, artificially, the common background that in old, rural society is provided by tradition. . . ."

Few educators, or few United States citizens for that matter, would question the desirability of the Americanization function. In this century, United States society has implicitly or explicitly rationalized entrance of foreigners by assuming that at least their children would move into and up in American society rapidly—that they would be assimilated—as they practiced the knowledge, skills, and values (culture) so diligently taught them in the classroom. Whether the school was principally responsible for the rapid acculturation and relatively easy entrance into American society of earlier and diverse ethnic groups, or whether an epoch of expanding opportunities was responsible, remains an unanswered but increasingly serious question in the contemporary context.

MEXICAN AMERICAN ACHIEVEMENT AND PARTICIPATION IN SCHOOL

How well has the Southwestern school performed its societally assigned functions? In other words, has the school been successful in teaching the Mexican American "our way of life," by aiding him to move into society? No definitive answers can be given. However, certain kinds of data indicate that the Mexican American minority in the Southwest has resisted acculturation and does not fully participate in Southwestern society or its educational institutions. This chapter presents this evidence. The following chapters attempt to explain why.

Academic Achievement. Schools very consciously attempt to teach the dominant culture to all children and especially to ethnically distinct groups. In fact, the curriculum (the content, sequence, and method of instruction) is merely culture as defined by and found in the school. A number of methods are used by educational institutions to test or sample the degree to which an individual or group has internalized the culture taught (the knowledge and skills of the parent society). These methods include all forms of achievement tests—IQ or mental maturity tests as well as less formal, more subjective measures in the form of grades. In this book "intelligence" tests are considered to be measures of learned items of culture and not indicators of intellectual potential or capacity. An IQ test tends to measure how much of "average culture" has been internalized and can be elicited by the proper stimulus—that is, the degree of group acculturation or individual enculturation.

Perhaps more has been written about Mexican American low academic achievement and IQ than about any other educational topic. There have been literally hundreds of studies comparing Mexican American group achievement scores to those of Negroes and Anglos, or to their own individual "capacity" as measured by various psychometric instruments. (For an extensive bibliography of early IQ studies see Blackman, 1939.) While individual studies vary in innumerable ways, a rather clear picture of the group's tested IQ and school achievement is evident. Interviews corroborate the general picture. Mexican Americans as a group fail to achieve well on standard tests of academic achievement, and they do not do as well as their Anglo counterparts in the more subjective evaluations of achievement. The grade-point average of the Mexican American group is generally lower than that of the Anglo group within the same school or district. Needless to say, there are numerous individual exceptions who violate these generalizations. There is also the real possibility that some schools "grade up" Mexican Americans. There are substantial differences among geographic areas, schools, rural and urban locales, and social classes.

In the area of language arts, Mexican Americans achieve at a rate substantially lower than national norms or their local Anglo counterparts. The ability to read is perhaps the most crucial skill learned in school, and in this area Mexican American children fail to reach the level of proficiency generally acquired by others. Since the American culture is carried in the English language, such low performance indicates low group acculturation. In no aspect of reading are they "normal." While general ability in language arts is low, two areas are reported to be exceptions: in spelling and the fundamentals of grammar, Mexican American children do better and some approach local or national norms.

Achievement in arithmetic is also low; however, it is generally higher than in the language arts. When total arithmetic achievement is broken down into "problem solving" (involving language skills) and "fundamentals," differences are found. The Mexican American group does relatively well in the "fundamentals," approaching local norms, but is far below local norms in areas dependent on language ability.

Mexican American children start out in school fairly close to Anglos in measured achievement of all kinds. Although they fall slightly more behind the Anglos with each grade, the two groups remain in about the same relative positions through the third or fourth grades. After the beginning intermediate grades, the Anglos continue their upward climb, approximating the national norms. Some time in the intermediate grades the Mexican American group begins to fall progressively and drastically further and further below the Anglo achievement norms. According to all reports gathered in the field, "mental withdrawal," as manifest in boredom, failure to work, inattentiveness, and discipline problems, begins some time from the third to the sixth grade. Usually Mexican American boys are reported to withdraw mentally earlier than girls. Because such a disproportionately large number of Mexican Americans physically drop out or "transfer," it is almost impossible to construct a meaningful graph comparing the achievement of the two groups over the 12 years of school. For example, some educators interviewed contend that a graph of average Mexican American and Anglo general achievement would not be as described above for their particular school. They state that minority and majority group achievement would be close in both the primary grades and the last years of high school. Considering the extremely high Mexican American dropout rates in the schools they are talking about, this becomes perfectly understandable. The Mexican Americans who do reach the last years of high school are indeed similar to the Anglos; the divergent ones have long since dropped out.

Factors Related to Achievement. In two recent research efforts, a wealth of data has been collected concerning Mexican American school achievement and the factors related or associated with it. The two studies were somewhat different, but their findings do tend to support each other.

The Los Angeles School Study[1] found, as anticipated, that a number

1. A substudy of the Mexican American Study Project (see page 2). C. Wayne Gordon and others studied sixth-, ninth-, and twelfth-grade Mexican American and majority-group students in selected Los Angeles schools.

of home-related factors were associated with achievement as variously measured. The same factors were related to both Anglo and Mexican American school performance, although the degree varied. These factors include the following (quotations from Gordon *et al.*, 1968, pp. 134–135): (1) "Parental aspirations for pupils' educational attainment." Of particular importance among the Mexican Americans were the mother's aspirations. (2) Pupil attitudes and values (perhaps a measure of home acculturation to middle-class orientations). (3) Language spoken at home. "The exclusive use of English contributes consistently and positively for Mexican American pupils at all grade levels" (again a measure of home acculturation). (4) Family economic level, which "contributes less to the performance of both ethnic groups than does family educational level," the influence being greater for Anglo than for Mexican American pupils. These home or cultural factors tend to support a general thesis of this book: the academic success of a Mexican American child depends on the degree to which his home has been oriented to Anglo middle-class culture.

The recently published national study, *Equality of Educational Opportunity* by Coleman and his associates, provides additional information on the subject of the school achievement of ethnic and racial groups (Coleman *et al.*, 1966). While numerous criticisms of this report have been made (see for example Boules and Levin, 1968), mostly questioning the research methods used, the study's findings correspond to the bulk of other research. Of the six racial or ethnic groups ranked on achievement tests in the Coleman study, the Mexican Americans ranked fourth. Puerto Ricans and Negroes scored lower; Anglos, Orientals, and American Indians were higher. If Mexican Americans were rated against Anglos, 85 percent would fall below. The reading-comprehension deficit of Mexican Americans was marked at all levels. By the ninth grade the Mexican American was three and a third years below the "white" sample of Northwestern America. Verbal ability fell below "white" norms by two years in the sixth grade and three and a half years by the twelfth. As with other minority groups, the Mexican American falls progressively more behind as he continues in school. However, there is a slight closing of the gap toward the end of high school—undoubtedly attributable to the high dropout rate of low achievers.

In regard to attitudinal and aspirational variables, the Coleman report found that Mexican American children: (1) strongly desired to stay in school, be good students, and attend regularly; (2) planned to go to college less commonly than Anglos; (3) held high occupational aspirations, (4) seemed to be slightly more self-depreciating than Anglos or Negroes; (5) indicated feelings of poor ability to control their environments. These factors may be important in regard to school achievement, but the direct causal relationships have not been established.

The staff of the United States Office of Education analyzed the Coleman report vis à vis Mexican Americans and concluded the following (Mayeske, 1967): "(1) family background is most important for achievement; (2) the association of family background with achievement does not diminish over the years; (3) the influence of school facilities, curriculum, and staff that is independent of family background is small; (4) teachers' characteristics account for most of the differences in school factors that are related to achievement; (5) the social composition of the student body is more highly related to achievement, independently of the student's own social background, than is any school factor; (6) attitudes concerning control or responsiveness of the environment are highly related to achievement, but variations in school characteristics have little influence on these attitudes." A number of perplexing questions are raised in the preceding quotation; the following chapters of this book attempt to shed more light on them.

School achievement, as measured by whatever standard, is closely related to social class and to home background. This seems to hold true regardless of the criterion used to judge socioeconomic status. Parents with more education, income, higher status jobs, and so forth, produce children who generally perform well in school. Higher status Mexican American homes tend to be less "Mexican," more "American" or acculturated. The more the child is like what the school expects, the better he will achieve—that is, the more acculturation, the higher the achievement.

As a general rule, children entering Southwestern schools directly from Mexico are reported to achieve better than the average local Mexican American. School personnel often are particularly proud of the performance of such children, who seem to learn English rapidly and well. The older the immigrant is, the better he appears to do in school. Many explanations are offered for this phenomenon, which appears to violate the relationship between acculturation and achievement. Among the more common are that such children are middle class or from upwardly mobile families, and that Mexican schools are becoming quite good, and the child is well-prepared there (he has learned to study and so forth). A much less common explanation is that the immigrant child is treated as something special and that teachers have high expectations for such "foreign students." There is no one reason given for the reported high achievement; each school and geographic area has a different answer.

If IQ scores could be assumed to measure potential and achievement, Mexican American children would tend to achieve academically about as well as their potential would indicate. In other words, as a group they would not overachieve. Since IQ scores are low for the group, it is argued that Mexican Americans are doing just about as well as can be expected—there is about the "normal" percentage who overachieve and underachieve. (For additional achievement reports, see Cline, 1961a; 1961b; Coleman, 1966, pp. 265, 268; Jensen, 1961; MacMillan, 1966; Mahakian, 1939; Manuel, 1965; McDowell, 1966, p. 24; Sánchez, 1932, p. 225; Colorado State Department of Education, 1967.)

When low achievement is coupled with a school's rigid standards for promotion, Mexican American children fail to move ahead as fast as others their age and soon are older than the proper age for their grade level. Rigid grade-level requirements were general throughout the Southwest in the past. Today, Texas seems to adhere most closely, and California least closely, to such requirements. In California, being overage is no longer a severe problem for Mexican American school children. Social promotions allow most of them to progress with their "age mates." In Texas, the tendency is to keep them back, and thus they progress with their "achievement mates." Being overage is a contributing cause to dropping out. The problem is being dealt with differently in different states, but its root remains the same: Mexican Americans as a group do not achieve well in school.

Enrollment in School. The degree of assimilation, or structural integration, of a group can be measured in a number of ways. One important indicator is the group's participation in the dominant society's institutions. Mexican Americans have not participated previously and do not now participate in formal educational institutions in the percentages appropriate to their number in the general population. The

TABLE 1: Median Years of School Completed by Spanish-Surname Adults 25 Years and Over Compared with Other Groups in Standard Metropolitan Districts in Five Southwestern States, 1950, 1960

	1950		1960			
	Total population	WPSS*	Total population	Anglo	WPSS	Nonwhite
ARIZONA	10.0	6.0	11.2	12.1	7.0	7.0
Phoenix	10.6	5.3	11.6	12.1	6.1	8.5
Tucson	11.2	6.5	12.1	12.3	8.0	7.8
CALIFORNIA	11.6	7.8	12.1	12.2	8.6	10.6
Bakersfield	9.9	6.5	10.8	11.4	7.3	8.5
Fresno	9.8	5.6	10.4	10.7	6.1	8.8
Long Beach–Los Angeles	12.0	8.2	12.1	12.3	8.9	11.1
Sacramento	11.3	7.9	12.2	12.3	9.1	10.9
San Bernardino–Riverside–Ontario	10.9	6.7	11.8	12.1	8.0	9.8
San Diego	12.0	8.1	12.1	12.2	8.9	10.7
San Francisco–Oakland	12.0	8.9	12.1	12.3	9.7	10.2
San Jose	11.4	8.1	12.2	12.4	8.3	12.0
Santa Barbara	11.8	7.0	12.2	12.4	8.3	9.9
Stockton	9.1	7.2	10.0	10.7	7.5	8.2
COLORADO	10.9	6.5	12.1	12.2	8.2	11.2
Colorado Springs	11.7	8.4	12.3	12.4	10.1	12.1
Denver	12.0	8.0	12.2	12.3	8.8	11.4
Pueblo	9.1	6.3	10.2	11.0	8.1	9.2
NEW MEXICO	9.3	6.1	11.2	12.2	7.4	7.1
Albuquerque	11.7	7.7	12.1	12.5	8.7	10.9

past history of low Mexican American participation in the Southwest's schools is demonstrated by the extremely low median for years of schooling completed by adults.

Table 1 shows the almost unbelievable "underschooling" of the minority, as well as the startling differences in years of schooling from

	1950 *Total population*	*WPSS**	*1960* *Total population*	*Anglo*	*WPSS*	*Nonwhite*
TEXAS	9.3	3.5	10.4	11.5	4.8	8.1
Abilene	10.1	—	11.7	12.0	4.0	8.8
Amarillo	11.3	4.7	12.1	12.2	8.1	9.5
Austin	10.9	3.5	11.7	12.3	4.4	8.6
Beaumont–Port Arthur	9.7	7.0	10.8	11.7	8.7	7.1
Brownsville–Harlingen–San Benito	6.3	2.7	7.9	12.3	3.9	9.5
Corpus Christi	9.4	3.2	10.1	12.2	4.5	8.0
Dallas	11.0	4.4	11.8	12.1	6.4	8.6
El Paso	9.2	5.2	11.1	12.4	6.6	11.7
Fort Worth	10.7	5.4	11.4	11.9	7.7	8.7
Galveston	9.4	4.9	10.3	11.3	6.9	8.3
Houston	10.4	5.2	11.4	12.1	6.4	8.8
Laredo	5.4	5.2	6.7	—	5.4	—
Lubbock	11.0	1.7	11.6	12.1	3.1	8.3
Midland	12.1	1.8	12.4	12.6	3.7	8.8
Odessa	10.4	3.9	11.4	11.8	4.6	8.8
San Angelo	10.2	2.9	10.7	11.5	4.0	8.0
San Antonio	9.1	4.5	10.0	12.1	5.7	9.4
Waco	9.4	2.9	10.3	11.0	5.5	8.2
Wichita Falls	—	—	11.4	11.7	6.3	8.7
ALL FIVE STATES	10.6	5.4	11.6	12.1	7.1	9.0

Source: Grebler (1967, Table 1, Table 6). *White Person of Spanish Surname.

region to region—differences that are difficult, if not impossible, to account for by either the availability of schools or their quality.[2] Variations should be expected, but such extremes must find their explanation either in the conditions outside school or in some combination of factors. Mexican Americans themselves certainly do not vary according to area enough to account for these differences. In Texas they are in the lowest position, relative to schooling of all groups, and in California they are in the highest. In some communities, the levels of schooling for Mexican Americans are truly appalling. However, it must be remembered that the adults living in a given area have not necessarily gone to school there. Migration of the better educated adults to other areas may partially account for low medians in some areas.

Differences between the sexes in schooling are also reported (Grebler, 1967, p. 8): "Contrary to the conventional notions about the role and upbringing of women in traditional Mexican culture, the average schooling of Spanish-surname females was about the same as for males." This is true for younger as well as older groups. Differences between urban and rural residents are also evident: the rural "farm" or "nonfarm" Mexican American population has fewer years of schooling than the urban. Again, the differences may partially be accounted for by migration (Grebler, 1967, p. 10): "Those who migrate may have above-average schooling and may be more motivated to seek better opportunities in urban environments." This situation, referred to later in this book as the rural-to-urban "brain drain," is reported by educators in the field. Even in the rural population, where the culture can be assumed to be more traditional than in urban settings, women have higher median levels of schooling. In the case of the "rural farm" population over 25 years old, women have a median of 5.2 years, while men have only 3.6. This can be assumed to be the most "traditional" group, yet the difference in favor of the females is greater than in any other age group or in any other demographic category (Grebler, 1967, p. 10).

The schooling status of Mexican Americans can also be contrasted

2. In Table 1 and other tables in this book, the abbreviation WPSS stands for White Person of Spanish Surname, a category used by the United States Census. It is roughly equivalent to Mexican American.

with that of other ethnic groups by analyzing enrollment in given grade levels of school or in different age groups.

Analysis of the United States Census data on percentages of given groups enrolled in school indicates to Manuel (1965, p. 55): "In nearly every age bracket the percentage of Spanish-surname persons enrolled in school is less than the percentage of the total population enrolled in school. The percentages for the two groups are closest in New Mexico, where the Spanish-speaking population is a larger part of the total than in other states. The early dropout from school of Spanish-surname children begins to be evident at the age bracket fourteen to fifteen and is quite marked at the age bracket sixteen to seventeen. At every age bracket from five to nineteen the lowest enrollment ratio for Spanish-surname children is found in Texas." Grebler (1967, p. 21) says: "When school enrollment is examined for more narrowly defined age groups, a definite pattern emerges. . . . Enrollment of Spanish-surname pupils compared to all pupils is low in the 5 to 6 year bracket. In other words, schooling typically begins later. Enrollment is about balanced in the 7 to 13 year group. . . . The differential between Mexican American and total enrollment widens increasingly with each successive age group. . . ."

Table 2 demonstrates the high attrition occurring at the crucial 16 to 21 age bracket. Mexican Americans start school late and drop out or are forced out early and at substantially higher rates than the total

TABLE 2: Percentages of Population by Age Groups Enrolled in Schools in Five Southwestern States, 1960

	ARIZONA		*CALIFORNIA*		*COLORADO*		*NEW MEXICO*		*TEXAS*	
Ages	*Total*	*WPSS**	*Total*	*WPSS*	*Total*	*WPSS*	*Total*	*WPSS*	*Total*	*WPSS*
5-6	57.5	55.0	82.8	79.9	69.3	63.9	50.9	49.6	39.0	34.5
7-13	96.9	96.2	98.2	97.6	98.1	97.4	96.8	96.4	96.9	94.5
14-15	92.9	90.2	96.3	92.9	95.2	89.4	93.4	93.3	91.6	82.7
16-17	79.1	68.3	83.3	73.7	83.5	68.0	81.5	76.3	76.3	58.6
18-19	45.4	36.6	40.8	33.1	48.0	34.0	41.6	41.7	41.9	31.1
20-21	21.4	10.1	21.5	12.1	26.3	12.4	17.6	14.5	20.2	11.9

Source: Manuel (1965, Table 19).
*White Person of Spanish Surname.

population. There is a higher attrition rate in rural areas than in urban. The disparity between Mexican American enrollment and Anglo enrollment could be assumed to be greater than it is between Mexican Americans and the total population.

Figures on the enrollment of Mexican American children by grade level are almost impossible to procure. It is rare for districts to keep records separating ethnic groups and rarer still for them to be made available. However, some examples of districts that have high concentrations of Mexican Americans can be cited, as well as some figures for Texas. A special study prepared by the Texas Education Agency (1957) compared enrollment of Spanish-surname and total-population students by grade level for the 1955–56 school year. The report stated (p. 3): "The ratio of the number of first grade pupils to the number of pupils in grade twelve is about 3–1 for all pupils in the State. . . . For pupils having Spanish surnames the ratio . . . is about 12–1. . . ." Such ratios are not valid descriptions of attrition. Many factors, including ages of the respective population groups, may distort the picture, but these figures are generally conceded to be a crude dropout rate.

The Brownsville (Texas) school system reports dropouts by comparing the enrollment of a given year, twelfth grade, with the enrollment of the same class in the fourth grade. Brownsville's school population is about 75 percent children of Mexican descent. In 1960 a 65 percent loss was reported between fourth grade and twelfth grade; this improved gradually (with some reversals) to the 1966 school year, which had only a 51 percent loss (Brownsville Consolidated Independent School District, 1967). In another Lower Rio Grande Valley school district, which has about 80 percent Mexican American students, the picture was similar. Fifty-three percent of the fourth graders did not reach the twelfth grade in 1966. In still another valley system that has a similarly high percentage of Mexican American students, only 267 twelfth graders were left in 1966 out of 524 seventh graders. Such differences between seventh and twelfth are very common in Texas schools that have high percentages of Mexican Americans. Estimates of Mexican American dropout rates in the valley vary greatly: one educator estimates that 1 out of 6 present Mexican American first graders will complete high school; others estimate that 30 percent will survive.

The Governor's Committee on Public School Education in Texas has recently concluded its study and published the findings (1968). This report is even more pessimistic than the statements of most people interviewed for this book, as indicated in Table 3. If it could be assumed, looking at Table 3, that 100 percent of all Mexican American ("Latin") students were enrolled in the seventh grade and that the percentage losses were as indicated, the total cumulative drop for Mexican Americans would be about 65 percent. Naturally the dropout rate cannot be computed this way, without taking account of the number of students either entering or leaving the school system—the transfer students. However, it is probably a fairly accurate picture, since it is certain that 100 percent were not enrolled in the seventh grade. The percentage of loss between a six-year elementary school and junior high school may be greater than it is between sixth and seventh grades in an eight-year elementary school. In one system in rural California, there was a loss of approximately 10–15 percent between eighth grade and freshman year in a four-year high school located in a separate school district.

The Governor's Committee report gives projections of percentages of high school graduates up to the 1978–79 school year. Table 4 shows these projections, and the magnitude of the Mexican American ("Latin") dropout rate is evident. The picture is not quite so grim in other Southwestern states.

Schools with high percentages of Mexican Americans in metropoli-

TABLE 3: Estimated School Dropout Rates by Grade Level, Texas (in Percent of Enrollment by Grade)

Grade	*Anglo*	*Latin*	*Negro*	*Total*	*Cumulative*
7	4.8	17.6	7.2	9.3	9.3
8	7.0	17.1	8.9	10.6	19.9
9	15.0	22.5	19.2	18.1	38.0
10	28.5	23.2	26.7	26.4	64.4
11	27.4	13.7	23.6	22.3	86.7
12	17.4	5.9	14.4	13.1	99.8
TOTAL	100.1	100.0	100.0	99.8	

Source: Governor's Committee on Public School Education in Texas (1968, p. 38).

tan poverty areas have exceedingly high attrition rates, but it is possible only to suggest what the degree of loss in these schools may be. In a large Texas junior high school, which has particularly rigid behavioral standards, there were only 276 ninth graders left in 1967 out of 516 seventh graders. This school is 100 percent Mexican American; other junior high schools in the same system had only a 10–20 percent loss. In the same district, a predominantly Mexican American high school had a ratio of 5 tenth graders to 3 seniors, while the ratio for the district as a whole was approximately 5 to 4. In another large Texas district, which has about 60 percent Mexican American concentration, the high schools that serve very low socioeconomic areas have a ratio of about 2 tenth graders to 1 twelfth grader. The ratio in the district as a whole is about 5 to 4; some predominantly Anglo schools are approximately 7 to 5. Regardless of the exact figures, there is no doubt that the dropout rate for Mexican Americans is extremely high (see Manuel, 1965, pp. 61, 62).

It seems reasonable to say that perhaps 60 percent of the children of Mexican descent who begin Texas schools do not finish high school. Other states would average somewhat better, California and Colorado perhaps reaching only a 40 percent dropout rate for the group. Arizona and New Mexico, in that order, would probably follow California and Colorado in percentages of dropouts. No data to support these estimates conclusively are available. Differences among states are great,

TABLE 4: Projected High School Graduates, Texas. Cumulative Percent Graduating by Age 21

Group	*1966-67*	*1970-71*	*1974-75*	*1978-79*
All groups	62	67	71	75
Anglo boys	66	70	74	78
Anglo girls	68	73	78	83
Negro boys	52	58	63	68
Negro girls	52	57	61	65
Latin boys*	40	45	50	55
Latin girls*	40	45	50	55

Source: Governor's Committee on Public School Education in Texas (1968, p. 16).
*Mexican American.

but there is perhaps as much variation among schools within states.

There seems to be a relationship between the percentage of Mexican Americans in a given school and its student attrition rate: the higher the Mexican American percentage, the more the loss (see Sheldon and Hunter, 1964; and Gordon *et al.*, 1968). If this is a causal relationship, which this author assumes it to be, it would follow that the highest dropout rate would be in the state that has the greatest degree of segregation in its schools. There are no statistics to prove it, but Texas certainly appears to be most segregationist.

Mexican American enrollment in institutions of higher education can be considered a crucial indicator of Mexican American advancement to middle-class status. Reliable estimates of Mexican American enrollment in college-level institutions are very difficult to make. For this study, an effort was made to determine the Mexican American population in selected colleges and universities in the Southwest, and almost insurmountable problems were encountered. The counting of Spanish surnames presented its normal difficulties, besides the fact that unknown numbers of these belong to students from Latin America. Differences among schools in method of reporting years of college, majors, and even sex of students, compounded the problem. However, enough relatively good information was collected to provide a basis for fairly valid estimates.

Percentages of Spanish-surname student populations at The University of Texas at Austin have been available since the 1928–29 academic year. Manuel collated other studies and added his own, bringing the data for the university up to the 1958–59 academic year. Table 5 duplicates Manuel's work but adds data collected for the present study for the 1966–67 school year. Whether the slightly lower percentages for 1966–67 represent the beginnings of a trend is unknown. In contrast to the university's main branch in Austin, the new branch in El Paso (previously named Texas Western College) is reported to have a Spanish-surname population of approximately 30 percent. In the case of Austin, which presumably draws students from all over Texas, the percentage of the Spanish-surname student population is about one-sixth of the percentage of Mexican Americans in the state. El Paso's percentage of Spanish-surname students is about half of the percentage of Mexican Americans in the area.

TABLE 5: Enrollment of Spanish-Surname Students Compared to Total Enrollment in The University of Texas at Austin

Year	UNDERGRADUATE			GRADUATE			GRADUATE AND UNDERGRADUATE		
	Total students enrolled	Spanish-surname students		Total students enrolled	Spanish-surname students		Total students enrolled	Spanish-surname students	
		Number	Percent		Number	Percent		Number	Percent
1928-1929	5,390	57	1.1	465	1	0.2	5,855	58	1.0
1938-1939	10,103	152	1.5	818	3	0.3	10,921	155	1.4
1948-1949	16,356	395	2.4	2,177	37	1.7	18,533	432†	2.3
1958-1959*	15,533	518	3.3	2,229	49	2.2	17,762	567†	3.2
1966-1967*	22,559	634	2.8	4,786	126	2.6	27,345	771†	2.8

Source: Manuel (1965, Table 22).
* Early in fall semester only.
† In the 1948-49 fall semester 139 students from Latin American countries were enrolled; most of them are probably included in the Spanish-surname count. There is no count available of the foreign students who may have been included in the figures for other subsequent years.

Manuel (1965, p. 60) reports that 5.7 percent of the 1958 freshmen in 146 Southwestern colleges had Spanish surnames: ". . . The percentage of Spanish-speaking [Spanish-surname students] entering college in 1958 was little more than half of the percentage of the Spanish-speaking group in the general population (11.8 percent in 1960)." The California State Department of Education (1967a, pp. 15–16) has released statistics for 1966 describing enrollment according to ethnic groups in junior colleges. These figures describe both freshmen and sophomores, instead of just freshmen, but the findings tend to corroborate Manuel's. According to the California study, 7.42 percent of junior college students enrolled in "graded classes" (regular credit courses) in the fall of 1966 had Spanish surnames. The percentage attending "adult classes" at junior colleges was 9.71, somewhat closer to a proper representation. (With their high attrition rate in high school, Mexican Americans still make up 13.30 percent of all pupils in California elementary and secondary schools.) Even in the inexpensive and extremely numerous junior colleges of California, this minority group is severely underrepresented.

While the Spanish-surname minority start the freshman year at percentages approximating 50 percent of their percentage in the local population, they apparently suffer from a higher attrition rate than other groups. Table 6 lists the Spanish-surname populations of seven

*TABLE 6: Spanish-Surname Populations in Seven Colleges and Universities, 1966-67**

	MEN		*WOMEN*	
Class	*Number*	*Percent†*	*Number*	*Percent***
Freshman	610	15.60	396	10.13
Sophomore	423	10.82	229	5.86
Junior	562	14.38	248	6.35
Senior	531	13.59	228	5.83
Graduate school	450	11.51	181	4.63

*Total combined enrollment of Spanish-surname students at University of Arizona, University of California at Riverside, University of Colorado, California State College at Los Angeles, Northern Arizona University, The University of Texas, New Mexico Highlands University.

† Percentage of all men enrolled. ** Percentage of all women enrolled.

Southwestern colleges and universities, all of which draw students from areas with high percentages of Mexican Americans. These percentages suggest that women do not survive so well as men, and they point up the high attrition rate. A low dropout rate would be indicated by approximately equal percentages at each level. The high percentage at the junior-year level is probably attributable to the influx of transfers from junior college, especially in California. Table 6 corroborates Manuel's earlier finding that the ratio of Mexican American men to Mexican American women in college is about 2 to 1 in favor of the men (1965, p. 60).

SUMMARY AND CONCLUSIONS

The undereducation and low socioeconomic status of most Mexican Americans have been recognized in a generalized way for years. However, it was not until the publication and subsequent analysis of data collected in the United States Census of 1950, and especially in the Census of 1960, that specific information concerning the disadvantaged status of the group was widely disseminated (see Fogel, 1965; Grebler, 1967; Manuel, 1965; Samora, 1963; Sánchez, 1940). Today the average educator is becoming aware of the dire social and economic situation of this ethnic group.

A number of facts stand out when the Mexican American group is compared to other ethnic groups in the Southwest. Analysis of the census data reveals the following. (1) The median years of schooling completed by White Persons with Spanish Surname is lower than for any ethnic group in the Southwest except the American Indian. (2) Income is associated with years of schooling. Mexican American median income is substantially lower than income for the Anglo or total population, but it is not so low proportionately as would be expected from their very low years of schooling. This fact suggests that Mexican Americans may face less discrimination in employment than do other ethnic groups (Fogel, 1965, p. 9). (3) The difference between the median years of schooling of Anglos and the Spanish-surname population (the "schooling gap") is narrowing. (4) The younger generation of the Mexican American population is going to school longer. "While Anglos of 25 years and over have a higher educational attainment than those 14 to 24 years, the reverse is true for the Spanish-surname and non-white population" (Grebler, 1967, pp. 5, 7).

The economic position and years of schooling of the group are slowly improving. Perhaps the most encouraging report is that the younger generation, even though many have not finished their schooling, have already surpassed those older than 25 in median years of school completed.

Mexican Americans apparently fail to take advantage of the schools, and vice versa. What are the reasons for their evident low academic achievement and poor participation in school? Why have the schools failed to acculturate and assimilate this group? All aspects of Mexican Americans' interaction with the schools seem to be slowly improving (although only teachers' observations support improving levels of achievement), but why does their position relative to other ethnic groups remain unchanged? The situation pleads for explanation.

TROY

Chapter 2:
Failure of the Culture

The vast majority of educators interviewed for this study and most of the relevant literature argue that Mexican American children are culturally deprived or disadvantaged, that their home environment does not provide the skills, personality characteristics, or experiences necessary for a child's success in school. This view provides most schoolmen with plausible explanation for the failure of Mexican Americans in school. Many school officials accept some part of the responsibility, however, saying that given the disadvantaged condition of so many minority-group children, the school has indeed been negligent in its efforts to overcome the influence of the home. Some see the school as remiss in not providing substitute experiences, remedial programs, or skill-building activities in order to make over Mexican American children into facsimiles of the middle-class children with whom the school sees itself as successful. This chapter explores the concept of cultural deprivation; Chapter 5 describes the numerous types of school programs designed to compensate for the initial disadvantage of birth into a Mexican American family.

A small but significant and increasingly vocal group of educators, social scientists, and school critics contend that while the Mexican American child may well be culturally different, difference does not imply deficiency. They argue that many contributory causes of failure are to be found within the school itself. The two following chapters examine this view. It has seemed appropriate for the purpose of this book to separate discussion of the influences of the culture and of the school, in order to minimize repetition and enhance clarity. In reality of course the home culture, the personality of the child it produces, the practices and policies of educational institutions, and the nature of the community are a complex intertwining of causes and effects. A few educators recognize this complex interrelationship and attempt to give attention to all factors in combination, promoting programs to deal with cultural difference as well as to overcome the inadequacies and injustices of present school practices and policies. Unfortunately, all too many activities intended to rectify the situation have overly simplistic rationales.

THE THEORY OF CULTURAL DEPRIVATION

Explicit in the concept that some children are culturally deprived is the idea that certain nurturing cultures do not provide the necessary influences to make children successful in school or acceptable in the majority society. The concept implies that the principal role of the school is to act as the first of a chain of influences that cause disadvantaged children to accept middle-class culture—that is, the school's function in society is to reeducate the culturally distinct, both the poor and the foreign. Also implicit in this concept is the assumption that the school is essentially satisfactory as it now exists, and that it is a valid representation of American culture.

Most of the authors of contemporary literature on this subject and certainly most of the school people interviewed in the course of this study would agree with the following definitions (Johnson, 1966, p. 9): "'The disadvantaged is anyone who cannot participate in the dominant culture.' Another definition is 'one who is handicapped in the task of growing up to live a competent and satisfying life in American society.' A definition from the viewpoint of the teacher is 'the child who has difficulty achieving in school because of his background.'" In other words, the disadvantaged child—or the "deprived" child—is one whose home background and experiential base are substantially different from those of the middle-class child. The strong implication is that these differences are the prime cause of the disadvantaged child's lack of success in school.

In order to determine the "causative differences or deficiencies" of disadvantaged children, researchers have used what practically amount to mathematical formulas. Many studies have been conducted of lower-class, poverty, or Mexican American homes and children. The conclusions of these studies, while sometimes confusing and contradictory, provide a generalized description of Mexican American life-style and personality characteristics. (For competent surveys of the pertinent research see Bloom, Davis, and Hess, 1965; Gordon and Wilkerson, 1966.) This generalized description can then be subtracted from an equally generalized (but more widely researched) description of the middle class and the personality characteristics of its children. The differences are the "lacks" of the disadvantaged child—by implication, those failings of home and neighborhood socialization that the school must change, remedy, or eradicate.

These manipulations provide the basis for school action "to meet the needs" of disadvantaged children—that is, to make them like other "successful" (that is, middle-class) children. Reissman (1962, pp. 4–5) lists the conventional reasons given for school failure of underprivileged children as these: ". . . lack of an 'educational tradition' in the home, few books, etc. Insufficient language and reading skills. . . . Inadequate motivation to pursue a long-range educational career and poor estimate of self. Antagonism toward the school, the teacher. Poor health, improper diet, frequent moving, and noisy, TV-ridden homes." These are the differences noted after the educational subtraction described above has taken place.

Implicit in the concept that there are disadvantaged cultures, and in the statements of many of its adherents, is a derogation of the poor and foreign and their life-styles that is suggestive of racism. The implied argument that a child's failure in school or society is due to deplorable conditions, and that cultural difference equals deficiency, is not shared by all who use the argument as a base for action. Some educators vehemently deny any derogatory implications and argue that Mexican Americans are "equal" to middle-class Americans but that they are "different." These educators do not see the Mexican American home environment as lacking in significant experiences but contend that although Mexican American cultural traits may be desirable within the subgroup, they are inadequate for success in school or the dominant society. This kind of educator also usually wants to reeducate disadvantaged children.

The rest of this chapter is devoted to a description of the Mexican American home culture and the children it rears.

MEXICAN AMERICAN CULTURE

Few Anglo educators have been intimately exposed to Mexican American society and culture. While most of those interviewed for this study have dealt with Mexican American children for much of their careers, few speak Spanish and fewer still have firsthand, reliable information about the culture they are dealing with. Only the rare individual has the training, experience, or insight to enable him to interpret Mexican American behavior correctly. Yet, with few exceptions, educators have a rather clear idea of what the Mexican American is all about. What are the origins of this knowledge? A number of sources exist: Anglo society has developed quite clear stereotypes of the Mexican American. Although most educators decry adherence to such stereotypes, a strong case can be made that their perceptions are strongly influenced by them (see Simmons, 1961; Parsons, 1965). Having in mind a set of preconceived ideas concerning the "group personality," it is an unusual educator who does not find his expectations confirmed by his observations of Mexican American behavior. The stereotype strongly influences his analysis of the group and acts as a selector of observed behavior. He tends to remember or "see" those aspects of behavior that correspond with his belief pattern. The stereotype may also be confirmed and reinforced by his Mexican American acquaintances, who are likely to be in the group known as "good" or "high type" Mexicans. Many of these upwardly mobile Mexican Americans may well hold an equally stereotypic view of the lower-status group.

The most valid sources of information are studies of Mexican American communities, values, life-styles, and customs. Many such studies stress cultural differences rather than similarities. Many are dated, or are descriptive of very localized, often rural, situations. Unfortunately, such information is regularly assumed to be correctly descriptive of Mexican American culture in general. Another common assumption is that Mexican American personality and culture are similar to those of other minorities. The numerous studies of Negroes, Puerto Ricans, and poverty subcultures contribute to the educator's perception of Mexican Americans. Educators combining local stereotypes, descriptions of culture, value comparisons, and information on other minorities produce a rather precise picture. It is evident that the Mexican American culture shown in this picture is part myth and part fact, part stereotype and part reality. In a sense, the separation of myth and reality is unimportant for the purposes of this book. What is crucial is to understand that the authors of most of the literature in the field, and certainly the vast majority of educators, hold that the Mexican American culture is monolithic and constant throughout the diverse areas of the Southwest. Regardless of whether their description is valid or not, the significant factor is that most teachers and administrators describe the Mexican American home, culture, and child in the same specific, usually stereotypic, ways.

The "Folk-Culture" Concept. The Mexican American child is almost universally pictured as the product of a rural folk culture. This life-style is carefully described in numerous articles and is presented as gospel in teacher-education texts. There may be a certain amount of truth in these descriptions, especially in their treatment of certain isolated communities; however, their constant reiteration results in almost complete acceptance by school people. What may once have been a valid description of Mexican or Mexican American culture is becoming universally accepted as descriptive of the current culture. Contemporary Mexican American culture varies greatly with geographic area. It is strongly influenced by the social environment created by the dominant society and is modified also by the historical experience of distinct groups. Urbanization has caused much culture change. Yet the "folk-culture myth" persists. The older model almost universally serves as reality to most educators.

As is true in all human groups, the Mexican American family establishes basic patterns of behavior and personality. A patriarchal "folk" family is almost invariably described in teacher-education texts. Authors from the 1920s to the present, with a few notable exceptions, picture most Mexican American families as "under the firm authority of the father, while the mother assumes the traditional subservient and severely proscribed role of homemaker, model of purity, bearer and trainer of children" (Hayden, 1966, p. 20). A recently published teacher-education text, especially geared to inservice education, continues the theme: "Most Mexican American families are a tight patriarchal structure. The father has all the authority, although the mother is the center of the family. When the father dies, the eldest male child inherits the father's authority over the immediate family" (Johnson, 1966, p. 5). Educators interviewed for this study almost invariably saw the Mexican American family authority structure in such terms.

In addition to having a tight patriarchal structure, the family is usually characterized as including "not only members of the immediate family—parents and their children—but also grandparents, aunts, uncles, and *compadres*" (Johnson, 1966). In contrast to the average American family, which includes only immediate relatives, the Mexican American family is described as extended. Formal kin reside in the home or are closely tied to the immediate family. Informal kinship relationships are seen to be regularly established between one family and others—*compadre* (godparent) relationships unite individuals and families.

Children in the "folkish" family are usually described as learning their social roles early. Most educators see boys as being strongly influenced by the *macho* (male) role of the father and other male relatives. This role is seen as particularly influential (Johnson, 1966, p. 5): "The Mexican-American family structure very clearly provides the outlines for the roles of female and male members. Thus, Mexican-American children rarely have any doubts about their role. A boy is nurtured on the idea that he is developing into a man, and this means he is *macho* and must behave *a lo macho* (to be male) or *ser muy hombre* (very much a man). In other words, boys are encouraged from birth to develop those qualities that are clearly masculine. This accounts for the *bravado* in so many young Mexican American males, the need to defend honor, the urge to establish a masculine image before girls, etc. Mexican Americans have a word for this: *machismo*. This clear understanding of identity and the role of the male may also explain why so many female teachers have trouble disciplining Mexican American boys. It may also partly explain why so many Mexican-American boys drop out of school early; a boy is *macho* if he is working, earning money, and standing on his own two feet."

Machismo ("maleism") is a regularly used term by most Spanish-speaking peoples. Its interpretation is difficult; most contend it implies "Don Juanism" and masculine assertiveness. Professor George I. Sánchez of The University of Texas concurs that it may have such overtones but contends it is best understood by the American word "guts." *El es muy macho* would usually mean "he's got guts." To many educators, the *machismo* concept becomes a plausible explanation for diverse male adolescent behavior. Skipping school, liking girls, disliking school, being impudent, and getting bad grades were explained by some of the informants for this study as attributable to *machismo*. Indeed, it is probably valid to say that *machismo* is a characteristic of certain Mexican American populations. Unfortunately many, if not most, educators ascribe this cultural characteristic to the group in general. However, the exact meaning of the term appears to vary greatly by area and by individual, as indicated by its use to explain diverse behavior in the quotation above.

According to much of the literature and to most interviewees, the social role of the Mexican American girl is patterned after the "submissive mother": "Mexican-American girls learn their role early in life also. Essentially the role of the Mexican-American female is to perform all the duties that maintain the family: take care of the children, cook, clean, and perform all the other countless duties to keep the family going. In performing these duties, the female is always subservient to the male head of the family" (Johnson, 1966). Girls are perceived as being taught to be submissive and responsible. As with *machismo* it is extremely doubtful that such roles and role learning characterize all, or even most, contemporary Mexican American homes. Teachers seem to think that they do, however. It is interesting to conjecture that such female roles adhere rather closely to the picture of the ideal American woman as held by many conservative or traditional teachers.

The authors cited above, as well as most others, caution that the minority family is changing and that roles may no longer be firmly fixed. But the distinctive roles of the father, mother, and children are perceived by most school people interviewed for this study as being identical or very similar to the generalizations of the traditional "folk" family described.

Values. Schoolmen tend to perceive the world views and value orientations of Mexican Americans as being similar to traditional folk culture. As with their view of family authority structure and roles, their ideas about cultural orientations are strongly flavored by local operating stereotypes. Unfortunately the exceedingly limited hard evidence often tends to support these stereotypes also. Social scientists and others who have investigated orientations usually concur that children of Mexican American sociocultural background are prone to do the following (Zintz, 1963, quotations from pp. 200–202): (1) Devalue formal education, especially for girls. (2) See success more in terms of interpersonal relationships than in terms of material acquisition. (3) See "time as a gift of life to be enjoyed to the fullest—and to be enjoyed to the fullest it must not be postponed." The Anglo concept of wasting time is not understood. (4) Be fatalistic, feeling they have little control over their natural or social environment: *lo que será será*—what will be, will be. Man's fate is seen to be in the hands of God, luck, or some other unseen force. (5) See change as unappealing and not motivating: "We may follow the old ways with confidence." (6) Be submissive to the status quo, patient, conformist, and perhaps apathetic. (7) See work only to satisfy present need. The Protestant work ethic is not accepted. The "work a little, rest a little" concept contributes to a low level of aspiration. "Be satisfied to follow in father's footsteps." (8) Attach little importance to time schedules and the Anglo concept of punctuality. "The expression for the clock runs translated from Spanish is the clock walks. It has been said that this explains the *mañana* attitude. . . ." (Actually, the Spanish word *andar* means "run" in the mechanical sense, as well as "walk" in the normal sense.) (9) Attach much importance to nonscientific explanation of natural phenomena (sickness and so forth).

For additional information on the folk culture concept, see: Burma (1954), Campa (1962), Clark (1959), Heller (1966), Sister Mary Immaculate (1959), Madsen (1964), McDonagh (1949), Sister Francesca McGarry (1957), Sánchez (1940), Valdez (1961, 1962). As mentioned, these sources may validly describe a local situation, but unfortunately most educators see them as describing Mexican Americans in general.

The "folk" orientations described above are seen as being contrary to the Anglo's desire to master natural forces, be punctual, work hard for future success, postpone present gratification for a future reward, practice thrift, and so forth. Since these values are expected, if not demanded, by the school, different value orientations are seen to be detrimental to success.

Two Mexican American value orientations are seen by many schoolmen as being particularly disadvantageous. One is the Mexican American orientation toward time, especially in regard to punctuality. Children must conform to the school's "well-run-ship" policies. The *mañana* attitude must be modified if the child is to fit in with the demands of school and society. The other value orientation that concerns teachers is fatalism. In their view, Mexican American children place too much emphasis on unseen forces instead of stressing the individual's ability to control his own environment as well as his own fate.

There is some current empirical evidence that bears on these life orientations. This author studied ninth graders in a semirural and castelike agricultural area of California. About two-thirds of the 288 high school freshmen studied were Mexican Americans. About 90 percent of the Mexican American children were from low-social-class homes; the majority of their fathers were nonmigrant agricultural workers. The Anglos were quite normally distributed in social class and fathers' occupations. The students responded to a number of written statements. Items that gave information on fatalism involved future planning. Fifty-five percent of the Mexican Americans, as contrasted with 22 percent of the Anglos, agreed that "planning ahead makes a person unhappy, since plans hardly ever work out." Approximately 19 percent of each group were undecided; 4 percent did not respond. Given the statement "The best thing to do is live for today and let tomorrow take care of itself," 41 percent of the Mexican American group and 25 percent of the majority group agreed, 16 percent of Mexican Americans and 11 percent of Anglos were undecided, and the rest did not respond. These two items tend to support the notion that the minority-group youngsters studied were primarily concerned with the present and that planning ahead is not seen by them as useful, apparently because of intervening and uncontrollable forces. Whether such orientations are attributable to "Mexicanness" or lower-class "culture" is unknown. The school staff was also interviewed.

About 90 percent of the teachers contended that fatalistic attitudes characterized the vast majority of their Mexican American students, but in no case did the "vast majority" of Mexican Americans studied respond in ways indicative of fatalism.

In the Los Angeles School Study researchers asked their samples of sixth-, ninth-, and twelfth-grade students to react to three statements relative to their expectations of the future (Wenkert, 1966, p. 108). These statements were: "People should not expect too much out of life so they won't be disappointed." "Planning only makes a person unhappy since your plans hardly ever work out anyway." and "The wise person lives for today and lets tomorrow take care of itself." In this study the children were separated into socioeconomic categories on the basis of father's occupation. At each grade level, and within each socioeconomic group, "a higher percentage of Mexican American than Anglo students agreed" with the statements. "In sum, Mexican American students tend to be less optimistic about their future, and about life in general, than Anglo students."

In the recent research of Coleman *et al.* (1966), three questionnaire items were assumed to measure twelfth graders' perceived ability to control their environment. These items tested to what degree the individual "feels that his environment is capricious, or random or beyond his ability to alter" (p. 288). The percentages of response, comparing "white" (Anglo) youth to the Mexican American sample are reported in the first part of Table 7. The response to all three items indicates that a slightly larger percentage of Mexican Americans do perceive their environments as less controllable than do their Anglo counterparts. As the researchers point out, high percentages of agreement on these items in the Mexican American group may reflect their correct interpretation of reality. Indeed, minority groups and the poor do not have the same control over their lives that is exercised by the majority. Whether this characteristic is attributable to ethnic or minority status, or to low socioeconomic class, is an intriguing question. However, the responses certainly do not indicate that Mexican Americans, as a group, are "fatalistic." If anything, they indicate that a small percentage of both ethnic groups are. They also indicate that Mexican Americans are more undecided, as well as that Mexican Americans who make it to the twelfth grade are very similar to Anglos. The "traditional" or lower-class minority-group member is all too often a school casualty long before his senior year.

TABLE 7: Twelfth-Grade Responses to Questions on Control of Environment and Self-Concept (in Percent)

CONTROL OF ENVIRONMENT	*Agree*		*Not sure*		*Disagree*		*No response*	
	A*	MA*	A	MA	A	MA	A	MA
Good luck is more important than hard work for success	4	11	5	12	87	68	4	9
Everytime I try to get ahead, something or somebody stops me	13	23	20	22	63	46	4	10
People like me don't have much of a chance to be successful in life	4	12	11	19	80	59	5	11

SELF-CONCEPT (OF ABILITY)	*Agree*		*Not sure*		*Disagree*		*No response*	
	A	MA	A	MA	A	MA	A	MA
I sometimes feel that I just can't learn	39	38	13	18	44	33	5	11
I would do better in schoolwork if teachers didn't go so fast	25	28	24	25	47	37	5	11

Source: Coleman *et al.* (1966, Tables 3.13.12; 3.13.13; 3.13.14; 3.13.15; 3.13.16).
*A: Anglo (white) in Southwest metropolitan areas. Southwest in Coleman's study includes Oklahoma, Texas, New Mexico, and Arizona. Metropolitan is used by Coleman as defined by the United States Census. MA: Mexican American total Coleman report sample.

To test the validity of the hypothesis that Mexican Americans adhere to traditional "folk values," Romero devised a value-orientation instrument and administered it to 348 secondary school students in Colorado and northern New Mexico (1966, pp. 47–50). His sample included approximately equal numbers of Spanish-surname and Anglo youths and was administered in both rural and urban areas. Testing the degree of adherence to "traditional Spanish" and dominant American values, in essence the degree and nature of acculturation, he concluded that the two groups were very similar. No significant difference between Mexican American and Anglo acceptance of the dominant American value system was evident. The fact that the two ethnic groups in Romero's study were similar in these aspects opposes educators' arguments. If such children generally subscribe to "American values," the argument that the traditional value system impairs school motivation is open to question. It also points up the possibility of wide variation of value orientation among Mexican Americans in the Southwest.

Romero also studied teachers' knowledge of sociocultural differences between the two groups. Teachers indeed had a knowledge of the stereotype of Mexican American (Spanish-American) culture. The results of his "teacher awareness scale" were that there exists ". . . a general teacher sensitivity to, and awareness of, socio-cultural differences of the two ethnic groups, namely, the Spanish-American and Anglo. This teacher awareness of socio-cultural differences could very well be superficial and not based on real knowledge of what constitutes a culture value system. In addition, cultural sensitivity may result from attitudes formed from operating stereotypes. Under these conditions a lack of *real* sensitivity could, in fact, exist" (Colorado State Department of Education, 1966). (See also Ulibarri, 1958.)

This summary statement was clearly corroborated by interviewing in the field for this study. Schoolmen do have a superficial picture of the value orientations of Mexican Americans. The stereotype was repeated throughout the widely diverse Southwest; little recognition of the diversity of the ethnic group was evident. The purpose of this study is not to question the validity of descriptive statements or empirical studies but to indicate that generalizations have instilled in the minds of most educators a picture of a typical Mexican American and a stereotype of a homogeneous folk culture. The product of this culture is usually seen by educators as a "standard ethnic child," almost predetermined to failure in school and ultimately in general society. As one California junior high school principal put it: "The very nature of their culture, their present time orientation, their fatalistic attitude, being part of the total Latin culture, almost prohibit their accepting the long-term rewards of the secondary schools."

MEXICAN AMERICAN CHILDREN

According to the adherents of the concept of cultural deprivation, most Mexican American children, through no fault of their own, are nurtured in sociocultural circumstances that fail to prepare them for success in school and society. This nurturing leads many educators to ascribe numerous characteristics to Mexican American children, most of which are seen as deficiencies that are in dire need of remediation.

Health and Nutrition. The concept of personal cleanliness and hygiene, with its multitude of moral corollaries, is deeply ingrained in Anglo middle-class culture. No wonder being dirty is seen by many educators as a principal failing of Mexican American children. Attempts to encourage acceptance of American "cleanliness" have, perhaps, expended more teacher energy in the Southwest than any other single educational effort, with the possible exception of language teaching. Descriptions of Mexican American health and sanitary conditions represent a significant part of early literature on Mexican Americans, as beautifully exemplified by this quotation: "The personal hygiene of these people is deplorable. Many do not have the facilities for cleanliness of the body, but if they did, the majority would still be dirty. They believe bathing will make them sick. The lack of personal cleanliness accounts for the many skin diseases for which these people are noted. When girls reach adolescent age, they try to cover up this dirt with paint, rouge, lipstick, and brilliant fingernail polish. The boys at this age clean up a little and take on a chic appearance, but all refuse to take a bath except on Saturday night, and then it is not a very thorough one" (Carpenter, 1935, p. 41).

"Dirty Mexican kids" are not the problem today they once were. Yet the bugaboo of dirtiness prevails in the minds of many teachers and administrators. Needless to mention, health conditions, disease, and contagion do present real problems. In most areas where Mexican American income is relatively high, obvious health problems are disappearing. In economically depressed areas, which usually have less acculturated populations, problems persist. In areas of extreme poverty, especially among migrants, the school correctly recognizes the need for improvement.

Cultural differences are clearly recognized as principal factors in the area of health and nutrition. Many school people perceive the Mexican American lack of cleanliness and hygiene as due to superstitions and the nonscientific nature of the explanations of natural phenomena that are assumed to be characteristic of the minority culture. Whether in reality superstitions and folk-medicine concepts are held in any local population would have to be determined by objective study in each community. Since most educators are neither equipped for, nor interested in, testing their perceptions of "folk culture," such studies are not likely ever to be undertaken, and the beliefs of most schoolmen will probably persevere long after any such Mexican American practices and beliefs disappear.

The failure to eat "a good breakfast" is deemed another great deficiency. Here, culture is not so much the culprit as is poverty. However, it is interesting to note that having an "American breakfast" is almost as close to being a core value of the dominant group as is cleanliness: "How can you expect these children to do well in school if they have a *tortilla* and coffee for breakfast?" Malnutrition exists and is a real factor in school attentiveness, but a serious question must be raised about the effect of a "Mexican breakfast" on an otherwise adequately nourished child. Some teachers see failure to have a large "American breakfast" as being an apparently sufficient explanation for classroom inattention and academic failure.

Intellectual Capacity. Lower innate intelligence is generally no longer ascribed to Mexican American children. Although IQ scores may be low, most schoolmen explain this phenomenon in terms of environmental factors, or the inadequacy of available psychometric instruments, or both. Nevertheless, the long history of belief in genetically determined lower intelligence still finds adherents. As one California principal stated, "Given time and library resources, it would be possible to make a strong case that racially these people are inferior."

Three principal types of evidence are seen as supporting low intellectual ability: (1) The results of widespread testing. (For a summary of relevant considerations for professionals using standardized tests with minority children see Fishman *et al.*, 1964.) (2) The disproportionate percentage of Mexican Americans in "slow" and mentally retarded classes. (3) The obvious failure of Mexican Americans to achieve in school. Confusion over the nature of IQ is as understandable as it is widespread. Many educators still consider IQ to mean innate capacity or potential—a constant, not varying significantly over time. Most modern information on the subject, however, contends that it is a "construct" that does not measure innate potential. At best, IQ is now seen as an accurate predictor of school success, measuring the type of learning expected by the institution and demanded for academic success.

A common reason offered to explain low group IQ, and the disproportionate number of Mexican American children placed in "slow" tracks or in special classes, is the inadequacy of psychometric instruments. Wolman (1962, pp. 454–455) says that culturally different children have: ". . . considerable difficulty in answering test items correctly. Many of the test items include vocabulary or situations unknown to them. This would be particularly true of children who come from homes of very low socioeconomic status, where no English or only little English is spoken, and where the cultural heritage is entirely different from the majority group." The vast majority of school people would agree. A significant minority argues that the tests adequately assess innate intellectual potential and that Mexican Americans are correctly placed in "slow" classes, an argument that supports the genetic determinist position.

Bilingualism. While teachers' perceptions of Mexican American children's lack of cleanliness and genetically determined mental inferiority are slowly changing, other images of deficiency are widely held. Most prevalent among these is the concept that bilingualism is detrimental to intellectual functioning and thus to success in school. Until recently, research tended to support this theory. Peal and Lambert reported from their search of the literature (1962, p. 1): "A large proportion of the investigators have concluded from their studies that bilingualism has a detrimental effect on intellectual functioning. The bilingual child is described as being hampered in his performance on intellectual tests in comparison with the monolingual child. A smaller proportion of the investigators found little or no influence of bilingualism on intelligence in that no significant difference between bilinguals and monolinguals on tests of intelligence was apparent." Many studies appear to be methodologically inadequate. Many are inconclusive—for example, a study conducted with Spanish-speaking people in Arizona (Arizona State University, 1960). No significant relationship was demonstrated between intellectual functioning and bilingualism, but significant relationships were found between sociocultural factors, school success, and test performance. The methodologically sound Arizona Study and its findings add credence to the idea that many other studies of bilingualism fail to control social factors adequately and, all too often, report differences between high-socioeconomic-status monolinguals and low-status bilinguals.

Perhaps the best-controlled study of bilingualism currently available is Peal and Lambert's (1962). After widespread testing with careful control for sociocultural factors, they concluded (p. 22): "The effects of bilingualism on intellectual functioning are explored in this study. A group of monolingual and a group of bilingual ten year old children from six Montreal French schools were administered verbal and non-verbal intelligence tests. . . . Contrary to the previous findings, this study found that bilinguals perform significantly better than monolinguals on both verbal and non-verbal intelligence tests. Several explanations are suggested as to why bilinguals have this general intellectual advantage. It is argued that they have a language asset, are more facile at concept formation, and have a greater mental flexibility. The results of factor analysis applied to the data supported the hypotheses that the structures of intellect for the two groups differ. The bilinguals appear to have a more diversified set of mental abilities than the monolinguals." (For additional summations of research on bilingualism and the Mexican American see Colorado State Department of Education, 1967. See also Jones, 1960, pp. 71–77; MacNamara, 1967; Tireman, 1941.)

The purpose of this study is not to examine the validity of bilingualism studies or to make an additional comprehensive study of the literature, but only to point out that confusion exists. Although current empirical evidence seems to argue against the idea that bilinguals have lower mental functioning, the majority of school people interviewed subscribe to the idea.

Most older teachers see bilingualism as a liability, and as a source of mental confusion, perhaps reflecting the fact that they were trained when the idea was more widely accepted. Most of these same teachers argue on the other hand that it is an asset to speak two languages in adulthood, a sign of a "cultured person." A strong suspicion exists that the argument about mental confusion originates in teachers' own difficulty in learning a foreign language in school or college. As one teacher interviewed for this study contended, "It is confusing because one has to translate one language into another." Another said, "You have to think in two languages and translate from one to the other." Traditional foreign language learning for them probably posed such difficulties. They assume similar processes and problems for young children.

Another interesting, although not common, view is that a child has to relearn every concept while learning a new language. A Texas school librarian said that if she were to learn Spanish, she would have to relearn the Dewey Decimal System. This kind of notion may provide the justification for a program designed for monolingual speakers of Spanish newly arrived from Mexico. One Texas school system places such children, regardless of their age or level of schooling in Mexico, in segregated second-grade classes with the regular primary curriculum, plus special English instruction. It is interesting to note that this district was the only one in which the interviewees for this study contended that immigrant Mexican children did not achieve as well, or better, than average Mexican American children.

Regardless of the reasoning, bilingualism is still deemed a mentally confusing liability by many, if not the majority, of the teachers and school administrators interviewed. Sánchez comments in reference to this point (1966, p. 15): "Still I was amazed at the persistence of the assertion that bilingualism is bad, that a foreign home language is a handicap, that somehow children with Spanish as a mother tongue were doomed to failure—in fact, that they were *ipso facto* less than normally intelligent."

Language Ability. Another point of view relative to the "language problem" is the widely held belief that many Mexican American children are essentially alingual, not truly speaking any language. Whether they are monolingual in Spanish or English, or bilingual, language ability is considered deficient. Research on the language patterns and usage of children who come from low-status homes and are English monolinguals at school entrance may be pertinent (see Bernstein, 1961; 1962). There is little doubt that the language spoken in low-status Mexican American homes, whether it is Spanish or English, is indeed different from that spoken by "educated" people. However, rarely do studies of social class and language usage take the stance that many educators do—that is, that language difference is language deficiency. Rather, such studies describe the situation. Schoolmen imply that the "language problem" is a prime determinant of school failure, instead of recognizing that school practices demanding standard (middle-class) English ability are at least partially responsible. As one authority argues, the child has no language problem, the school does—that is, it expects, if not demands, rapid language growth from a base that often is quite different from that of the average middle-class child.

Some teachers stated that some children had a problem not so much because they spoke Spanish as because they spoke no language at all at home—that is, that they were truly nonverbal and alingual. A California education executive stated in referring to the Mexican American child, "They have minimal communication in two languages." This condition was deemed proven by the fact that many young Mexican American children did not talk in school. In one case, preschool children were reported to respond with a simple yes or no to questions addressed to them in either language by teachers. After such comments were heard in the course of this study, an effort was always made to observe the children concerned at free play: they were invariably noisily verbal in Spanish, English, or some combination of the two.

Many interviewees regard Mexican American Spanish as deficient: "The language spoken at home is *pocho,* 'Tex-Mex,' or 'wetback Spanish,' really nonstandard dialects." Such comments as these were commonly encountered: "Their Spanish is of such an inferior quality that it does not warrant classification as a language." "The child's Spanish provides a meager base for future learning in even that language." No

Anglo speaker of Spanish made this kind of comment. Many Mexican American teachers saw the local Spanish as grossly inferior; English monolinguals tended to agree. These patterns lead one to assume that most interviewees are influenced by prevailing stereotypes. However, of particular interest is the Anglo Spanish speakers' response: perhaps these individuals have freed themselves from such influence and are judging the quality of locally spoken Spanish on a more factual basis than are either the Mexican American or the monolingual Anglos. While arguments continue about the nature and quality of the Spanish spoken in the Southwest, it is interesting to note that an inferior status is usually ascribed to the local vernacular. Opinions concerning the language of others are usually full of judgments reflecting the education and social status of the evaluator. A serious research study of the Spanish spoken in different geographic regions or by Mexican Americans in different social levels would undoubtedly conclude that differences exist. The researcher, unless he had a vested interest in "proper Spanish," would only describe and analyze the differences, but the layman, and many educators, assume that difference is deficiency.

The home language of Mexican American children, and the experience on which it depends, are almost invariably perceived as detrimental to school success. Bilingualism, lack of verbal experience in any language, inferiority of the local Spanish, or a combination of these factors are seen as predetermining school problems. Needless to say the inability to communicate in English initially discourages school achievement and grade promotion. However, where bilingual organization, English-as-a-second-language programs, or flexible curricular policies exist there need be no or only slight disadvantage to the child. It can be strongly argued that speaking two or more languages enhances achievement and learning.

Negative Self-Concept. Self-derogation is seen by most schoolmen as being characteristic of a disproportionate percentage of Mexican American children, especially adolescents. Self-concept usually implies the internalization by the individual of the expectations, values, or opinions of persons significant to him—"significant others." As social scientists delve into and measure personality characteristics, they see a relationship between self-concept and school achievement. It is difficult to determine which is cause and which is effect.

Does school failure cause the negative self-concept or vice versa? At any rate, the factor is of great interest to educators.

There is little doubt that self-concept of ability can functionally limit a child's ability to achieve: ". . . for the expectations of others to be functional in a particular individual's behavior, they must be internalized and become a part of the person's conception of himself. . . . If the child perceives that he is unable to learn mathematics or some other area of behavior, this self-concept of his ability becomes the functionally limiting factor of his school achievement" (Brookover and Gottlieb, 1964, p. 469). For example, it can be assumed that failing a subject, if he values it highly, and the judgments of the teacher, could make a child internalize his failure and thus limit his future success in that subject.

The study by Coleman and his associates (1966) reported on the self-concept of ability of Mexican American twelfth graders. Two of their questionnaire items are of particular relevance. These are not specifically related to a particular academic activity; they report on general self-perceived ability to learn. Table 7 on page 45 shows the percentages of agreement and disagreement of Anglo and Mexican American respondents. The response percentages in all categories are quite similar for both ethnic groups. However, in response to both statements, Mexican Americans appear slightly more self-depreciating as well as more undecided or give no response.

In another of Coleman's items, twelfth graders were asked to indicate "how bright they think they are in comparison with other students in the same grade." In response to this, 8 percent of the Mexican Americans and 13 percent of the Anglos perceived themselves to be "among the brightest," 22 percent of the Mexican Americans and 38 percent of the Anglos saw themselves as "above average," and 53 percent of the minority group and 45 percent of the majority saw themselves as "average." Ten percent of the Mexican Americans and 3 percent of the Anglos saw themselves as falling below average. While fewer Mexican Americans than Anglos perceived themselves in the "bright" category, the difference in percentages was not great, nor was it substantially out of balance in the other direction (Coleman *et al.*, 1966, p. 287). Whether this item measures self-concept of ability to the degree of the other two statements is questionable. It is perfectly possible for a student to say that he is of average ability and perhaps mean only that he receives C grades. These twelfth graders were possibly referring to school success as measured by grades. To what degree sixth and ninth graders would respond similarly is unknown.

Educators interviewed generally saw a much more diffuse negative self-concept as characteristic of an excessive percentage of Mexican American children. The logic of their arguments proceeds in this manner: "Growing up in a family that has inherited the cycles of poverty, living in an environment that includes failure, being rejected by society, and being confronted with his own inadequacies in the school—in other words, possessing all the 'bad things' of our society—the disadvantaged pupil learns to look upon himself with contempt. Furthermore, his negative attitude of himself is continually reinforced" (Johnson, 1966, p. 10). Mexican American poor, like other disadvantaged groups, are seen to internalize the dominant society's perception: "Many Mexican-American students are aware of the stigma of second class citizenship. Early in their development, they have realized the role assigned to them by many members of the Anglo-American society, and feeling the discrimination, have reacted with a mechanism behavioral scientists call ethnic self-hatred. This complex or characteristic shows itself in the youngsters assigning to themselves the inferior position given to them by the dominant society" (Hernandez, 1967). Hernandez sees the outcome of negative self-view as being aggressive behavior, a position regularly taken by educational practitioners.

The cultural marginality of many Mexican Americans contributes to problems of self-identity and causes more than normal self-derogation. DeLeon (1959) argues that: ". . . the partial disintegration of the parent culture and the fact he has been taught, through social pressure, to be ashamed of, and even to disown his ethnic ancestry, has made the Mexican-American a victim of confusion, frustration, and insecurity." No careful observer would deny the marginality of many Mexican American children (see Madsen, 1964; Ramirez, 1967a). Surely school curriculums and practices do affect how children see themselves, as well as what they think of education and school personnel (see Chapter 4 of this book). However, hard data in this area are lacking.

The majority of the people who gave information for this study believed that a high percentage of Mexican Americans suffer from an almost debilitating, generally negative self-view. It is necessary to suggest that many Mexican Americans may not think of members of the dominant society as "significant others" and may disregard the opinions of teachers, principals, policemen, and so forth. They may internalize instead the views of "significant others" from within their own adult or peer society. Relative to this point I administered a semantic differential questionnaire to 190 Mexican American and 98 Anglo high school freshmen, asking them to give their opinions of their own intelligence, power, goodness, and happiness. The distribution of responses of the two groups was almost identical: the majority of the Mexican American children appeared to be doing a magnificent job of maintaining a positive view of themselves against the onslaught of the beliefs of the Anglo and the judgment of the school (Carter, 1968).

To many schoolmen, the Mexican American negative self-concept provides plausible explanation for all kinds of behavior. Interviewees for this study were asked how they knew that minority-group members perceive themselves negatively. The reasons given were that Mexican Americans have low educational and occupational aspirations, speak English poorly, don't get along well with teachers, fear authority, lack ambition, are poor, have few positive role models at home, "overrespect" authority, and receive poor grades in school. According to the educators interviewed, the home contributes to the child's negative self-perception. Parents see themselves negatively also, as shown in various ways: they are dominated by Anglos at the PTA, they are ashamed of their living conditions (they won't answer the door when a school official makes a home call), they use poor English, and they are poor or lower class. These, and other examples of assumed manifestations of negative self-concept given by schoolmen, may well be misinterpretations of Mexican Americans' behavior.

As is the case with so many other aspects of educators' perceptions of Mexican American children, factual information is scarce: whether large numbers of the group's children suffer from self-devaluation or not, has not yet been determined. Yet the belief that they see themselves negatively is almost universal, and those who believe it usually use patronizing or pitying tones when they are describing this condition. It is possible that the belief may not be based solely on Anglo misinterpretation of behavior but may stem from a somewhat questionable assumption: middle-class people tend to assume that anyone who is poor sees himself as a failure and therefore sees himself negatively. Educators may make a similar assumption, seeing Mexican Americans as failures and assuming that they see themselves in similar manner.

Apathy. Mexican American children are characterized by most of the school practitioners interviewed for this study as apathetic and noncompetitive. The regular activities of the school, including extracurricular activities, do not involve most Mexican American youngsters. For explanation, many rely on their picture of the Mexican American home, as described earlier. Docility, apathy, and self-satisfaction with one's role in life are seen to have deep roots. The belief is widespread that years of servitude and subjugation have produced a people who have essentially given up. According to an early author: "The Mexicans, as a group, lack ambition. The peon of Mexico has spent so many generations in a condition of servitude that a lazy acceptance of his lot has become a racial characteristic" (Graeber, 1938, p. 97). The almost universal acceptance of the folk-culture concept, with its fatalism and orientation toward the present, provides additional support for the alleged apathy.

In school, apathy is seen to manifest itself in "poor motivation." Educational jargon is sometimes difficult to translate; however, these words appear to mean that the child: (1) doesn't desire to learn, isn't interested in school, doesn't do well in school, doesn't work up to ability; (2) has low educational aspirations; (3) is unable to perceive grades, promotion, or other school rewards as socially significant; and (4) is unable to postpone reward until completion of school. A whole syndrome of behavior is subsumed in "poor motivation." Perhaps it is best to conclude that anyone who doesn't do well in school may be said to be poorly motivated.

The inability of Mexican American children to find reward within school is part of this problem. School is assumed to be a rewarding and motivating experience, on the grounds that middle-class children achieve well in school and enjoy it. It could be argued that little in the school academic experience of most children is personally rewarding, intellectually stimulating, or even pleasurable. However, middle-class children in general put up with it and graduate. Low-status Mexican American students, perhaps finding school equally "punishing," tend not to achieve or persevere, so educators assume they are "poorly motivated." Many low-status Mexican Americans do not see any reward available to them in their community if they graduate from school, and thus the very thing that may keep middle-class youngsters at an acceptable academic and behavioral level is lacking.

Coleman *et al.* reported on the general motivation of twelfth graders (1966, pp. 279–286). They found little difference between Mexican Americans and Anglos from Southwestern states in their desired rank in scholarship, the average time they spent studying outside school, the number of days they did not attend school because they didn't want to, and the number of books they read in the summer before twelfth grade. Slight differences were reported in relation to future plans and steps to reach them. Although the two groups were still close, fewer Mexican Americans than Anglos desired to finish college or go into the professions, had read a college catalog, or had communicated with a college official concerning admission.

Descriptive studies reiterate that the Mexican American home culture does not support desire for change. Personal advancement is reported to be seen negatively. The ability to delay gratification is not taught at home; Mexican American children learn to live for the moment. The little objective data available seem to indicate that low-status parents do have high occupational and educational aspirations for their children and do push them but that they do not always know the appropriate steps necessary to encourage perseverance and success in school. Other factors tend also to defeat the "motivated" child, as discussed in the following chapter on school practices.

Poverty. Economic factors are deemed by many as responsible for many Mexican American children's withdrawal, lack of interest, and low achievement in school. In addition to other cultural factors, the exigencies of living in poverty force the child to seek employment as soon as he is "mature." The roles taught by the Mexican American family are seen to insure that boys will go to work early. Girls drop out of school in order to help care for younger brothers and sisters. Necessity lowers educational and occupational aspirations and precludes success in school. Schoolmen argue that even if children have high aspirations they are forced to lower them as they become aware of their social circumstances. Economic deprivation is seen as characteristic of all but a few Mexican Americans. Undoubtedly many of these factors actually are reasons for withdrawal in school. However, the assumption that Mexican American families have low educational and occupational aspirations as a result of economic deprivation is open to serious question. In fact, most of the interviewees for this study no longer hold to this view but state instead that the Mexican American families instill high but "unrealistic" aspirations in their children.

Ability in Art and Music. All aspects of Mexican American culture are not negative; some are very positive. Genetically inherited or culturally determined artistic and musical abilities are seen as highly developed in Mexican American children.

Of these, musical talent is believed to be especially well developed, and this belief has a long history of acceptance. In 1934, one educator stated: "Music is the sixth sense of the Mexican race. The musical feeling of the Mexican is extraordinary and his interest in it is greater than in any other art" (Hayden, 1934). In 1944, a teacher-training manual stated: "For Latin Americans, singing is a natural means of music expression; their sense of rhythm is acute, making it possible for them to learn quickly music involving complicated or difficult rhythms; their natural feeling for harmony is obvious" (Southwest Texas State Teachers College, 1944b, p. 228). About half of the informants for this study seemed to concur. Many felt that the school fails to capitalize on such talent: "After all, it is one of the few areas where Mexican Americans excel."

Artistic ability and manual dexterity are likewise perceived by many teachers as special gifts bestowed by culture or genes on Mexican American children. According to many teachers, brilliant colors, unusual color combinations, and bold and expressive use of form characterize the art work of these children. High achievement and creativity in art, photography, and shop classes in secondary school are reported.

However, the results of empirical studies testing artistic and musical ability generally report no significant difference between Anglo and Mexican American children (see Garth and Candor, 1937; Marcoux,

1961; Manuel, 1930, pp. 21–33). Educators adhering to the "special talent" argument confirm their beliefs by pointing out that Mexican American children do especially well in art, music, and vocational classes. Many apparently do achieve well in these activities. But approximately half of the school people interviewed for this study disagreed with the idea of special talent. Some of them contended that if the children do well in these activities, it is because teachers expect them to and subsequently praise and reward them for their achievement (implicit in this argument is that teachers' expectations are indeed fulfilled). Others argued, perhaps realistically, that art, music, and shop activities are outlets in which excellence is not determined by school learning, and that Mexican American children, in contrast to Anglos, have few such outlets in which they can excel.

SUMMARY AND CONCLUSIONS

American educators, pressed to explain the failure in school of low-status and minority-group children, rely heavily on the theory of "cultural deprivation." The fault is seen to lie in the socialization afforded by the home and neighborhood, and it is assumed that the child must be changed, not society or its educational institutions. Serious questions must be raised about the adequacy of this theory, and the effectiveness of school programs based on it. Critics of the theory pose a number of rather embarrassing questions. Clark (1965, p. 131) has this to say: "To what extent are the contemporary social deprivation theories merely substituting notions of environmental immutability and fatalism for earlier notions of biologically determined educational unmodifiability? To what extent do these theories obscure more basic reasons for the educational retardation of lower-class children? To what extent do they offer acceptable and desired alibis for the educational default: the fact that these children, by and large, do not learn because they are not being taught effectively and they are not being taught because those who are charged with the responsibility of teaching them do not believe that they can learn, do not expect that they can learn, and do not act toward them in ways which help them to learn?"

In the first section of the above quotation, Clark implies that the cultural-deprivation theory may be little more than the traditional biological determinist position, with modern trappings, and that the present approach is similar to older arguments based on the genetic inferiority of racial groups—for example, the arguments that Negroes as a race are inferior and their position in society is a result of racial characteristics, that since race is immutable so is social status, and so forth. Strong overtones of this sentiment were evident among the interviewees for this study, although very few took an overtly racial determinist position. There can be no doubt that numerous educators, especially in more conservative areas of the Southwest, believe that Mexican American children are inferior—that they are inferior because they are so obviously Mexican. Implicit in this belief is that Mexicans are culturally, if not racially, inferior.

It is assumed by many educators and other observers that a person from a lower-class segment of American society is incompetent and leads an unsatisfactory life, that the conditions of his life are somehow negative and bad. As Leacock suggests (1960, pp. 30–32): "All too often, the concept carries with it the uncomfortable implication that middle-class norms are *ipso facto* desirable, that 'lower-class culture' is merely a subtraction from middle-class culture and has no positive attributes of its own on which to build learning, and that our goal should be to have all children reject any deviation from middle-class standards." The ready acceptance of the cultural-deprivation theory is understandable, since it provides justification for educators' preconceived views of lower-class or "foreign" cultures.

From recent research concerning the school in an American Indian community, Wax *et al.* contend that the cultural-deprivation concept is equivalent to what they refer to as the "vacuum ideology of education" (1964, pp. 67–70). They state that schoolmen perceive "that the Indian home and the mind of the Indian child are meager, empty, and lacking in pattern." The perception of the Mexican American child and home held by educators is not dissimilar. The vast lists of Indian deficiencies encountered by these researchers have their equivalents in the prevalent descriptions of the Mexican American. Wax *et al.* state that "The vacuum ideology is a rationalization for the educator's defeat . . . given their pathetic image of the Sioux child, then surely it must be a miracle if the school manages to teach him anything." The use of the cultural-deprivation argument in relation to Mexican Americans can be seen as such a rationalization. In the course of this study, for example, one California teacher interviewed said, "What can you expect the school to do when you know the children's home and background?"

The inadequacies of the Mexican American home become the Mexican American child's educational "needs," arrived at by the pedagogical mathematics described in this chapter. Unfortunately, the cultural characteristics regularly ascribed to Mexican American children correspond all too often to the rather clearly defined and widely accepted Southwestern stereotype of "Mexicans" in general. "Mexicans" are categorized as being lackadaisical, individualistic (noncooperative), self-satisfied with their subordinate role, lazy, and imbued generally with a *mañana* attitude. Much of the information available to teachers supports this stereotype, thus adding a measure of "scientific" verification to their ideas. Certain aspects of the picture of Mexican American culture in the minds of schoolmen are founded on valid older descriptions of Mexican American life-style, customs, and values. Few educators are able to test the pictures in their minds against reality. Few have the knowledge or skills necessary, and few interact on anything but a superficial level with their Mexican American students or the minority community. The superordinate role of the educator, in his relations with Mexican American children and their community, encourages belief in his own superiority. His position almost guarantees it: if he weren't superior, obviously he would not be in authority.

The near stereotype of the Mexican American child and culture is not destroyed by exceptional cases. A few low-status children do succeed in school and society. These usually share, or are assumed to share, middle-class values or have some personality characteristics expected or admired by school people. In spite of the exception to the rule, the stereotype of the Mexican American child remains unmodified in its essentials. Unfortunately, teacher-preparation institutions probably do more to support stereotyping than to destroy it. Even as additional empirical evidence that refutes the stereotype becomes available, it is doubtful that it will substantially modify educators' perceptions. The findings of Romero (1966) and others, if widely circulated, would probably be discounted. "Contrary evidence is not admitted or allowed to modify the generalizations; rather, it is perfunctorily acknowledged but excluded" (Allport, 1954, p. 23).

To what degree belief in the stereotype so well established in the Southwest contributes to teachers' pessimism about educating Mexican Americans can only be speculative. However, the stereotype does provide a plausible and sufficient explanation for the behavior and failure in school of Mexican American children, as well as justification for the school programs established to overcome their real or imagined deficiencies: educators tend to argue that since the problem lies with the home culture, no fundamental changes are required of the school. The educational status quo is thus perpetuated.

Chapter 3: The Default of the School

Some educators take the position that much of the school curriculum and many school policies and practices inhibit learning and promote culture conflict, emotional problems, and the eventual flight of children from school. They believe that the school is at fault because of its inability to adjust realistically to serve culturally different groups, that there is nothing per se bad or deficient about Mexican Americans, but that the school has failed to capitalize on the "good and sufficient" child. These educators denounce the argument that Mexican American children are culturally deprived and see their background as full of meaning, order, and significant experiences. Recognizing these points, Lopez stated in an address to schoolmen concerned with the education of Spanish-speaking people (1964, p. 16): "I take exception to the word 'problem' when referring to the Mexican American community or the youngster, or so referring to any youngster regardless of his racial background. It is not a minority problem . . . not a problem of the child and so forth. It is a problem of the school, of the total community, of society. So, consequently . . . as we seek solution to these problems, let us not look within little Juan—let's see if we can find the solution to his problem within us."

While it is true that the school, as an institution, reflects or mirrors its parent society and probably has little effect on changing the nature of that society—the school cannot build new industries, destroy castes, eliminate racial or ethnic discrimination, change the roles of men or women, change power distribution, and so forth—it is not unreasonable to assume that the school can eliminate or modify practices that are detrimental to certain children. Whether or not the elimination of school practices or conditions that discourage Mexican American children will ultimately affect the nature of the local society must await the passage of time.

Following the same theme, but concentrating on institutional factors, a prominent Texas school administrator argued that the "traditional school" has "crippled" many Mexican American children: "We have expected the impossible of the Mexican American child when he comes into our school system. In the first grade we have always spent a great deal of time preparing a child for formal school experience in reading. We call this reading readiness, but we have not taken into consideration that the Mexican American child, coming from a different cultural and language background, is completely unable to benefit from the little nice things we do because he is unable to conceptualize in the Anglo culture and language. From the day he enters school he begins to lag behind in acquiring information because the only medium of communication is English. Eventually if he sticks it out he arrives at junior high school two to three years overage. If something isn't done at this age the child will not tolerate too many frustrations and becomes a dropout. These are the kids we have crippled because of the bungling methods we have used in attempting to instruct them in the traditional American school." Few take as strong a stand. However, a significant number of educators would generally concur; many advocate radical institutional changes.

The present school is inappropriate for many Mexican American youngsters. Factors particularly disadvantageous are de facto segregation, isolation in its various forms, the dependence on English, and inadequate teachers. Less obvious factors include rigidity of school practices and policies, curricular irrelevancy, culture conflict, and the negative perceptions of educators. The aggregate of these factors produces a generally negative school social environment or climate—a factor recognized as crucial to school survival and success. Social climate includes every aspect of the environment in which a child "learns" and "lives" in school. "School environment of the child consists of many things, ranging from the desk he sits at to the child who sits next to him, and including the teacher who stands in front of his class" (Coleman, 1966, p. 37). These things are difficult to measure objectively. The on-site observations, teachers' comments, interviews, and findings reported in the few objective studies that have been done are all open to question. However, a description of the school environment for many Mexican American children is attempted in this chapter.

SEPARATION AND ISOLATION

Many Mexican American children attend schools where they form the ethnic majority. While de jure segregation has been declared unconstitutional, isolation of minority-group children from sustained contact with other groups continues. The school does little to promote full and equal-status interaction among ethnic groups and reflects instead the ethnic separateness of the community.

De Jure and De Facto Segregation. No Southwestern state legally provided for the segregation of Mexican American children, yet the widespread practice had the force of law. In the mid-1940s, this Southwestern form of de jure segregation was terminated by recourse to the courts.

Separate "Mexican schools" were maintained in the past on the grounds that the separation was beneficial to Mexican American children. Reasons for segregation espoused in official school pronouncements included the Mexican American child's language handicap and his need to learn English, his need to be Americanized before mixing with Anglos, and his slowness in school, which would hinder the progress of Anglos. Mexican Americans were reported to be dirty and disease-ridden and to have low moral standards. Separate schools gave Mexican American children the opportunity to overcome these deficiencies and protected them from having to compete with Anglos and thus feeling inferior, as well as from the Anglo practice of "hazing" and other discriminations reported prevalent before the 1950s. (See Carpenter, 1935; Clinchy, 1954; Taylor, 1934.)

Segregation practices, however, implied other reasons than those given by educators. Although no definite or uniform practices were evident, certain actions and conditions raised the question of motives. These included: (1) The tendency for "Mexican schools" to have vastly inferior physical facilities, poorly qualified teachers, and larger classes than Anglo schools. (2) The practice of placing all Spanish-surname children in segregated schools, even though some were fluent in English. The fact that Negro children were sometimes assigned to "Mexican schools" suggests a racial rather than language basis for segregation. (3) The lack of effort to enforce the often weak attendance laws. (4) The failure to demand enrollment and attendance of Mexican American children while counting them on the school census. This Texas practice was abolished when the state shifted to "average daily attendance" as a basis for financial support. (5) In numerous cases the discouraging of individual children from attending school at all, especially in secondary-level institutions. Such practices were not universal in the Southwest, but they were common. Some still are. (See Calderón, 1950; Ceja, 1957; *Common Ground,* Winter 1947; Rubel, 1966; Strickland and Sánchez, 1948; Taylor, 1934; Trillingham and Hughes, 1943.)

The amount of Mexican American de jure segregation and its quality are difficult to assess. Little, in his 1944 study of Texas school districts he assumed to be representative, found that segregation was widespread but was not always practiced at the same grade levels. The large percentage of districts segregating at the higher grade levels, as shown in Table 8, is another encouragement to the belief that reasons other than "the language problem" and "pedagogical justifications" were behind segregation practices.

Attitudes revealed in public pronouncements and conversations indicated strong racist and economic biases on the part of both edu-

TABLE 8: School Segregation at Different Grade Levels, Texas

Number of districts segregating	*Grades segregated*
9	1-2
16	1-3
23	1-4
27	1-6
13	1-7
17	1-8

Source: Little (1944).

cators and laymen. Comments like these were reported commonly: "If the Mexicans get educated, they will go to the cities where they can get more money. Some Mexicans are very bright, but you can't compare their brightest with the *average* white children. They are an inferior race. . . . Most of the schools here take the money out of the Mexican allotment and use it for the whites" (Taylor, 1934, pp. 196, 200, 203). In general, segregation seemed to be maintained out of fear of intermarriage with inferior people and a feeling that if Mexican Americans were educated, they would not be so easy to manipulate and would no longer work for low wages. Such attitudes still prevail and probably underlie the widespread desire to maintain neighborhood schools and de facto segregation.

As in other sociopolitical areas, World War II stimulated Mexican Americans to demand change. Becoming more aware of their rights, privileges, and duties as American citizens, they demanded an end to separate schools and other discriminatory practices. Although it was illegal in all Southwestern states, segregation of Mexican Americans had gained the force of law and required legal action to terminate it. In 1946, with Mexican American organizational support behind them, a group of Mexican American parents initiated legal action against four Southern California elementary school districts. In *Westminster School District et al.* vs. *Mendez et al.*, the plaintiffs, on behalf of their minor children, claimed that the school districts discriminated illegally against children of Mexican descent by maintaining separate facilities. The plaintiffs contended that such practices violated their Constitutionally guaranteed rights to "due process and equal protection of the law." They did not argue that "Mexican schools" were inferior; rather, they agreed that they were as good as the Anglo institutions or perhaps superior to them. The court ruled in favor of the parents and enjoined the districts from segregating. The decision was appealed in a higher court, but the lower court decision was sustained. This case laid the groundwork for subsequent desegregation decisions in the 1950s, which were argued also on the basis of the First, Fifth, and Fourteenth amendments to the Constitution. (See Cooke, 1948, pp. 417–421; Sánchez, 1951.) In 1948, legal redress was sought to end school segregation of Mexican Americans in Texas. In *Delgado* vs. *The Bastrop Independent School District*, a federal court ruled that such segregation was illegal. The decision, like that in California, was based on Constitutional guarantees. Legally sanctioned segregation was ended.

De facto segregation continues. Schools are ethnically and racially out of balance in metropolitan areas, as well as in smaller urban and rural areas, because housing patterns continue to influence the placement of new schools and of the boundaries within which children must live to attend them. The end of legal segregation has not markedly affected concentrations of low-income Mexican American children in segregated schools. As families that become better off economically move from the traditional *barrios*[1] to mixed neighborhoods, the group that remains becomes more homogeneously poor and culturally disadvantaged. Those who leave are replaced by new rural or Mexican immigrants. Few Southwestern towns or cities are without their Mexican American sections. The situation is changing somewhat, but residential segregation remains the common pattern (see Moore and Mettelbach, 1966). With few exceptions, schools reflect this segregation.

California is the only Southwestern state to publish statistics relative to the concentration of ethnic groups in schools. In October 1966, the State Department of Education collected data from all but six of California's 1,162 school districts. Racial imbalance was found to characterize many of the schools. Although this fact had long been recognized, the degree of ethnic isolation was somewhat startling. For the purpose of analysis, school districts were divided according to size of enrollment. The eight largest districts, with enrollments of 50,000 or more, and a representative sample of 56 smaller districts were analyzed separately. A method to determine whether a school was *majority, minority,* or *mixed* was established: "A simple integregation scale was applied to each of the 2,340 schools in the study groups, comparing each school's percentages of the three largest racial and ethnic groups (Spanish surname, 'other white,' and Negro) with the corresponding percentages of the districts in which the school is situated. Allowing a deviation of as many as 15 percentage points above or

1. *Barrio* is a term used in many ways in the Southwest. "Neighborhood" is perhaps the best translation. It does not necessarily mean a slum, but it has this connotation in some areas. In this book it means simply Mexican American area or neighborhood.

below the appropriate district percentage, it was possible to classify each school as high concentration, mixed, or low concentration with respect to each of the three racial or ethnic groups. When the basis of comparison was 'other white' percentage, the term *majority* school, *mixed* school, or *minority* school could be substituted" (California State Department of Education, 1967a, p. 10).

The California survey indicates that Negro children are more segregated than Mexican Americans in both the largest and smaller districts of the state. In the eight largest districts, 57 percent of Spanish-surname children attend *minority,* 28 percent *mixed,* and 15 percent *majority* schools. Eighty-five percent of Negroes attend *minority* schools, 12 percent *mixed,* and 3 percent *majority.* In the smaller districts 30 percent of the Spanish-surname students attend *minority,* 63 percent *mixed,* and 7 percent *majority* schools. In these districts also, Negro children are more segregated.

These figures are perhaps adequate for the statewide picture, but they distort the real situation. There are fewer minority secondary schools than minority elementary schools, and to lump them together is misleading. The recent study by Coleman *et al.* (1966) of educational opportunity sheds some light on the elementary–secondary school differences: "A substantial number of Indian-American and Mexican American first graders are in schools in which they are the majority group. This is not true at the 12th grade" (p. 41). The report also says (p. 212): "While the average Negro elementary child is in school where 16% of the students are white, the average percentage of white classmates is . . . 53% for Mexican-Americans. At the secondary level, the average Negro is in a school where 24% of the students are white, while the average percentage of white classmates is . . . 68% for Mexican-Americans. . . ."

An educational executive in Texas commented: "I would say that more Mexican American children generally attend elementary school with other Mexican American children and when it's not that way, generally the ratio will be decidedly in favor of the Anglo—the proportion will be much larger Anglo." This informant implied that there are two types of schools. One is almost exclusively Mexican American, the other almost exclusively Anglo. Mexican American children generally are not interspersed with Anglos, but when they are, Anglos predominate. This situation is quite common in elementary schools throughout the Southwest. The "Mexican school" serves the lower social class; the mixed (but usually predominantly Anglo) school serves the middle class.

The California survey (1967a) indicates that in minority schools one finds overrepresentation of compensatory education programs: "On the integration scale, 27 percent of the Title I (ESEA) target schools . . . in the 56 district sample are *minority* schools, and 2 percent are *majority* schools: 79 percent of the Title I target schools in the eight largest districts are *minority* schools, and 1 percent are *majority* schools. Funds from a special California compensatory education act go also almost exclusively to *minority* schools . . . 81 percent of the Senate Bill 28 [a California compensatory education program] special aid schools in the sample are *minority* schools . . . 92 percent of the Senate Bill 28 special aid schools in the eight largest districts are *minority* schools. . . ." (pp. 12–13). Specifically mentioning Mexican Americans, the survey says: "In compensatory education target elementary schools (Title I–Elementary and Secondary Education Act), Spanish surname pupils comprise 54% of the enrollment. 48% of all Spanish surname elementary pupils in the State attend these target schools" (p. 5). Mexican Americans tend to go to minority elementary schools, and these schools receive a disproportionate share of compensatory education funds. Mexican American poverty and minority schools are associated.

In the Los Angeles School Study it was found that the composition of the school population was of great importance to the success in school of Mexican American children. A number of elementary schools and junior and senior high schools were categorized according to the number of children in various ethnic and socioeconomic groups. The categories are roughly analogous to the minority, mixed, and majority categories used in the California survey. It was found that: "School type contributed substantially to the performance of Mexican-American elementary and junior high levels, but not at senior high levels" (Gordon *et al.*, 1968, pp. 134–135). In other words, if other factors are constant, minority-group children perform better in schools that have a low percentage of minority-group pupils. However, "The performance of Anglo pupils is not affected by school context at any level." Although tentative, these findings strongly suggest that mixed or majority schools improve Mexican American academic achievement.

In spite of the law, theoretical arguments, and some empirical evidence against segregated schools, there is a strong and widespread desire to retain neighborhood schools (see Coleman *et al.*, 1966). While few educators interviewed for this study were overtly segregationist, most defended the neighborhood-school concept and contended that the closing of "Mexican schools" would work to the disadvantage of the children. Their arguments are similar to those previously used in defense of de jure segregation: ". . . the Mexican children are often at a disadvantage . . . in segregated schools Mexican children experience no such invidious comparisons. They compete against other Mexican children, with far better results ensuing. Even Mexican parents who have been opposed to segregation have been converted to its merits. For the first five grades, segregation is advocated . . . on the ground that the children make better progress and have a chance in that time period to learn the English language and thus to compete with American children on a fairer level than would be the case in an earlier grade level. They acquire a confidence in their own abilities, which helps them to go ahead creditably with American children" (Bogardus, 1928–29, pp. 276–283). Another frequently heard argument for maintaining "Mexican schools" is that parents are perfectly content with the status quo; there have been few pickets or objectors—"Mexican Americans like to be among their own kind, just as Anglos do."

California, responding to pressure from the civil rights movement, is moving to desegregate its schools. The California School Boards Association stated in 1965 that school districts should be "encouraged to analyze the extent of racial imbalance in their district and take steps to ameliorate any imbalances which are found to exist" (California School Boards Association, 1965, p. 4). The California State Department of Education also is encouraging the ending of racial imbalance. Schoolmen are generally aware of this imbalance in their schools and, encouraged by Department of Education consultants, are proposing plans for desegregation.

A number of California cities, including Sausalito, Garden Grove,

Berkeley, Livingston, and Riverside are implementing plans to overcome ethnic imbalance. Riverside is desegregating its minority-group children by sending them by bus to assigned schools. Two schools almost exclusively composed of Mexican American and Negro children were closed in the fall of 1966; a third, a *barrio* school, was closed in the fall of the following year. Some members of the Mexican American community served by the *barrio* school were in favor of keeping their neighborhood school. The movement to desegregate Riverside and other California schools was first led by Negro elements, but now Mexican American leadership is also vocal. However, Mexican American and Negro advocacy of desegregation may be lessening, as more members of these groups stress ethnic and racial "nationalism" and separateness. This trend will undoubtedly be supported by many middle-class Anglos who adhere to racial isolation and perhaps to a racist ideology.

A seven-year study of the effects of desegregation on the achievement, attitudes, and behavior of children of all three groups has been undertaken. An interdisciplinary team from the University of California at Riverside, and members of the staff of the school district, are collecting data from children and parents. The findings of this study have not yet been published (see Singer and Hendrick, 1967, pp. 143–147).

In spite of governmental pressure in California, much reluctance to desegregate is still evident among educators and within both the majority- and minority-group communities. Pressure probably will eventually cause districts to modify the status quo. However, the percentage of educators interviewed for this study who desired to end segregation was higher in California than in Texas. Many Texas Mexican American teachers desire desegregation but feel that it is utterly impossible for the present. Anglo Texas schoolmen interviewed say that they are trying to do their best with the present school programs, that desegregation may some day be forced upon them, but that community opinion is strongly opposed to "mixing the races." This attitude may be assumed to characterize also those areas of New Mexico and Colorado that are under strong Texas influence (see Chambers, 1949). Barring massive protest by Texas minority groups, or strong state-level intervention, continued de facto segregation for many years may be foreseen. California and Colorado may be slowly moving toward desegregation and probably will continue to do so, perhaps with increasing resistance from many sources. Advocates of all positions, with varying degrees of influence, are found in all five Southwestern states. School systems and staffs of each area strongly reflect the local social environment.

Mexican American School Districts. History and geography have isolated Mexican Americans from contact with Anglos. In all five states there are districts that are predominantly Mexican American; in many the percentage is over 85, and in some it approaches 100. These districts are concentrated in counties along the border, in California's rich agricultural valleys, and in northern New Mexico and southern Colorado. Extremely high percentages of Mexican Americans are particularly evident in the small Texas cities along the Rio Grande River, especially in Starr, Kennedy, and Zapata counties. Describing this in 1957, a Texas Education Agency report stated (p. 1): "The heaviest concentration of Spanish surname pupils was reported from the counties bordering Mexico . . . a total of 31 counties, about 12% of the total number in the State, reported an enrollment of 50% or more Spanish surname pupils. Schools in eight counties reported more than 75%, and one county, Kennedy, reported 100%." In many cases, the percentage of Mexican American children in school would be higher if it were not for the large number of them who drop out.

In some communities, two school districts exist: one Mexican American, the other either mixed or predominantly Anglo. Del Rio, Texas, and Las Vegas, New Mexico, are examples. Las Vegas is two incorporated cities, each with its own school district. Del Rio is one city with two school districts. While there are other and different kinds of reasons for the existence of the two school systems, strong segregationist overtones are evident. A number of school districts visited are virtually 100 percent *pura raza* (Mexican American).

Free-Choice Policies. Many school officials interviewed commented that their districts have a free transfer plan. This plan allows for free choice of school by parents; those desiring to place their children in predominantly Anglo schools are permitted by school policy to do so. Educators argue that this is a step toward compliance with the "spirit of desegregation." The function of this policy may be seen two ways:

it permits Mexican Americans to attend predominantly Anglo schools and allows Anglos to flee from schools with large percentages of Mexican Americans. It appears that very few lower-class Mexican Americans transfer to other schools, because of their lack of desire, their lack of knowledge of school procedures, or because of intimidation by school officials. In order to transfer, students usually must have permission from either the school board or the superintendent. One Texas interviewee replied to a question on this point as follows: "The parent says, well, look, I don't want my kid going to this school where I live. He can apply for a transfer, and then the transfer comes before the Board of Trustees and they say, 'What's the reason for the transfer?' 'Well, I don't like that school.' 'What's wrong with it?' Who among these people [low-status Mexican Americans] is going to push a request of that type?" Responding to a question about whether middle-class Mexican Americans would have any problem, the same informant stated: "They probably wouldn't live in that area. I know some who have done it and they know their way around. They come in, it's no problem for them. They're accepted every year."

On the other hand, a sociologist, a specialist in Mexican American affairs, commented on the flight of Anglos: "They do have a free transfer policy; for example [a certain high school], up until five or six years ago was the high school of the elite. This is the school to which the wealthiest families and the old families sent their children. Then in the last 10 years, you had a very heavy movement of Mexican Americans into the geographical area covered by [this school] so at the present time, perhaps the Mexican Americans number more than 60 percent of the student body. The wealthy Anglo American families now transfer their children to [another school]." Whether the free-choice policy maintains segregation or encourages mixing of the groups remains to be seen. However, it appears evident that the "good Mexican" has little difficulty in gaining permission to transfer his child, and that de facto segregated minority-group schools are becoming more homogeneously lower class. What was once segregation according to ethnic group is increasingly becoming separation according to social class. The bottom social group in much of the Southwest is made up of Mexican Americans, who remain isolated from "better off" Mexican Americans, as well as from Anglos.

Brain Drain. As movement of rural Mexican Americans to the cities continues, another form of isolation may be developing. In one school district in rural northern New Mexico administrators discussed what they called the "brain drain": ". . . there is a kind of cycle, a continuum of migration from the rural areas to the more urban and this drains off the more qualified people at all levels so that the more qualified semi-urban are moving to Albuquerque and the more qualified of the unqualified rural are moving to the small city, so that you constantly are faced with a lowering quality of aspiration [etc.]. The intelligent, relatively speaking, the well-educated, the ambitious, leave the more rural areas [etc.]. But what it means to teachers and superintendents in the small city is that they are constantly dealing with children of a less ambitious group of people or less upwardly mobile." Whether the effect on the quality of students is as described is open to question. Logically, it might be assumed to be so. Whether this is reality or educators' perception of reality may be of little importance: it can be argued that because they think it is true teachers' expectations are lowered and efforts lessened.

Roman Catholic schools may act as a brain drain also. It is reported that parochial schools principally enroll Mexican American children of upwardly mobile or middle-class families. Comments by informants for this study varied greatly on this point. Each parochial school is different, as is each community and its public schools. The degree to which Catholic institutions take the best academic prospects must be determined by local study.

Mexican American Teachers. The assignment of Mexican American teachers to minority schools functions to isolate children from contact with Anglos. It is strongly argued that, having gone through a similar life pattern, Mexican American teachers understand their charges and are the best possible role models for their group's children. Mexican American spokesmen encourage school administrators to hire bilingual teachers and to assign them to "Mexican schools." "Bilingual" is almost invariably translated as "Mexican American" by administrators. A Colorado source states: ". . . given equal academic or even lower academic qualifications, the Spanish-surnamed teacher applicant deserves special consideration because of two special qualifications he possesses . . . (1) his example or presence in the school can encourage Spanish-surnamed students, and (2) his ability to understand and give special counsel to many Spanish-surnamed students.... The second qualification may not always be valid. ... Mexican American teachers . . . from upper-middle-class-urban culture may have nothing in common with a poor working class Spanish-surnamed student" (Colorado Commission on Spanish-Surnamed Citizens, 1966, p. 62). In spite of qualifying conditions, this kind of statement is usually interpreted to mean that Mexican American teachers should be hired for Mexican American children. Administrators tend to comply whenever possible.

As rules of thumb it can be stated that Mexican American teachers are generally (depending somewhat on the state or area): (1) highly desired by districts that have large Mexican American populations; (2) employed in numbers proportional to the Mexican American population of the school in which they teach; (3) concentrated at the elementary level; and (4) rarely found in Anglo elementary schools (except as Spanish teachers).

Except in districts in which the population is almost wholly Mexican American, there are very few Mexican American administrators in any field. In the vast majority of districts, Mexican Americans fill only the teaching positions. The few administrators are almost invariably principals of predominantly Mexican American schools, or language (often Spanish) consultants. In a few districts there are district-level administrators in charge of business, physical education, health, school social workers, and federal projects. In general, Mexican American administrators are found at all levels in the almost purely Mexican American districts, are low-level administrators in Anglo-controlled districts—even where the majority of students are of the minority group—and are associated with activities that bring them into contact with the ethnic community. Regardless of the advantages, such practices tend to isolate Mexican American communities and children from contact with Anglos and vice versa.

One almost wholly Mexican American district reflects the type of placement pattern characteristic of such areas. "A" School District consists of 12 elementary schools, 1 junior high school, and 1 senior high school. Its total enrollment for 1966–67 was about 2,600. The central office staff of 16, the 5 board members, and the 14 principals were Mexican Americans, as were all counselors and assistant principals. Of the teaching staff of 126, all but 10 had Spanish surnames. The student population was about 99 percent Mexican American.

A large metropolitan district demonstrates another and much more common placement pattern. "B" School District contains 9 regular high schools, 20 junior high schools, and 79 elementary schools. Its total enrollment for the 1966–67 school year was approximately 74,000. The Mexican American school population was about 60 percent of that total. Table 9 indicates the staff breakdown for 1966–67. Almost half of the Spanish-surname teachers were assigned to schools that approximated 100 percent Mexican American enrollment; the others were sprinkled throughout the system. However, it is reported that the percentage of Mexican American teachers approximated the percentage of Mexican American children in the other schools. Of the 10 Spanish-surname building administrators, 8 were in *minority* schools.

"C" School District serves a smaller city. Although approximately 80 percent of the students in the district are Mexican American, its placement pattern is similar to "B" District. Of the 30 principals, assistants, and counselors, 3 have Spanish surnames; only 1 is in a secon-

TABLE 9: Spanish-Surname and Non-Spanish-Surname Staff Members of "B" School District

	Non-Spanish surname	*Spanish surname*	*Total*
Board of education	6	1	7
Central office administrators	32	1 (Reading consultant)	33
Business and other services	10	1 (Head nurse)	11
Secondary school principals, assistants, deans, and counselors	88	6 (4*)	94
Elementary school principals and counselors	72	4*	76
Teachers	2,625	289†	2,914

Source: "B" School District Staff Personnel Directory.

*Number employed in schools approximating 100 percent Mexican American enrollment.

†49 percent in schools approximating 100 percent Mexican American enrollment.

dary school in the capacity of assistant principal of a junior high. No central office administrator has a Spanish surname. Of the 425 teachers, 106 have Spanish surnames. These are concentrated in schools with large Mexican American student populations. No Spanish-surname teacher is placed in the one predominantly Anglo school (85–90 percent). Sixty-six percent of the Spanish-surname teachers are in elementary schools and 34 percent in secondary schools.

Districts "B" and "C" described above are representative of districts that are strongly under the control of the dominant Anglo society but are eager to procure as large a Mexican American staff as possible. While Mexican American teachers are hired and placed, few are promoted to the administrative ranks.

In California, during the 1966–67 school year, there were 3,866 teachers and 153 principals with Spanish surnames (California State Department of Education, 1967b). This represented 2.25 percent and 1.68 percent respectively of the state totals for these two categories (p. 8). Of the certified Spanish-surname teachers in the large districts, 51 percent taught in *minority,* 24 percent in *mixed,* and 25 percent in *majority* schools (p. 28). In the sample of 56 smaller districts, 66 percent of Spanish-surname teachers taught in *mixed,* 12 percent in *majority,* and 22 percent in *minority* schools (p. 29). Approximately 55 percent of the Spanish-surname certified personnel taught at the secondary level (p. 13). According to this California survey, "There is little likelihood that a Spanish surname student will be taught by a teacher of his own ethnic group"—since there are too few Mexican American teachers (p. 31). Yet, in most cases observed, the general rule holds: Mexican American teachers, especially elementary school teachers, are placed in schools that have high percentages of Mexican American students.

Colorado Spanish-surname elementary school teachers appear to be in larger percentages in districts that have smaller percentages of Mexican Americans. Whether such teachers are placed in predominantly Mexican American schools within these districts is not known. At the secondary school level, the tendency appears to be to concentrate Spanish-surname teachers in districts that have larger percentages of Mexican American students. In Denver, 1.33 percent of elementary school, 2.38 percent of junior high school, and 1.43 percent of senior high school teachers have Spanish surnames. However, their number is small. Of Denver's 3,687 teachers, only 65 have Spanish surnames; of these, 57 percent are at the secondary level. It is reported that most of these are probably Spanish teachers (Colorado State Department of Education, 1967, p. 61).

At the state department of education level, Mexican American educators fill numerous staff positions. In every state included in this study, Mexican Americans hold responsible positions; most deal with intergroup, migrant, compensatory, or related educational activities.

SEPARATION IN MIXED SCHOOLS

In ethnically mixed institutions, many minority-group students are nonetheless isolated from sustained equal-status interaction with Anglos. Naturally there are numerous exceptions. The *agringado* middle-class student usually mixes quite well with his Anglo peers. (An *agringado* is an Angloized Mexican American. The term is not used here in any depreciatory sense.) He tends to achieve and react in ways similar to other middle-class children, even though he may suffer from a more than normal identity crisis. The majority of Mexican Americans, however, have lower-class status and are not acculturated to middle-class orientations and norms; they are carriers of low-class (perhaps caste), traditional or transitional cultures. Even though these Mexican Americans attend mixed schools, in reality they may be isolated from their Anglo and *agringado* peers. School policy and practice contribute to this isolation, tending to reinforce the ethnic and social class cleavage that exists within most of the Southwest. The school reflects the community and tends to perpetuate the separation of Mexican and Anglo roles and expectations.

Ethnic Cleavage. In most of the Southwest, two separate castelike social structures exist. Two communities, the Anglo and the Mexican American, exist side by side. This castelike relationship is characterized as dominant-submissive: the Anglo segment is superordinate, the minority subordinate (Simmons, 1952). The school mirrors and is a microcosm of the community it serves. Whatever ethnic cleavage and castelike social structures are locally extant are present also in the community's educational institutions. Loomis (1943, p. 25) concluded in his early study: "The measures of cleavages used indicate strong tendencies for Spanish-American and Anglo students in the two New Mexico high schools studied to choose associates within their own ethnic groups. Some tendency was manifest from members of the minority ethnic group, whether English-speaking or Spanish-speaking, to reject the members of the majority ethnic group relatively more frequently than the reverse." Parsons reports that ethnic cleavage characterizes the small California farming community of "Guadalupe" and that the school reflects and teaches separate roles to the children (1965, pp. 386–387): ". . . ethnically differentiated social patterns and associated stereotypes are learned by village children quite early. After the second grade, Anglo and Mexican-American children increasingly restrict their social choices to members of their own ethnic group. By the time they reach the upper elementary grades, there is virtually complete social separation between the two groups. That the children are aware of Anglo dominance is reflected in their leadership and prestige choices. Both Anglo and Mexican-American children choose Anglos as sources of prestige and both groups made significant choices of Anglos for positions of leadership. One of the most impressive features of the Guadalupe social structure is the high degree of functional integration exhibited by its major institutions in the maintenance of the traditional ethnic patterns. Whether they are at home, in church, at school, on the playground, shopping with parents, attending scout meetings, or watching the artichoke festival activities, children are provided with examples of the social positions they are expected to occupy and the roles they are expected to play. They are frequently shown that Anglos are best in everything and the Mexicans are the worst. Mexican-American children are rewarded in school and in church when they look and act like Anglos and punished (or ignored) if they look and act like Mexicans."

To what degree school personnel act to reinforce and perpetuate this cleavage differs with each institution and community. Interviewees support the contention, however, that teachers do reflect the stereotyping and expectations of Mexican Americans that characterize their community. Mexican American students interviewed report that teachers' behavior appears to reflect such attitudes. Students mention teachers asking the class "Why are you Mexican kids so lazy?" Others report that teachers show preference for Anglos and regularly choose them for school leadership roles. Parsons describes such a situation (1965, pp. 38–39). An Anglo boy was placed in charge of a small group of Mexican American boys after they had rushed from a classroom. He quotes his interview with the classroom teacher:

"Teacher: Usually the kids are pretty good, but that day those boys were in a hurry to get out to the playground. . . . I remember thinking that the Mexican boys were going to make trouble if I didn't catch them—you know, they just can't follow directions. You always have to tell them what you want done. They seem to have a hard time remembering the rules. Anyway, I thought that if I told Johnny [the Anglo boy] to take the lead, they would have a good example of how to act.

"Interviewer: Was there some reason why you chose Johnny specifically?

"Teacher: Yes. He was right there of course. Besides that, I think Johnny needs to learn how to set a good example and how to lead others. His father owns one of the big farms in the area and Johnny has to learn how to lead the Mexicans. One day he will be helping his father and he will have to know how to handle the Mexicans. I try to help him whenever I can."

Physical education activities also reflect the school's isolationist and separatist actions: teams are divided on ethnic lines. Teachers responding to questions concerning this procedure commented: "Most said that it was 'traditional' for the PE activities to be arranged along ethnic lines. Several said that '. . . most everything in Guadalupe is set up this way. It just seems like the natural thing to do. Anyway, the kids are more comfortable when they are playing with their own group.' Many agreed that there was likely to be less 'trouble' if the two ethnic groups were kept separate" (Parsons, 1965, pp. 300–301).

Parsons contends that teachers and administrators "share the general Anglo stereotypes of Mexicans and . . . use these as the basis for organizing their perceptions of, and programs for, the Mexican pupils." In the summary of his dissertation, he mentions the following practices, among others, that contribute to ethnic differentiation of pupils and stereotyping within the school (pp. 306–307): (1) posting achievement charts (there is a tendency for students to use charts as a basis for judgments about classmates); (2) sending Mexican American pupils who "smell" out of the room; (3) establishing and continuing formal teacher-student relationships between Anglo teachers and Mexican American students, in contrast to the less formal relationship between Anglo teachers and Anglo students; (4) placing the Mexican American students in a subordinate position to Anglo students by saying that Mexican Americans lack intelligence and need "the guidance of Anglos who know better" than they do. It is strongly recommended here that the Parsons study be read in its entirety for full understanding of its significance.

From recent observation and interviewing relative to interethnic relationships in school, one major, although perhaps unsurprising, conclusion can be reached: ethnic separation is general in Southwestern schools, its degree and nature determined by community social patterns and their reinforcement of educators. What control educators have over school intergroup relations reflects the views of the more conservative and powerful members of the Anglo community. Where contact is permitted in mixed schools, adolescents are experimenting in new relationships; perhaps these youth are responding to the national climate of ethnic acceptance instead of reacting solely to the local social climate.

Students are, with varying degrees of success and speed, reported to be breaking down ethnic distinctions. This is particularly true in regard to interethnic social contact between the sexes. Interviewees for this study commented that "serious" interethnic dating is increasing; adolescents seem to be more and more prone to date members of the other ethnic group. Mexican American-Anglo dancing is rarely openly discouraged by the school authorities, as it was reported to be formerly. Yet, the most "traditional" Mexican American students are reported to feel that such close contact is "bad." The same would be true of more "traditional" Anglo youth. A small number of Angloized Mexican Americans are acceptable as steady dates to the Anglos. Anglo boy and Mexican American girl (usually Angloized and "non-Mexican" appearing) is mentioned as being a common dating arrangement. Popular Mexican American boys date Anglo girls, but some stigma seems to be attached in this case. Even in the most castelike communities, "thrill dating" is reported to be practiced, usually as a clandestine activity that involves both sexes of both groups. Anglo girls test the "Latin lover" stereotype attributed to Mexican American boys; Anglo boys conversely investigate the "immorality" of Mexican American girls, a dating arrangement reported to be highly unacceptable to "traditional" girls. In spite of the increasingly permissive racial and sexual attitudes of today's youth, the majority of both ethnic groups seem to restrict their serious activities to members of their own group. Numerous teachers interviewed for this study mentioned their dislike of mixed dancing and dating. They contended that while the school can do little to discourage it, they themselves "take the offenders aside" (almost invariably the Anglo partners) and inform them of the stigma ascribed to such activities. Suffice it to say that boy-girl activities, perhaps the last stronghold of ethnic separation, are gradually changing. The more urban the environment, the more interethnic dating is evident.

Even in the communities that have the most rigid ethnic cleavage, there is a general acceptance by educators that any school-sponsored activity is open to all students. Academic and sports activities are rarely, if ever, closed to students because of their ethnic background. In only one school did an informant comment that certain sports activities were closed to "Mexicans": tennis was "lily white," but in other sports, Mexican Americans were welcomed. In this same school, until a few years ago, debate and drama activities were open only to Anglos, but these restrictions were broken down by ambitious Mexican American students. It must be stressed that it is rarely school officials who encourage the breakdown of ethnic barriers; it is usually the case that they respond belatedly to the fact that students have already destroyed the obstacles established by tradition.

Social class barriers still exist and appear to be replacing some ethnic distinctions. School policy requiring fees or expenses to enter certain activities discourages lower-class students. In one school, for example, band is reported to be an elite activity. The school provides instruction only on an advanced level, thus excluding children who have not had private lessons. In other schools, students are required to buy equipment before they can go out for certain sports. While poor Mexican American star performers may be given such equipment by local athletic buffs, often the beginner desiring to try out is not. Acceptance into the Anglo or middle-class ethnic peer groups is usually associated with acceptable dress, again discouraging the entrance of otherwise acceptable poor Mexican Americans. Because most Mexican American children in most areas come from lower socioeconomic levels, economic factors discourage their full integration in school and student life. The degree and nature of these conditions depend on the actions of educators and the local community social climate, and variations among areas are great.

A few Mexican Americans in every mixed school are breaking down the ethnic barriers and are fairly well integrated socially. Even in many of the most conservative communities, these few children are on the fringe of acceptance into Anglo peer societies, but in some cases they remain essentially isolated or form small groups with equally marginal youngsters. In every secondary school observed during this study, however, clear lines of ethnic separation were visible in activities in which students were allowed free choice of associates.

Nothing stated or implied here is meant to refute the findings of those who have made empirical studies of ethnic cleavage in schools. Educational institutions continue, explicitly and implicitly, to teach children to conform to the expectations of the community. The previous paragraphs merely report that some of the more obvious sanctions of the school are probably disappearing. Implicit sanctions against ethnic "togetherness" are still evident; their full exposition must await detailed study of individual school and community situations.

Separation by Special Curriculum. Educators speak of the "special needs" of minority-group children and establish school programs to meet them. Most such needs are met by special classes or programs to overcome the "deficiencies" of Mexican American children. Such special compensatory education (usually remedial) programs are becoming almost universal in Southwestern schools. Because of institutional practices, however, some compensatory programs are tracks that tend to cause the isolation of Mexican American students. Compensatory classes that require attendance for a period or so a day (the child remains in regular mixed classrooms the rest of the day) are the most commonly encountered. This kind of program does not isolate the child to an unwarranted degree. Other compensatory programs do substantially isolate Mexican American children, who then tend to associate with their Mexican American peers and, in essence, attend a subschool within an ethnically mixed institution. Institutional organization and procedures can discourage or prohibit breaking out of such sections or groups.

Tracking. One of the prime functions of the school is to help society allocate status and role—that is, to separate individuals and treat them differently in order to fill the ever recurring social and economic slots. Few would argue that this sorting and sieving process is not essential. However, many educators and social scientists believe that present sorting practices are merely perpetuating status at birth—that members of the low social class leave school prepared to enter low-status social slots little different from those of their parents. If this is true, the school is indeed granting status on ascription rather than proscription, a situation that is counter to the values professed both by the school and by American society. Tracking is becoming an almost universal sieving device to treat students differentially. Great concern is manifest that the manner in which children are sorted into tracks, and the treatment they receive in them, almost predetermine their low achievement in school and their ultimate exit from school prepared only to assume low status.

In one form or another, rigid ability grouping is widely and increasingly practiced in Southwestern schools. For the purpose of this paper, a distinction is made between *grouping* and *tracking*. *Grouping* as used here refers to the practice of temporarily placing children in groups of like ability or interest—for example, "reading circles" within otherwise heterogeneous classrooms. These tend to be temporary and under the exclusive control of the classroom teacher. *Tracking* is an extreme form of ability grouping involving the permanent assignment of children to classrooms or sections (tracks) composed of individuals assumed to have like abilities, interests, or other characteristics. Tracking involves formal institutional decisions, planning, and curriculum organization; grouping does not. Grouping tends toward flexibility and student mobility and tracking toward inflexibility and student immobility. Track placement is usually institutionally determined on the basis of grades, teachers' observations, results of achievement and intelligence tests, counselors' observations, behavior records, or some combination of these factors. However, appraisal of intellectual capacity and achievement, whether by standardized tests or other means, is usually the principal determinant of track assignment. In these measured characteristics, Mexican American children tend to fall below school or national norms. The relationship between socioeconomic class and track placement is obvious; with few exceptions, families in lower socioeconomic classes rear children who score below average on the instruments that are used to predict or measure school achievement or intelligence.

Mexican Americans are greatly overrepresented in the lower-ability tracks of every mixed school I have observed; Anglos are overrepresented in the middle- and high-ability tracks. In one Texas "Mexican" high school, which serves very low income families, only the low and average tracks were found. In other district schools three or more tracks exist, including the accelerated. Tracking at the elementary school level is increasing; secondary school tracking is general and well established. Many tracked or homogeneous first-grade classes were observed. According to the Coleman report (1966, pp. 13–14), 37 percent of Mexican American children attend elementary schools where tracking is used, compared to 48 percent of the majority-group students. In the Southwest, 79 percent of the Mexican American secondary school students, contrasted to 82 percent of the Anglo secondary school students, attend schools that are tracked. Coleman *et al.* indicate (p. 112) that the percentages of Mexican American children in the highest and lowest tracks are almost identical to the "white" student percentages. This finding is opposed to everything that was observed in this study or reported to it. However, the degree to which Mexican Americans overpopulate low-ability tracks can only be determined by careful study of individual institutions.

It is common practice to divide children into two, three, or more tracks when they enter junior high school. At this level, vocational, occupational, and academic aspirations and aptitudes are usually considered. Aptitude and achievement, regardless of how they are determined, are matched with college or vocational requirements. Tracks are well established and stable by the end of junior high school. As in elementary school, Mexican American children are found to be in disproportionately high percentages in vocational and low-ability tracks (see Hickerson, 1962; Parsons, 1965). High school continues the practice; there it becomes almost impossible to move out of a track, principally because of institutional rigidity and the differing curriculums within tracks. Once a student is tracked at any level, movement upward is difficult. However, a first grader has a better chance to change tracks than a tenth grader.

Few educators interviewed in this study argued against tracking, the vast majority perceiving it as the fairest and most efficient way to handle intellectual difference and encourage maximum achievement. The general complaint was that present techniques to determine track placement are inadequate. A few informants saw tracking as a most insidious form of segregation and as a damning and self-fulfilling prediction. Educational institutions rely heavily on the results of group and individual psychometric instruments to sort children into tracks. Yet almost every educator interviewed argued that such instruments were neither reliable nor valid for culturally different children. A paradox exists. Most teachers and administrators argue that the school and the students would be better off, or equally well off, if they stopped relying on such instruments. But their institutions, well-oiled and self-perpetuating, continue to make decisions that affect the life chances of children on the basis of tests often agreed to be of questionable value. The difficulty in determining correct track placement for all children is obvious. Serious questions must be asked about the techniques used in "sorting" culturally different children. If the ethnic imbalance found in school tracks reflects valid innate intelligence appraisals, it would have to be concluded that Mexican Americans are indeed an "inferior race." But if intelligence is equally distributed among all groups of people, the techniques of measurement and placement must be rigorously examined.

Most educators contend that the practice of assigning students to tracks encourages maximum academic achievement, that tracking eliminates extremes of ability, thus providing a more "comfortable" learning environment, and that in the tracking system the curriculum can better be adjusted to "meet the needs" of students as a group and as individuals. Others argue against tracking, some contending that it has adverse effects on the attitudes, aspirations, and self-concepts of students. Still others say that it discourages students from reaching their maximum potential. No research concerning the effect of tracking on Mexican American students was found during the course of this study; other research on the effects of homogeneous grouping on student achievement and attitudes has been generally inconclusive.

A comprehensive survey of research relative to the effects of tracking was recently conducted by Goldberg, Passow, and Justman (1966). After carefully examining experimental research in Europe, as well as the United States, they concluded that: "Many of the issues concerning grouping [tracking] remain unresolved, and most questions are still unanswered despite 70 or 80 years of practice and at least 40 years of study. Insufficient and conflicting data are being used to support partisan views concerning the consequences of grouping, rather than to resolve the persistent issues" (p. 21).

These researchers conducted their own carefully constructed and evaluated experimental study of elementary tracking in New York City. After analysis of the data collected, they stated: ". . . in predominantly middle-class elementary schools, narrowing the ability range in the classroom on the basis of some measure of general academic aptitude will, by itself, in the absence of carefully planned adaptations of content and methods, produce little positive change in the academic achievement of pupils at any ability level. However, the study found no support for the contention that narrow range classes are associated with negative effects on self-concept, aspirations, interest, attitudes toward school, and other non-intellective factors" (pp. 167–168). They concluded that tracking in itself is neither good nor bad: "Grouping can be, at best, ineffective, at worst, harmful. It can become harmful when it lulls teachers and parents into believing that because there is grouping, the school is providing differentiated education for pupils of varying degrees of ability, when in reality that is not the case. It may become dangerous when it leads teachers to underestimate the learning capacity of pupils at the lower ability levels. It can also be damaging when it is inflexible and does not provide channels for moving children from lower to higher ability groups and back again. . . ." (p. 168).

Statements like the above are of particular relevance to Mexican Americans in Southwestern schools. It is the contention of this author, supported by observations and interviews, that most tracking adversely affects both teachers' and students' expectations and their subsequent behavior. Goldberg, Passow, and Justman found that tracking did not significantly affect the self-concept, attitudes, or aspirations of their middle-class sample. They point out that this may be true because low-track students did not differ socially or ethnically from high-ability sections, "thus did not perceive their status as socially or racially segregated with a concomitant degradation which such segregation may imply" (pp. 165–166).

Regardless of the effect on academic achievement, the track system, as commonly functioning now in the Southwest, unduly isolates Mexican American youth from equal-status interaction with others. The low-ability track status of most Mexican American children reinforces existing stereotypes. Mexican American children learn their future subordinate role in society by practicing it at school; Anglos reaffirm their superordinate position and find proof positive that Mexican Americans are indeed dull-witted, as stereotyped. Ethnic homogeneity in tracks supports group cleavage and maintains cultural difference and may in fact slow the process of acculturation. Thus the track system may run counter to the almost universally professed desire to Americanize foreign groups through the schools. Any practice that keeps two cultural groups apart inhibits one from learning the culture of the other.

Tracking is an ethical and legal, as well as an educational, dilemma. Critics ask whether it is the prerogative of the school to predict, and perhaps predetermine, success or failure in school and society. If American society is based on the inalienable right to succeed, can this right be abrogated by the practices of schools? Concomitant with the right to success is an equally inalienable right to fail. Some critics argue that as long as the school impinges on neither, American democracy is served. The track system may not be Constitutional. In a recent landmark decision, a United States District Court enjoined the city schools of Washington, D.C., from the practice. The decision was based on provisions of the Constitution insuring "due process" and "equal protection of the law." The court found that the track system deprived poor people and Negroes of rights guaranteed them and was, by its very nature, discriminatory. The information collected during the hearings, concerning the practice of tracking in Washington schools, could equally well describe the practice in most Southwestern schools. After extended hearings, the judge, in his closing remarks, said: "Even in concept, the track is undemocratic and discriminatory. Its creator admits it is designed to prepare some children for white collar, and other children for blue collar, jobs. Considering the tests used to determine which children should receive the blue collar special, and which the white, the danger of children completing their education wearing the wrong collar is far too great for this democracy to tolerate" (United States District Court, Defendants' Civil Action No. 82–66, p. 177). The impact of this decision on tracking in Southwestern schools can only be conjecture. To what degree Mexican American organizations will attempt recourse to the courts for redress depends on a multitude of social and political factors.

The previously widespread practice of assigning all Spanish-surname children to "Mexican rooms" within mixed schools is disappearing. Such extreme tracking is, in reality, a form of segregation, popular in areas where no "Mexican school" is maintained. Samora reported in 1963 (pp. 2–3): "Many communities have had their 'Mexican rooms' for years and years. This is segregation on pseudopedagogical grounds, the reasoning behind being that children who come to school who are Spanish-speaking should be placed in a room by themselves in order to learn English. One community in Colorado had such segregation through the first four grades as late as 1950. A neighboring community in Southern Colorado just abandoned their 'Mexican rooms' last year, after pressure was brought about by the local Spanish-speaking citizenry."

Some "slow" tracks in mixed schools are 100 percent Mexican American. It is difficult to determine whether this tracking is established for ethnic or "ability" reasons. A recent case in point involved a school district in the eastern part of New Mexico, an area with a long history of attempts at isolation or segregation of its Mexican American school population. Pressure from the G. I. Forum and other Mexican American organizations was brought to bear; state education department officials investigated, and explanation and solution were forthcoming. A Mexican American organization officer interviewed for this study inferred that the district will probably attempt the reestablishment of "Mexican rooms." This interviewee contended that such rooms were the result of ethnic prejudice rather than ability tracking.

"Special education" classes—that is, classes for children who are classified as mentally retarded—are an extreme form of tracking. Mexican Americans are greatly overrepresented in such classes. In the 10 California counties that have the largest number of Spanish-surname students, there were almost twice as many Spanish-surname children in special education as their percentage in the total school population would indicate. These 10 counties had an average Spanish-surname enrollment of 15.35 percent, and 30.09 percent of special-education students had Spanish last names. This figure includes one county, Alameda, in which 10.14 percent of the enrollment was Spanish surname and only 13.03 percent were in special education, thus lowering the percentage for all 10 counties together. In the California counties ranked 39 through 48 according to number of Spanish-surname students, it was found that the average enrollment of Spanish-surname students was 2.76 percent and there was an average of 3.63 percent in special education classes. The counties ranked 49 through 58 had so very few Spanish surnames that percentages were not calculated. Apparently the larger the Mexican American percentage within schools, the more likely it is that the children will be considered retarded. Perhaps when the number is small, minority-group children are considered more individually, and when the group is large stereotypes have more influence on judgments concerning individuals. Undoubtedly, a multitude of other forces are at play. For California as a whole, 13.30 percent of the school enrollment are students with Spanish surnames, and 26.62 percent of special-education students have Spanish surnames (California State Department of Education, 1967a). Observations made and questions asked during this study regarding the percentage of Mexican Americans in special-education classes throughout the Southwest revealed similar disproportions, although statistics are unavailable.

Although Mexican Americans are overrepresented in classes for the educable mentally retarded, they are not overrepresented in the lower levels of retardation. Mercer and other researchers are carefully compiling data on mental retardation in a California metropolitan area assumed to be representative of the nation. To date, much of their research is unpublished, but a letter of inquiry brought the following reply (1967): "When ethnic group was studied alone, there were disproportionately large numbers of identified mental retardates of Mexican-American and Negro heritage. The numbers ran almost five times higher among Mexican-Americans and three times higher among Negroes than would be expected from their percentage in the population. . . . However, when the data are analyzed by IQ level, the disproportionately high numbers in the Mexican-American and Negro populations are all concentrated in persons with IQ's over 50. They have, percentage-wise, no more mental retardates with IQ's under 50 than does the Anglo-American population. It appears from these preliminary findings that the higher rate of identified mental retardation among Mexican-American and Negro populations is accounted for by the so-called 'undifferentiated' types of retardation—the cultural-familial varieties which are highly related to social and economic deprivation."

The failure of standard psychometric instruments to measure Mexican American children validly is recognized as a principal reason for the overrepresentation of that ethnic group in special education, as well as in other low tracks. However, Palomares and Johnson conducted an experiment that demonstrated the crucial role played by the psychologist (1966, pp. 27, 29). Each author tested and interviewed a number of Mexican American children who had been recommended for EMR (Educable Mentally Retarded) class placement. After testing the children with standard instruments, "The non-Spanish-speaking psychologist [Johnson] found 24 of his 33 pupils (73 percent) eligible for EMR classes and recommended their placement. In contrast, the Spanish-speaking psychologist [Palomares] recommended that only 9 of his 35 pupils (26 percent) be placed in EMR classes. Clearly, examiners, as well as tests, differ, even though the pupils tested are similar and the tests used are the same." After a discussion of the psychometric instruments used, the authors concluded: "The importance of the psychologist as a variable in the evaluation process has received less attention than the tests. The results of this study indicate that the examiner is a most important variable. Whether the examiner does or does not speak Spanish may aid in his establishing rapport. . . . [The] examiner's years of experience and his understanding of school problems and cultural handicaps presented by those pupils are more important than his fluency with the language." It is suspected that a larger-scale experiment would result in similar findings. As in so many educational endeavors, it is not so much a problem of the tools of the trade as it is a problem of the lack of understanding and skill of the workmen.

Teachers of special-education classes, and administrators in charge of such programs, were asked in the course of this study to estimate the number of Mexican Americans within such classes that were truly mentally deficient. Only one replied that all were; others estimated that from 50 to 80 percent rightfully belong in regular classes. An interesting point of view is espoused by a few educators, especially special-education teachers. While they recognize that most Mexican Americans in special classes are "sharp" and intelligent, they argue that it's better to allow them to stay where they are because in special education children receive the individual attention and psychological support lacking in regular classrooms.

CULTURAL EXCLUSION

Many educators in schools that have large percentages of low-status, non-Angloized Mexican American students believe in rigid exclusion of all things Mexican. The higher the percentage of Mexican Americans in a given school, the more rigidly their culture, or the culture they are assumed to have, is excluded. Cultural exclusion takes many forms; by far the most obvious is the prohibition of anything that seems "foreign," including the carrier of culture itself, the Spanish language. A more subtle form of exclusion is curricular rigidity; schools with high percentages of Mexican Americans tend to adhere most carefully to state or local curriculum guides and grade-level requirements. Few institutions can thus modify their curriculums to include elements relative to the lives, expectations, experiences, or values of Mexican American children.

The culturally "Mexican" child has and does present the school with an extreme challenge to Americanize him and acculturate him, and do it as rapidly as possible: "The philosophy of the State and local school systems is imbued with the traditional middle-class Anglo-American value that all minority and immigrant groups should be required to abandon their native languages and cultures, give up their identity, and become absorbed as individuals into the dominant group, usually on a lower-class level. If any group resists full acculturation, it is regarded as somewhat uncivilized, un-American, and potentially subversive. There is a complete unwillingness to accept the idea that a native born American who happens to want to speak Spanish, German, or Polish, and to retain many of the values of his native culture, might well be a loyal American. As a result, the full force of the educational system in the Southwest has been directed toward the eradication of both the Spanish language and the Spanish-American or Mexican-American cultures" (Knowlton, 1965). In order to accomplish this eradication, almost every vestige of "Mexicanness" is excluded from the school environment. Christian and Christian (1966, p. 304) say that the Mexican American has been thought to be "a thorn in the side of educators" and that the Spanish language and culture are "weeds to be uprooted so that English and 'our way of life' can flourish." To accomplish this uprooting a school must have a strong authority structure.

Authoritarianism. Schools with large percentages of Mexican American children tend to maintain order rigidly. "Mexican schools" tend to be less permissive than Anglo or mixed schools within the same district. Texas schools in general are more authoritarian than those of California, in part perhaps because California is less Southern in general attitude, its society is more open, and its educational philosophy is influenced to a greater degree by progressives.

The reliance on rigid control can be partially explained by recognizing that educators are insecure in their roles; their status is ambiguous or poorly defined. There is a perilous equilibrium of authority in the political structure of educational institutions. According to Waller (1932, pp. 10–11), the school "... is a despotism threatened from within and exposed to regulation and interference from without. It is a despotism capable of being overturned in a moment, exposed to the instant loss of its stability and its prestige. . . . The authority of the school executives and the teachers is in unremitting danger from (1) students, (2) parents, (3) the school board, (4) each other . . . the members of these groups, since they threaten his authority, are to some extent the natural enemies of the person who represents and lives by authority. . . ."

Culturally different students, especially adolescents, pose threats that are not encountered with other children. Their culture and language are unknown and "bad." It appears that the larger the percentage of Mexican American students the more necessary is the use of strong authority in order to control and "convert" them. Conforming behavior is insured by rigid sanctions against overt manifestations of "Mexicanness." Secondary school students are less tractable and more of a challenge than young children, and thus strong authority structures are most evident in junior and senior high schools.

The "No Spanish Rule." The Southwest has a long history of prohibiting the speaking of Spanish in school. Social scientists and critics make a strong case that this is inferred by Mexican Americans to be a prohibition or negation of their homes and culture. The school curriculum, with few exceptions, is carried in English. Some educators believe that prohibiting Spanish encourages rapid acculturation. Institutional arguments for the "no Spanish rule" are well known and regularly stated: (1) English is the national language and must be learned; the best way to learn it is to prohibit Spanish; (2) bilingualism is mentally confusing; (3) the Spanish spoken in the Southwest is a substandard dialect; and (4) teachers don't understand Spanish. Although schools are undergoing change, the prohibition of Spanish is still widespread. The argument that Anglo staff cannot understand Spanish and therefore it should be prohibited is prevalent. Such statements as "I can't understand them" and "It's impolite to talk a foreign language in front of a person who doesn't speak it" are common. To what degree the institutional prohibition of Spanish speaking reflects these feelings is unknown. Perhaps the truth is that Spanish speaking is an extreme threat to authority: those in power don't know what the Mexican Americans are saying. Are they being disrespectful, impudent, using foul language, urging their peers to riot and revolt? The enemy is seen to be using undecipherable code and thus violating the established conventions of war (school regulations).

The constant and increasingly loud criticism of the "no Spanish rule," as well as the widespread advocacy of bilingual instruction, should have eliminated this problem by now. It has disappeared in some schools, yet still persists in many others. Many schools no longer actively prohibit Spanish—instead, they encourage English. Whether encouraging English is not prohibiting Spanish depends on the local situation. The difficulty of determining what is truly happening is obvious. In one all Mexican American junior high school in Texas the teacher's manual says: "Encourage the use of English. All teachers are expected to correct students using Spanish on school property." From observation and interviewing in this school, it appears that every effort is made to prohibit Spanish but that it is almost impossible to do so.

Numerous examples of imposing strong sanctions against Spanish are encountered. One almost wholly Mexican American district did so until recently when it received a substantial private grant to experiment with bilingual instruction. A state department of education official commented that apparently a principal consideration in awarding the grant was that English speaking was rigidly enforced in district schools.

"Spanish detention" still exists. At one Texas secondary school, students caught speaking Spanish are punished; if they persist, they are suspended and ultimately may be expelled. This school is approximately 100 percent Mexican American and serves a slum area. Commenting on this particular situation, a local university professor said: "They have what they call Spanish detention and if the child is caught speaking Spanish he is usually held after school for an hour, an hour and a half. If he persists, he may be spanked by the principal." In another Texas city, similarly strong sanctions were imposed by a Mexican American high school principal on his 99 percent Mexican American student body.

The younger the child, the less strict the rules; secondary schools appear to exert more pressure than elementary schools. Numerous Southwestern elementary schools are encouraging the speaking of Spanish, and doubtless the majority of Southwestern institutions no longer actively prohibit it. Many educators interviewed for this study saw the prohibition of Spanish as an anachronism and expressed hope that it would be universally abolished. Federal educational assistance under the Bilingual Education Act may encourage the elimination of such practices.

Other Behavioral Controls. The "no Spanish rule" is part of a whole syndrome of behavioral controls imposed by Southwestern schools. Institutions observed, with few exceptions, tend to prohibit other manifestations of "Mexicanness." As such manifestations are most prevalent among the unacculturated and the poor, strongest sanctions are found in schools serving that population. At the secondary level, Mexican American students often appear to be the very model of modern, middle-class teenagers. Elementary school students are much less so. In attempting to convert Mexican Americans to "our way of life," the school inadvertently creates an environment that does not reflect the real American culture. Rather, the climate is ideal middle class: the "unsavory" aspects of American culture, its diversity and controversial elements, are excluded. The enforcement of strict behavioral standards promotes serious culture conflict. Children learn a culture (language, values, expectations, roles, and so on) in their homes or from their peers. The school enforces another and different culture. In order to persist in the school, the child is required to drop the other culture, at least outwardly, and manifest the cultural characteristics demanded by the institution. Many cannot do this and flee the hostile school environment, removing themselves mentally in the elementary school years and physically as soon as local law or practice permits. (For more information about culture conflict and education see Allinsmith and Goethals, 1956; Spindler, 1963; Henry, 1960, pp. 267–305.)

Space does not permit full explanation of this rarely discussed topic. Suffice it to say that a rather extreme form of culture conflict may be apparent between the home and the school. The product of this conflict is usually the rejection of the new school values and mores, while the child remains essentially what his own culture dictates. However, with two sets of rules imposed, some children react negatively. Caught between two cultures, a significant number manifest signs of personal disorganization: "The conflict in directives is perhaps the source of the most serious difficulties in larger, less homogeneous societies, where the total educational process includes schooling as well as training in the home. Serious conflicts and deep-seated maladjustments may result from education [schooling] received at the hands of persons whose cultural or sub-cultural frames of reference differ" (Herskovits, 1957, p. 315). The student rejects one culture or the other; few can live with the internal conflict generated by two sets of values and mores. Since he has to live in a real society, he will often reject what he sees as the meaningless, artificial, and inappropriate culture taught at school.

Many subtle aspects of culture conflict affect Mexican Americans in school; examples of a few can be cited. Every culture or subculture teaches children what kind of man or woman they are expected to become. In some cases the male role learned by Mexican American boys is diametrically opposed to the behavior demanded by the middle-class-oriented school. Most secondary schools stringently prohibit boys from having long hair, sideburns, mustaches, wearing tight pants or shirts with more than the collar button open. Boys are suspended for violation of this code. Rubel (1966), in his study of a Mexican American community in Texas, indicated that rigid dress behavior is required in the local junior high school. An administrator stated that each Mexican American child is screened before he is permitted to enroll, and "if he wants to stay, he has to get a good haircut, cut off the sideburns." Another educator interviewed by Rubel concurred (p. 11): "We try to get kids' hair cut, get 'em to look like the rest; cut off the *pachuco* style . . . down in old Mexico they go around with their shirt unbuttoned all the way down to the navel, and then they tie it around their waist. They think it makes them look sexy. We can't have that here."

Rigid codes are enforced in most Southwestern schools. In a California junior high the vice-principal cut a seventh grader's long black locks: "Shame-faced and almost in tears, Mexican-born John Garcia took his seat in class. His head was bald in spots. He tried to hide the black tufts of hair that stuck out all over. There was an awkward silence. Garcia's humiliation was to serve as a warning to the other boys. Haircutting never works [John's English teacher commented later]. All this does is force them out of school; they've had this kind of treatment since the first grade. Why should they want to stay in?" (Industrial Union Department, AFL-CIO, 1966, pp. 18–19). The teacher pointed out that Anglo children are never given such treatment.

Children are regularly suspended, and ultimately excluded, for "non-American" physical appearance. A school social worker in Texas interviewed said this: "One of the biggest problems that I have in my job is to go and ask a father to tell his son to cut his hair in an Anglo-ized way, with the short sideburns and no bush on top, and the father is wearing his hair exactly like the son. About the only thing you can tell him is that, 'Look we don't like this at school because children don't dress like that and we don't want the children to look like adults.' This is really stepping on eggshells." The implications of conflict are obvious. The school enforces a kind of conformity that may violate what some Mexican American boys accept as manliness. As dress codes appear to be more rigorously enforced in lower-social-class schools, the brunt of this practice falls on those most prone to adhere to divergent dress or grooming.

Psychologists say that a child's name is perhaps a first touchstone of self-identity. Yet schools continue to change the Spanish given names of children as they enter. Many parents do desire to use English names, but many see nothing improper about the Spanish Christian names conferred at baptism. Teachers apparently do. *Jesús* is almost invariably changed to Jesse; after all, good middle-class teachers couldn't say "Jesus, I want you to be quiet and sit down." One does wonder, however, why they couldn't use *Jesús*. *María* becomes Mary, *Juan* John, *Roberto* Bobby, and so on. Although it may seem unimportant, it can be argued that the Angloization of Spanish Christian names may do psychic harm. Such practices reflect the way the school sees the Mexican American child and are part of the syndrome of culture conflict as encouraged by the school in its attempts to obliterate things Mexican. A question concerning Anglo perception of Mexican culture must be raised. If a little French boy named *Pierre* entered a Southwestern school, would teachers change his name to Peter? Probably not, on the grounds that the French are "cultured people." Mexican Americans are not and must be transmuted as soon as possible into full-fledged Americans.

Modesty, of a very special nature, is taught in some traditional Mexican American families. Girls learn not to expose their bodies. Medical examination by male doctors is abhorred, as is nudity in front of other females. Group showering is required in practically all secondary school physical education classes. To force a Mexican American girl who has been taught this kind of modesty to disrobe and shower in the presence of others is a direct affront to strongly ingrained beliefs. Girls are reported to form circles around their disrobing peers and use other devices and ruses to protect their modesty. In this case, the Anglo core value of cleanliness, institutionalized, confronts traditional Mexican modesty.

Ramirez and Taylor conducted research relative to the influence of identification with traditional Mexican American culture and student "success" in northern California junior high schools and senior high schools. In a preliminary report, Ramirez (1967b) contends that there is little doubt that some Mexican American negative feelings toward school and some of their poor achievement in school are attributable to culture conflict. He states: "By assessing attitudes toward education and reviewing the cumulative files of 300 Mexican-American students, the researchers were able to identify those students who are experiencing most difficulty in adjusting to school setting and, thus, seemed to be those most likely to drop out in the near future. . . . These students were interviewed, observed in class and were asked to tell stories relating to pictures depicting students, teachers, and parents interacting in a school setting. The stories told to these pictures were very revealing in terms of value conflicts and their effect on the adjustment of the student and his attitude toward the school." While finding that all Mexican Americans do not hold traditional ethnic values, Ramirez did demonstrate that culture conflict was apparent in some students. With these students, the value orientations that cause the most conflict with the school's expectations include those previously mentioned plus the fact that the traditional culture: ". . . teaches the adolescent to be loyal to his family group. This frequently results in subordination of the student's educational goals when the family is in need of help. . . ." Ramirez concludes that traditional Mexican American students bring: ". . . values with [them] to the school which in many cases are in direct opposition to those of their teachers, counselors and principals. Not only must the bicultural student face conflicts at school; he also meets conflicts in the home when the values he learns at school are opposed by parents. He is thus continually faced with the ominous choice of conforming or quitting. This usually results in feelings of insecurity and eventually in negative feelings toward the school which he comes to see as the source of his frustration and ambivalence."

The previous examples of conflict induced or encouraged by school policies and practices concentrate on children reared in the "traditional" Mexican American family. These families are becoming less common in much of the Southwest; perhaps most Mexican American children grow up in families that are themselves transitional. Minority-group families run the gamut from the traditional to the highly *agringado*. Between these poles, all number of possible variations of transitional culture exist. With the possible exception of the *agringado,* who meshes quite well with the school's expectations and often with his Anglo peers, traditional and marginal children manifest a strong proclivity to form tight ethnic peer groupings. Mexican American children reaching adolescence and caught between quite divergent cultures at home and at school tend to place great reliance on their peers for psychic support, value orientation, and roles. In a sense, these peer societies form their own transitional subcultures. The ethnic peer group exerts a tremendous influence on many Mexican American teenagers' lives and on their success in school. For many Mexican American youngsters, the peer group is a primary agency of socialization. The outward manifestations of peer-society membership are likely to be bizarre: new argots, unusual dress, "peculiar" behavior, and so on.

The ethnic peer group functions in numerous ways. It provides sanctuary and protection in schools, establishes acceptable and unacceptable behavior, ameliorates certain kinds of anxiety, defines male and female roles, and carefully prescribes the types of academic success and school participation deemed acceptable. Robles' 1964 study of a California junior high school that draws its Mexican American students from a *barrio* elementary school clearly describes how the ethnic peer group affects the upwardly mobile Mexican American student's school behavior. As a result of strong peer allegiance, there is: ". . . a noticeable lack of participation, avoidance and lack of interaction with the total student life of the school . . . this behavior stems from . . . peer group pressures because most of the mobility oriented students show a higher aspirational level [and more interaction] when the peer group is not present" (pp. 66–67). The effect of the ethnic peer group is often to set low school aspiration levels and thus adversely affect grades and achievement. Robles points out that conscientious school personnel can accomplish much to modify such situations if they understand the total social function of the ethnic peer group.

Attitudes and actions relative to ethnic peer groups vary in the Southwest. Most educators interviewed during this study indicated that they saw such groups as negative and detrimental to the school and the individuals involved. In most cases, the schoolmen see their role as suppressive, and strong regulations against outward manifestations of membership in these groups are exercised. In many secondary institutions there is literally a hot war in process between ethnic peer groups and the school. In many cases efforts are made to destroy, rearrange, or modify the groups; they are often held to be delinquent or involved in some form of antisocial behavior. Little understanding of the role such groups play in the lives of culturally marginal Mexican American adolescents was demonstrated by the schoolmen interviewed.

The ethnic peer group may be seen as another threat to stability and the authority structure of the school. The more divergent the group's behavior, the greater the threat is seen to be. The middle-class peer group, although it is not totally acceptable to school management, is not so threatening as the ethnic peer group so characteristic of urban slums: "While cars, dates, and athletic success are far more valued than scholastic competence, even in middle-class schools, still teachers find it easier to maintain order within the schoolroom and the children do manage to acquire more of the subject matter taught there. The big difference between the situation of slum and suburb is not the literacy of the parents, but the meshing of values of parents and teachers. By providing an understanding support of their children in school, parents reduce the necessity of the child to rely so heavily on his peers in his struggle with educational authority" (Wax, Wax, and Dumont, 1964, p. 97). The values of many Mexican Americans do not mesh with those of the school, and low-status Mexican American parents do not lend the essential support.

The roles, values, languages, and so forth learned from the ethnic peer society, like those learned in the "traditional" home, are regularly prohibited by schools, since the newly learned peer culture is often diametrically opposed to the middle-class expectations of many teachers and administrators. Again, conflict results: what is meaningful to the child is prohibited by the institution. Some institutions attempt individual counseling to "save the better youngsters" from their peers. This attempt, usually a you-know-what-is-right-and-good-for-you appeal by counseling staff, fails to recognize the tremendous social and psychological pressure on the child. The school's rigid prohibition of the outward manifestation of peer-group membership creates an intolerable situation for some adolescents. Rather than treat such manifestations of marginality as normal and useful, the school declares open warfare. In so acting, it denies or contradicts what the child is doing to find his place in society and learn his own identity. It drives the peer group underground and often drives its members from school.

Some educators, however, do see the strong ethnic peer group as normal, understandable, and useful. Counselors at one California high school visited are making a sustained effort to use the peer group itself as a tool to raise achievement and increase "positive" school participation. They are attempting through nondirective counseling techniques to reorient the groups without destroying their integrity.

Even in the most authoritarian institutions, some traces of Mexican culture are permitted and sometimes encouraged; items encouraged usually reflect the controlling Anglos' acceptance and perhaps idealization of certain aspects of the Mexican culture. Music, art, the celebration of certain Mexican festivals and holidays, and so on are often promoted. Thus the educator's stereotype of the quaint or picturesque Mexican culture is sustained, and Mexican American children are encouraged to become what educators think they already are.

The lower the social class of the student body, the more rigidly the child is expected to conform to the educator's image of the perfect middle-class Anglo teenager. The predominantly Mexican American secondary schools in Texas observed were extremely rigid in their prohibition of all but "perfect" (idealized middle-class) behavior. California schools were much less so. Yet, in all states visited, *minority* or *mixed* lower-class schools appeared more restrictive than middle-class institutions. Many Texas slum minority schools are ultraconformist, tending to operate by the book. Classroom discipline is rigid, children speak when spoken to, halls and playgrounds are patrolled and rigidly controlled, gum chewing can lead to suspension, dress codes are strictly enforced, hair is short, dresses long. The Mexican American teenager who cannot or will not conform is pushed out early in his junior or senior high school career. The rest of the children appear to be "ideal" middle-class teenagers. Unfortunately, rigidity of behavioral standards and the conflict such standards engender drive many traditional, transitional, or low-status Mexican Americans from school.

The Curriculum. The three components of the school curriculum—its content, method, and sequence—are drawn from the culture carried by a society. The content is drawn from the history, knowledge, skills, values, expectations, roles, laws, and so forth of parent generations. Teaching methods reflect how members of a given society commonly teach children, as well as how they teach their children to learn. Sequence is made up from analyses of the stages of development at which the children of a given society are exposed to and internalize certain cultural items.

In American society, school curriculum is based on an analysis of the middle class. The curriculum is usually somewhat dated, even for middle-class children, but it does appear to approximate at least the "ideal" culture of the average home. When this same curriculum is employed with culturally divergent children, severe reactions can be anticipated. What may well be relevant to the "normal" or "standard" American child may be irrelevant to another subsociety's child. In extreme cases, what is taught the "standard" child is directly contrary to what has already been learned by the "different" child. Many educators believe that the failure of the school curriculum to reflect and supplement the home curriculum (culture) is responsible for many Mexican Americans' failure in school.

A number of comparisons can be made between disadvantaged, predominantly minority, schools and more advantaged Anglo or mixed schools. Differences pertaining to behavior have already been cited. In general, the lower the social class and the higher the ethnic density in the school, the more rigidly teachers adhere to state or local curriculum guides and texts. Difference is equally apparent between high- and low-ability tracks within the same school. The lower the track level, the more bookish, less oral, more rote, more dogmatic, more memoristic the techniques of instruction appear to be. The higher the social class of the school, the more progressive the approach (or at least the more acceptable in contemporary education theory). The learning environment of many predominantly Mexican American schools or classes can best be characterized as dull and uninspired. Many Mexican American classes observed in this study consisted almost exclusively of recitation of facts, truths, values (the fable of the ant and the grasshopper is popular for young children). At high schools, numerous "discussions" were observed; in reality they were usually only recitations.

Rigid adherence to local or state grade-level requirements contributes to the narrowness of the curriculum content so obvious in many disadvantaged classrooms. If it is required that certain first-grade texts must be read, for example, a supreme effort is usually made to get each child to read at that level. The skills of reading are emphasized and the time for other activities reduced. If a certain number of "concepts" must be learned in order to move to the next grade, memoristic methods are often resorted to almost exclusively. If an average child is deemed to need x number of words to be promoted to second grade, teachers tend to teach only these words. The long-established practices of inflexible grade-level requirements contribute to curriculum rigidity and memoristic teaching, and cause a large number of Mexican American children to repeat grades and thus become overage.

If it is thought essential to devote maximum time and effort to teaching those skills on which grade level and promotion are based, little time remains for teaching anything else that might be relevant and intrinsically rewarding. What little intrinsic reward in the form of relevant learning experience may be found in high-ability or middle-class classrooms is all too often lacking in the lower tracks. Low-status children are overrepresented in low-ability groups; in many areas, the lowest-ability group is the Mexican Americans, and they thus suffer most from the "good intentions" of teachers and the system.

Couple the above situation with the fact that learning experiences in school may be out of sequence for low-status minority-group children, and another problem is evident. The sequence of the curriculum is based on analysis of the children of the dominant society; Mexican American children may be learning cultural items in their subsociety at a different period in their lives. It may be true that middle-class children, as a group, are "ready" to read English at six but that Spanish speakers are not, and it may be true that many low-status children are "ready" to learn the decimal and money systems at five while middle-class children are not ready until later. Yet curriculum sequence is rarely substantially modified for culturally different learners. When the content is out of sequence for a group, the school inadvertently reduces the relevancy of the learning experience, making such "learning" unnatural and exclusively dependent on the rewards school or teacher offers. Intrinsic reward for school learning is reduced. It appears that this situation is all too common.

Regardless of the general rule, numerous oral, spontaneous, and exciting schoolroom situations were observed. However, these exceptions neither prove nor disprove the rule. Texas schools are again the extreme example; few such very "traditional" classes were observed in California and the other states. Yet, in all states visited it was generally true that the higher the ethnic density of the class, the more traditional the teacher-learner relationship and the more rigid the adherence to set curriculum.

Lack of connection between home and school culture has long been recognized as a problem. Curricular irrelevancy was seen as a principal problem to be solved as early as 1941: "Such subject matter as geography, history, and health, is taught in terms that are foreign to the [Spanish-Americans]. During the school year of 1939–40, the pupils of El Cerrito [a small rural New Mexico community] worked out posters and other projects based on such subjects as transportation in Boston and importance of navigation in the growth of Chicago. Under such a curriculum as this, it is small wonder that pupil interest is at a minimum and that progress is slow" (Leonard and Loomis, 1941, p. 53). Many educators continue the theme today, contending that low-status children's lack of interest in school is partially due to the fact that they see little or no connection between what they learn in school and live at home. As has often been reported, school readers tell stories about families of different color and culture. For example, stories about fathers going to the office and children returning to beautiful bedrooms and homes are seen as irrelevant to low-status children. Attempts are being made to rectify this situation, and many new texts and primers are being published. Admirable as this is, it is only a superficial remedy for the problem of irrelevancy and culture conflict. The curriculum of the school is rarely substantially modified by using "paint their faces brown" texts. To change the curriculum radically, to incorporate relevant and nonconflicting items from the Mexican American home culture may actually be impossible for the average middle-class teacher or school system. Many schoolmen would see incorporating culture they consider to be "bad," negative, or foreign as supporting the very life-styles they and their schools are dedicated to eradicate. A real quandary exists.

The curriculum is permeated with the assumed ideals, not necessarily the mores, of middle-class culture. Extreme cleanliness, respect for the law, unfamiliar manners and morals, and so forth continue to confront Mexican American children in school. They are expected to learn (memorize) these things in order to gain a grade or teacher approval. Perhaps such exercises are only irrelevant to the child and what is so learned will soon be forgotten. However, certain conflicts are created. For example, a Head Start teacher interviewed was appalled by the lack of respect for the police manifest in her Mexican American children. To overcome this, a large blue "Policeman Sam" some five feet tall was constructed of cardboard. Children were drilled on how Sam helped them, protected them, and was a friend of the family. The children observed seemed eager to please the pleasant teacher and were rewarded for their recitations of how good Sam was by her acceptance and praise. Policemen may be seen in a totally different way at home, and a child might be severely punished for his school-taught reply to his father's question about what he is learning in school. Children are taught the same nursery-rhyme stories that are used with middle-class children; the maxims of Anglo middle-class culture are drilled and drilled. Many of these are probably irrelevant; some may be conflicting.

Cleanliness is an obsession with many teachers, Mexican American as well as Anglo. It is taught to minority-group children by explaining the reason for it (to wash away germs), by having them constantly wash their hands, by drill in brushing teeth, and by rote memorization of information and maxims reinforcing cleanliness. Clean is translated into *limpio* (with little understanding that *limpio* does not carry the same cultural meaning as *clean; limpio* means clean in the scrubbed way while *clean* involves a whole set of moral connotations). No stone is left unturned to insure the Americanization of Mexican American children in this regard. One elementary school teacher interviewed advocated the forceful bathing of "dirty Mexican kids because it will teach them how nice it feels to be clean," a very doubtful result. A school social worker commenting on his district teachers said: "We have the type of teacher that wouldn't let a Mexican child hug her without looking at the hair to see if there are lice."

Nutritional practices of the children are causes for indignation and elicit strenuous efforts to modify food preferences. A Texas school principal, complaining about the children's refusal to eat vegetables, commented that beans and carrots seemed to be the only vegetables they would eat. In the same school, children were prohibited from access to hot pepper sauces; only the teachers' table had such condiments. "We don't serve children such highly seasoned food because it's bad for the digestion," commented the principal. The central cafeteria of a large district, about 85 percent Mexican American, served half an avocado and a carton of milk on the same lunch to its thousands of students. In this area, many believe that these two foods eaten together cause *empacho* (a digestive upset). Understandably, many children left one or the other item. The consternation over the waste can be imagined. An Anglo home economics teacher was observed in a junior high school as she explained a well-balanced dinner to a group of Mexican American girls. The children were confounded that the menu included a "hot" and a "cold" food, a practice they had been taught was guaranteed to produce *empacho*. The girls questioned the teacher concerning this and were answered with an "I never heard such superstitious nonsense" argument. This teacher as well as the others mentioned above seemed totally unaware of the influence of culture on the stomach. Proper dinner service is emphasized, as are table manners: "A person just can't eat with a *tortilla* among nice people." This may be in considerable conflict with what "nice people" do at home.

Inflexibility and rigidity of school practices and curricular irrelevancy or conflict are seen as interrelated aspects that function to the detriment of culturally different Mexican American children. Ungraded, or multilevel, primary grades are becoming increasingly popular as a solution to grade-level rigidity. Whether in fact this reorganization significantly modifies the present situation requires analysis of each school. If nine levels with rigid set requirements are substituted for the previous three grades, it is doubtful that any substantial change is made. However, if there are flexible requirements for the levels, there may be real change. A Texas superintendent interviewed implied that his newly instituted upgraded primary system was, in essence, a subterfuge. He said that it was essentially a tracking device, one of its advantages being that parents do not attach as much stigma to their children's repeating a level, or remaining there longer than normal, as they do to failing a grade and being retained.

An obvious aspect of rigidity is the traditional school year. The September-to-June calendar precludes many migrant and other agriculturally dependent families from sending their children to school for the full academic year. This fact, coupled with rigid grade-level requirements, is partially responsible for the large number of migrant children who fail to be promoted. Only recently are schools beginning to adjust to the migrants' calendar, but most migrant schools observed for this study appear not to be adjusting their regular grade-level requirements, curriculum, or school policies and practices.

Few educators interviewed are aware of the ramifications of curricular irrelevancy and conflict. However, many recognize such obvious problems as that the American history taught in school may be in serious disagreement with the history of Mexico and the Southwest taught at home. Many see the inherent problems of a curriculum taught solely in English, especially if little is done to teach Spanish-speaking children the language of the school. Unfortunately, thoughtful analysis of the effect on Mexican American children of curriculum, policies, and practices is rarely evident. The failure of most educators to recognize the influence of conflict on personality and behavior as well as the conditions permitting one cultural group to accept innovations from another causes a tremendous loss of time and energy. The school sees the children that won't accept "our way of life" as "stubborn," failing to understand the massive support of the diverse Mexican American subsocieties and subcultures that reinforce this "stubbornness."

DIFFERENCES IN PERCEPTIONS AND FACILITIES

Great differences exist among educational institutions in the Southwest as well as among schools within the same local administrative structure. This section delves into some of these differences. Little hard evidence can be presented in some of the areas discussed, and therefore much that is written here relies on impressions gained from observations.

Teachers' Views. Teachers are not unlike other middle-class citizens. They almost universally see their role and the school's to be one of encouraging the poor and foreign to become full-fledged middle-class Americans. They genuinely and willingly desire to help Mexican Americans, but they don't necessarily like them or like or accept them as they are. Friedenberg contends that (1967, pp. 194–195): "Between the traditions and staff of the public school, on the one hand, and the 'culturally deprived' among its clientele, on the other, there is real conflict and often enmity. It is frustrating to deal with these children who ignore, reject, or misinterpret the school's effort to transform them, who find its offerings meaningless, and are unmoved or annoyed by the arguments it offers on its own behalf; who cheerfully shrug off its pretentions. . . ." Indeed the "culturally deprived" and many Mexican Americans do reject institutional endeavors. They may be openly hostile to the school and what it teaches, and they may find its curriculum irrelevant. Many reject the best efforts of the institution by removing themselves mentally in the intermediate grades and physically at the earliest practical moment.

Such rejection encourages teachers' frustration and often covert dislike. Teachers, being human, tend to blame the student for his failure to "learn" what they "teach." Either the peculiar (abnormal) personality characteristics of the individual or the equally strange cultural characteristics of the group are seen to prohibit internalization of the curriculum presented or the social norms taught. Some teachers see the rejection of school as personal failure—they have not "reached the child." The two views are equally frustrating. On the one hand, the child is seen to reject the school because of his home culture or personality, two things exceedingly difficult to modify. On the other, the teacher sees herself as failing, which is particularly damning because she may feel she has conscientiously tried everything. The frustrations inherent in the attempt of one individual or institution to teach another person or group to modify values, modes of life, language, and so forth, can easily be translated into contempt. Poverty and foreignness are acceptable as long as they go away. It is exceedingly difficult to understand, accept, like, or treat as social equals the natives who reject the sincere efforts of the missionaries.

Two major views of the Mexican American exist among Southwestern teachers. The "failure of the culture" idea is gaining wide acceptance, as discussed earlier in this study. A few educators are able to grasp the full implication of the influence of the home culture on children's personality and school performance; but most use the concept of cultural difference to justify the school's failure. The other most common perception involves an undifferentiated view of all children.

Many teachers contend that children are generally alike, regardless of their backgrounds, and that school is equally meaningful to all. Many of these teachers have had little experience with diverse ethnic or poverty groups, nor has their training provided insights into such matters. In 1959, Ulibarri questioned teachers in New Mexico about their awareness and sensitivity to cultural differences and found that teachers generally manifest little real awareness of the differences among Mexican American, American Indian, and Anglo cultures or of the influence each has on children. Most teachers expressed the opinion that school was equally significant and meaningful to children of all three groups (Ulibarri, 1959, pp. 103–105). To what degree a repetition now of Ulibarri's formal research would reach the same conclusion is unknown, but many of the teachers interviewed for this study demonstrated practically no real knowledge of the influence of culture on children's personality and behavior.

The views that Mexican Americans' problems in school may be caused by their individual personalities, by the failure of the culture, or by the failure of teachers, all lead to frustration. The first two views tend to encourage continued and intensified efforts to modify the child; all encourage the development of the common teacher attitude that Mexican American children just can't learn. Too many well-intentioned teachers have given up, contending that failure will continue until the home environment changes, and that until that time there is little hope for all but the exceptional lower-class minority-group child. The pervading atmosphere of almost every school with a high concentration of Mexican Americans that was visited in this study was one of pessimism. Others have received similar impressions. Knowlton (1965, pp. 3–4) reports comments that Mexican American children lack the ability to learn. He writes that teachers have said "Look, so many Spanish-American children have to repeat the first grade two or three times. They just can't learn as fast as Anglo-American children. They lack the native ability to do schoolwork. If you don't believe me, just check their test scores." Many educators have reached this point of view after years of sustained effort. As one California junior high school teacher interviewed for this study phrased it: "We will keep trying . . . but there is nothing you can do with these kids, they can't discuss, they can't talk, all you can do is give them seat work to keep them busy and keep them under control." This perspective often provides justification for rote methods used, as well as for the rigid classroom control so often observed.

Only recently has empirical research tended to corroborate the widely held belief, or suspicion, that teachers' perceptions of children's ability is a crucial factor in academic achievement. Previous experimental evidence has indicated that animals perform better on tests of learning when the experimenters are falsely informed that certain animals have been bred for intelligence. Drawing on earlier research with animals and such phenomena as the placebo and Hawthorne effects (that is, the influence of nonspecific factors on behavior), Rosenthal and Jacobson (1968) studied the effect of teachers' high expectations on children's academic behavior, as measured by standardized instruments. A random sample of children in a south San Francisco low-social-status elementary school were falsely predicted to make dramatic gains in IQ and general class work. Only the teachers, not the parents, were informed of the "blooming" or "spurting" predicted for individual children. The researchers' carefully controlled study rather clearly demonstrated that the false predictions were self-fulfilling and that the experimental groups of children did make substantial gains in IQ.

In addition to the general findings of the rise in IQ for the "spurters," a number of points made in the Rosenthal and Jacobson study (pp. 174–178) are of special interest here.

(1) The expectancy advantage—the degree to which IQ gains by the "special children" exceeded gains by the control group children—was particularly evident among younger children (first and second graders).

(2) Older children who may have been more difficult to influence (did not demonstrate the same degree of expectancy advantage as younger children) may have been better able to maintain their advantage autonomously.

(3) While it was anticipated that slow-track children (the school divided children into three tracks) would be most affected by teachers' expectations, it was found that the middle-track children "spurted" the most. However, the other tracks were not much behind during the first year.

(4) "After the first year of the experiment and also after the second year, the Mexican children showed greater expectancy advantages than did the non-Mexican children, though the difference was not significant statistically. One interesting minority-group effect did reach significance, however, even with just a small sample size. For each of the Mexican children, magnitude of expectancy advantage was computed by subtracting from his or her gain in IQ from pretest to retest, the IQ gain made by the children of the control group in his or her classroom. These magnitudes of expectancy advantage were then correlated with the 'Mexican-ness' of the children's faces. After one year, and after two years, those boys who looked more Mexican benefited more from their teachers' positive prophecies. Teachers' pre-experimental expectancies for these boys' intellectual performance were probably lowest of all. Their turning up on a list of probable bloomers must have surprised their teachers. Interest may have followed surprise and, in some way, increased watching for signs of increased brightness may have led to increased brightness."

(5) "In addition to the comparison of the 'special' and the ordinary children on their gains in IQ it was possible to compare their gains after the first year of the experiment on school achievement as defined by report-card grades. Only for the school subject of reading was there a significant difference in gains in report-card grades. The children expected to bloom intellectually were judged by their teachers to show greater advances in their reading ability. Just as in the case of IQ gains, it was the younger children who showed the greater expectancy advantage in reading scores. The more a given grade level had benefited in over-all IQ gains, the more that same grade level benefited in reading scores."

(6) "All teachers had been asked to rate each of their pupils on variables related to intellectual curiosity, personal and social adjustment, and need for social approval. In general, children who had been expected to bloom intellectually were rated as more intellectually curious, as happier, and, especially in the lower grades, as less in need of social approval. Just as had been the case with IQ and reading ability, it was the younger children who showed the greater expectancy advantage in terms of their teachers' perceptions of their classroom behavior. Once again, children of the medium track were most advantaged by having been expected to bloom, this time in terms of their perceived greater intellectual curiosity and lessened need for social approval."

(7) "When we consider expectancy advantages in terms of perceived intellectual curiosity, we find that the Mexican children did not share in the advantages of having been expected to bloom. Teachers did not see the Mexican children as more intellectually curious when they had been expected to bloom. There was even a slight tendency, stronger for Mexican boys, to see the special Mexican children as less curious intellectually. That seems surprising, particularly since the Mexican children showed the greatest expectancy advantages in IQ, in reading scores, and for Mexican boys, in over-all school achievement. It seemed almost as though, for these minority-group children, intellectual competence may have been easier for teachers to bring about than to believe."

The importance of this study cannot be overstated; however, as with other research, the questions raised are as important as those investigated. The specific items concerning teachers' expectations of and behavior toward Mexican Americans (especially boys) are particularly loaded.

Teachers' pessimism varies with the grade and the subject they are teaching and with the environment or morale of the particular school. Primary-grade teachers tend to be quite optimistic concerning Mexican American children's ability to learn; intermediate and secondary teachers more commonly have given up. Indeed during the primary years, minority-group children do tend to perform fairly well, appear to be quite "well adjusted," and seem to be "happy" in school. In the upper elementary grades, rejection of the school begins and "adjustment problems" become more evident. Teachers' pessimism is often allayed by introducing new curriculums or perhaps modifying the curricular content or teaching techniques. Teachers often respond to these changes with enthusiasm and optimism. Regardless of the nature of the innovation, a placebo effect may be engendered; if the children become involved in the experimental atmosphere, a Hawthorne effect may be implemented. If teachers' optimism persists, school social climate may well be modified to the benefit of the children's achievement. However exciting such situations are, they happen only exceptionally.

Other points of view discourage teachers' efforts and optimism. A few teachers take what might be called the "happy slave" perspective, arguing that the school should not attempt to modify Mexican Americans substantially since they are perfectly content with their way of life and their low socioeconomic status. They argue that the social distance between Anglos and the minority group is the natural order and should be maintained. Such teachers don't dislike "Mexicans"—they "understand" them and their "childlike" ways. Individuals subscribing to this view think that outside interference disrupts the natural order inherent in their castelike society. As one Texas school counselor interviewed for this study said: "Only a few days ago a teacher told me that these Mexican American children don't know their place: 'Why they are just the rowdiest people I've ever seen—they don't act typically Mexican. Since you got all those Federal programs and all these aids, why they think they own this school.'"

According to the "happy slave" view, the school is a service to the Mexican American and the Anglo alike. The rudimentary literacy acquired by the average Mexican American is essential to his position as an efficient worker. The extreme variety of this view is blatant prejudice, dropping the "happy-go-lucky" idea and replacing it with strong convictions of racial or cultural inferiority. This kind of prejudice is not common, but it is encountered in some individuals, especially in areas strongly influenced by the Southern ethos. Neither of these two views encourages equal-status interaction between the groups; both encourage a fatalistic view of Mexican American children's potential in school or prospects for future "success" in society.

Tracking Mexican Americans into lower-ability sections encourages academic failing. Teachers' low expectations and subsequent rigid, rote, memoristic, and dull teaching promote students' rejection of school and what it teaches. Tracking encourages a ". . . sense of personal humiliation and unworthiness. [Students] react negatively and hostilely and aggressively to the educational process. They hate teachers, they hate schools, they hate anything that seems to impose upon them this denigration, because they are not being respected as human beings, because they are sacrificed in a machinery of efficiency and expendability. . . ." (Clark, 1965, p. 128). The track system fails Mexican American students, if not all students, and encourages them to reject the school. This rejection is usually rationalized by educators as the failure of the home and culture. Teachers argue that one can expect little from such backgrounds and react negatively and defensively to the hostility manifest in their students, a condition that in turn was at least partially engendered by such school practices as tracking. It is a vicious circle. Unfortunately, the most common teacher view of Mexican American children is at best one of pessimism and at worst one of contempt.

Mexican American Teachers. It would appear logical to assume that Mexican American teachers would, as a group, be accepting and understanding of their own group's children. Having gone through similar life situations, they would tend to understand the living and learning situations of their group's children. And it is logical to assume that Mexican American children would look up to such teachers and use them as social role models. However, observations of Mexican American teachers and interviews of students during this study encourage the questioning of such assumptions.

Spanish-surname teachers generally subscribe to the views of Anglo teachers. Even the racist position finds a few adherents who assume that the degree of Indian blood in an individual influences his intellectual capacity. Mexican American and Anglo teachers appear to be equally effective or ineffective with Mexican American children. While bilingual teachers are certainly needed, the fact that they are of Mexican descent appears to be of little consequence. The ability to understand, to accept, empathize with, and constructively cope with individual and cultural diversity are the characteristics necessary. Many Mexican American and Anglo educators take strong exception to this point of view. To what degree burgeoning "ethnic nationalism" on the part of the Mexican Americans and racial prejudice and desire for separateness on the part of the Anglos affect their respective positions is unknown, but it seems likely that they are strong influences.

Perhaps some light can be shed on this controversial topic by analyzing the roles teachers play in schools. Southwestern teachers, of all ethnic groups, appear to fit into three broad and naturally overlapping categories as they function within, and relate to, their respective schools and students. These are the conformist, the "expecter," and the "system beater." Each group has a standard and a super category within it, and it is suggested here that Mexican American teachers tend toward the super side of each group.

In order to persevere within a rigid and authoritarian school system, teachers must conform. Teachers with widely divergent personalities or philosophies from those extant within a system have two alternatives: either outwardly conform or flee. Either they must learn to adjust by keeping their mouths shut, teaching children what they are supposed to learn, and showing appropriate deference to authority, or they must seek a position in a different system or occupation. This school social system unfortunately discourages many creative individuals of all ethnic groups and tends to perpetuate the school status quo. Many teachers, especially women, cannot flee to other systems or jobs; many are tied to a locale by their husband's occupation, their family, their love of the particular geographic area, and so on. They have to conform to exist. Of these, some become institutional or status personalities, internalizing the norms of the institution. Some conform even to degrees not demanded by the institution. A large percentage of Mexican American teachers appear to be in this super conformist group. They adhere strictly and rigidly to institutional demands, apparently in order to gain whatever financial, social, or political rewards the system provides. The fact that so many minority-group teachers seem to be of this type is completely understandable. The number of alternative positions (economic slots) available to Mexican Americans is more severely limited in many communities in the Southwest than are those for the majority-group teachers. A nonconformist Mexican American teacher may incur the wrath of authority for his divergence more than his Anglo counterpart. Thus, a Mexican

American teacher may well be "forced" into conformity, because of the position afforded his group, or because of the expectations of those in educational power.

While adhering to the system's requirements and policies, many Mexican American teachers recognize the school's inadequacies. They understand many of the Mexican American child's school problems, but because of their precarious position they are unable to do anything to change the situation. Since few Mexican Americans reach authority positions within Anglo-dominated school systems, and fewer still who are promoted hold divergent views, another problem is created. The nonconformist Mexican American teacher, the one who wants change, has few advocates in power. These teachers are even less capable of fomenting change than are their Anglo peers within the conformist group. The vast majority of Mexican American teachers started their careers with zeal and determination to aid their group's children, but pressure from innumerable sources has dampened their enthusiasm. The few that can't conform flee to other occupations or become "system beaters."

Desire to help children and holding high expectations for them are characteristic of most teachers of all ethnic groups. Most teachers honestly want their students to excel in school and succeed in society. These characteristics seem especially applicable to the middle-class or upwardly mobile individual. Mexican American teachers with excessively high expectations for their group's children are encountered everywhere. Such teachers may honestly attempt to identify with their charges, contending that they are part of the same culture but have risen above it. This group seems to be super middle class. They seem to say "Look, you *chicanos,* I made it and you can make it too. The only thing wrong with you is your attitude." These teachers may also be conformists contending that there is nothing wrong with the system, only with the attitudes of their Mexican American students. Such Mexican American teachers seem to expect more of minority-group children and be harsher on them than are many Anglos, seeing this approach to be in the best interest of children.

Many Mexican American teachers are themselves the product of environments similar to their children's but are upwardly mobile, often accepting middle-class norms and values more thoroughly than their

Anglo counterparts. Some of these "expecters" may harbor very negative feelings toward their poor relations. Clark finds the same conditions to exist among Negro teachers, arguing that such attitudes are understandable, though regrettable. He states (1965, p. 132): "Many of today's scholars and teachers come from 'culturally deprived' backgrounds. Many of these same individuals, however, when confronted with students whose present economic and social predicament is not unlike their own was, tend to react negatively to them, possibly to escape the painful memory of their own prior lower status."

Whatever the cause, negativism in one form or another seemed to this author to be a characteristic of many of the Mexican American teachers interviewed during this study. This negativism may manifest itself in the excessively high expectations and rigid demands for conformity characteristic of a great many of these teachers. One Anglo Texas superintendent indicated that he would never again place a Mexican American principal in a *barrio* school. He commented that his district "has fallen flat on its face in moving Mexican Americans into principalships. They have no sympathy for Mexican American parents." One such principal "expected a great deal more of Mexican American parents than he would have of Anglo parents," and the school district almost had a revolution on its hands. Other informants reported that students were particularly resentful of rigid and high expectations from minority-group teachers.

"System beaters" exist in all ethnic groups. As in the other categories, Mexican Americans seem to overpopulate the super side of this group. In this author's opinion the system beater does the most for minority-group children. System beaters of Mexican descent seem particularly efficient in raising achievement, encouraging acceptable behavior, and so on, and may perform a truly significant role in their schools. These teachers apparently deliberately attempt to identify with their students and often seem to succeed. They stress the identical nature of their own and their students' background and in so doing develop a joint conspiracy with students to evade the full force of the system's directives and sanctions. A mutual protection association is formed between teacher and student, each encouraging the other to evade the system while incurring as little disapproval and as much reward as possible. Such teachers are often censured by administrators but help to provide the kind of support essential for certain kinds of Mexican American students.

Many Mexican American principals and teachers of course do a magnificent job. Some of the most patient and understanding educators interviewed and observed in the course of this study were Mexican American. One such principal in particular seemed to be the antithesis of the principal described by the superintendent quoted above. Some of the most spontaneous classes observed were conducted by Mexican American teachers (this was rare at the secondary level, however). But numerous mechanisms within both the school

TABLE 10: Selected Statistics on School Attendance, Graduation, and Expenditures per State in Five Southwestern States, 1965-66

AVERAGE PERCENTAGE OF CHILDREN AGES 5-17 ATTENDING SCHOOL DAILY

State	Rank order among all states	Percent
California	5	93.8%
Colorado	6	92.0
Arizona	21	84.7
New Mexico	22	84.6
Texas	24	83.3

NUMBER OF CHILDREN (AGES 5-17) PER 100 ADULTS (AGES 21-64)

State	Rank order among all states	Number of children
New Mexico	1	69
Arizona	12	58
Colorado	18	56
Texas	18	56
California	43	49

*ESTIMATED EXPENDITURE PER ADA**

State	Rank order among all states	Expenditure
California	9	$613
Colorado	22	571
Arizona	23	568
New Mexico	24	556
Texas	39	449

PUBLIC SCHOOL EXPENDITURE AS PERCENT OF PERSONAL INCOME, 1965

State	Rank order among all states	Percent of personal income
New Mexico	2	5.4%
Arizona	5	5.0
Colorado	10	4.6
Texas	24	4.0
California	32	3.8

and society appear to be operating to encourage overrepresentation of super conformists and super expecters. Changes in school hiring, placement, and promotion policies would undoubtedly affect this situation in a positive way.

Quality of Facilities. The allocation of financial resources to children through educational institutions can be an important, although terribly oversimplified, measure of educational quality. The five Southwestern states vary considerably in their ability or desire to support their school systems. Table 10 indicates the differences in financial effort and the results of that effort in the Southwestern states. No pre-

PUPILS PER CLASSROOM TEACHER

State	*Rank order among all states*	*Pupils*
Colorado	12	22.3
Arizona	22	23.8
New Mexico	26	24.4
Texas	31	24.9
California	44	26.7

ESTIMATED AVERAGE TEACHERS' SALARIES

State	*Rank order among all states*	*Salary*
California	2	$8,450
Arizona	15	7,230
New Mexico	20	6,630
Colorado	21	6,625
Texas	33	6,025

PUBLIC HIGH SCHOOL GRADUATES IN 1964-65, AS PERCENT OF NINTH-GRADE CLASS IN 1961-62

State	*Rank order among all states*	*Percent of ninth-grade class*
California	1	88.9%
Colorado	20	78.2
Texas	34	69.5
New Mexico	38	68.0
Arizona	47	62.6

PERCENT OF DRAFTEES FAILING MENTAL TESTS, 1965

State	*Rank order among all states*	*Percent*
Colorado	20	14.0%
California	25	15.3
Arizona	26	20.5
Texas	35	23.3
New Mexico	38	25.4

Source: National Education Association (1967, pp. 12, 21, 25, 29, 32, 54). *Average Daily Attendance unit.

cise conclusions can be drawn from this table, but certain differences seem obvious. In general, California spends the most money, pays the highest salaries, has the highest percentage of children attending school, appears to have the fewest dropouts, and is second only to Colorado in lowest percentage of draft rejectees. Texas is at the other extreme with the poorest school attendance, lowest teacher salaries, and lowest expenditures per pupil; it is in the middle range in number of dropouts and has the next to highest percentage failing mental tests for the draft. When it is understood that a large percentage of the dropouts and draft rejectees in these states are in minority groups, in some areas almost exclusively Mexican American, the magnitude of the school's failure in regard to the disadvantaged is evident. While California expends the most money per pupil, it is the lowest of the states in percentage of total personal income used for public education. New Mexico and Arizona, with the largest number of children per 100 adults, seem to be making a strong effort by allocating to the schools the largest percentages of total personal income. Differences within states are perhaps as great as between them. However, it seems evident that California and Texas are at extreme poles on most, if not all, aspects of school.

In general, making comparisons within states, it can be stated that the lower the socioeconomic status of students, the poorer the quality of physical facilities. Schools in rural districts, which tend in the Southwest to serve large percentages of poor Mexican Americans, generally have less adequate plants than schools in metropolitan districts in the same state. Differences in physical facilities between high-status and low-status schools are much less obvious in California than in the other four Southwestern states studied.

The terrible physical condition of "Mexican schools," as described in the early literature, is still encountered, but it is not so prevalent as in the past and rarely so bad. Sánchez' report on New Mexico school conditions in the late 1930s, Taylor's description of Texas schools during the same period, and other reports from California, Arizona, and Colorado, documented the plight of these Mexican American schools. All these reports demonstrated that physical plants were rundown, badly maintained, overcrowded, poorly furnished, and lacked equipment. In general, they clearly failed to compare with Anglo institutions within the same school district. (See Calderón, 1950; Corona, 1955; Holliday, 1935; Kibbee, 1946; Lehman, 1947; Manuel, 1930; Rubel, 1966; Sánchez, 1966; Strickland and Sánchez, 1948; Taylor, 1932; Trillingham and Hughes, 1943.)

Contemporary conditions are much improved, yet one still finds schools with high percentages of Mexican Americans in deplorable physical condition. In many sections of the Southwest, the contrast between the physical facilities of predominantly minority schools and the middle-class institutions is immense. The minority schools are poorly maintained and dilapidated, often lacking in landscaping and outside play facilities. The present practice is to replace these older, previously de jure segregated, buildings with new modern facilities. This accounts for the fact that in some communities the *barrio* schools have by far the best facilities in the district. If this trend continues, the difference in quality will be eliminated. Often schools for migrant children occupy the oldest and poorest plants within a district. Some of them are miserable almost beyond description, especially in certain areas of Texas.

In school districts with very high percentages of Mexican Americans, school plants are generally inadequate. In some of these districts, many buildings in present use were not constructed as schools; conversions were made from convents, old homes, or military facilities. It is probably impossible to tax the population at higher rates in most of these areas, which are economically depressed. However, the economic base in some of them is industrial agriculture, and in these higher taxation is possible, the local politico-economic power structure permitting.

A Texas school administrator interviewed during this study, recognizing the poor facilities afforded Mexican Americans in his area, described the feeling of some of his fellow educators, and perhaps the Anglo community. He commented that many feel it best to provide inferior facilities, arguing that placing such children in beautiful schools with exciting surroundings would raise their expectations and ultimately encourage frustration, since "so few Mexicans can ever reach such levels during their lifetime."

School plants do not guarantee high quality education. Some of the most exciting, creative, and apparently dedicated teachers observed were working in unbelievably poor physical conditions. However, it is difficult to deny that size of class, length of teacher service, qualifications of teachers, and so forth influence quality of education. As with other aspects of Mexican American schooling, previous reports indicated that past conditions were much worse than those observed today. However, in some cases, discriminatory practices in regard to teacher placement and size of classes continue. Schools with high percentages of Mexican Americans received, and still receive, a disproportionate percentage of poorly trained teachers. It is a common practice for noncertified teachers to gravitate toward, or be placed in, these schools. In an unpublished study of 1,650 elementary teachers in the lower Rio Grande Valley of Texas, Ramirez (1966) reported that 10 percent of the teachers had no bachelor's degree, 13 percent were serving with emergency credentials, and 30 percent were on provisional credentials; only 57 percent were fully certified Texas teachers. A Rio Grande Valley superintendent reported that he was forced to employ some teachers with as few as 60 college credits. In other areas, the situation appears to be much better. The Governor's Committee on Public School Education in Texas (1968) found a strong relationship between Spanish-surname percentages in the population and teachers who are practicing without a bachelor's degree. It can be inferred that the higher the percentage of Mexican Americans the fewer fully certified teachers are in the schools. The Governor's Committee found that one characteristic of districts that have teacher shortages seems to be a high percentage of minority groups. During the three-year period from 1964–65 to 1966–67, teachers who did not have degrees and were teaching with emergency permits made up more than 14 percent of the total teaching staff in 9 of the Committee's 158 sample districts. Table 11 clearly illustrates the magnitude of the problem. Since areas with high concentrations of minority groups have low socioeconomic conditions and thus low school revenues, the relationship of poverty and assumed quality of schooling is also demonstrated.

The shortage of qualified teachers throughout the Southwest particularly influences the quality of Mexican American schooling. Noncertified teachers are often placed in schools serving low socioeconomic areas where little reaction can be expected from the adult community. Teacher shortages have a more adverse effect on minority schools or districts than on Anglo. It is commonly reported, but undocumented, that minority schools serve as training institutions: beginning teachers are often assigned there, and those who do well are subsequently moved to higher status (more Anglo) schools (see Trillingham and Hughes, 1943; Condit, 1946, p. 5). This is rarely the case with Mexican American teachers, however. As mentioned in previous sections, they are usually kept in schools with high percentages of minority children. Most school districts place few such teachers in high-status Anglo schools, but many transfer good Mexican American teachers to mixed schools.

Teachers who are considered to be troublemakers by local school administrators are said to be "punished" by being placed in minority schools. A number of interviewees contended that while they could not prove such statements, they were quite sure it was the practice. In some cases, this could prove to be a positive action; some trouble-makers are creative nonconformists and work out very well in certain kinds of new settings.

Mexican American children tend to be in larger classes than their Anglo counterparts; the teacher-student ratio is higher. Although the nationwide statistics reported by Coleman *et al.* (1966) do not indi-

TABLE 11: Teacher Shortages in Texas Analyzed According to Population Characteristics, 1964-65 to 1966-67

District	*Permits to teachers without degrees*	*Total permits*	*Percent of teachers without degrees*	*Percent of Spanish surnames in district population*	*1966-67 salary base*
Edgewood [San Antonio]	591	1,024	57%	76%	$4,104
Rio Grande City	53	113	55	88	4,104
Brownsville	124	297	44	73	4,384
Laredo	85	204	41	82	4,204
Pharr–San Juan–Alamo	57	140	41	70	4,450
Harlingen	56	153	37	29	4,449
Harlandale [San Antonio]	76	302	25	40	4,504
Ysleta [El Paso]	190	1,048	18	36	5,000
San Antonio	135	995	14	45	4,900

Source: Governor's Committee on Public School Education in Texas (1968, p. 46).

cate significant differences, many excessively large Mexican American classes were observed during the course of this study. Such overcrowded conditions were reported to be very common in the past.

In metropolitan areas, differences in the quality of physical facilities for the two ethnic groups will probably disappear within the decade. Old "Mexican schools" are being replaced with new modern facilities. Nonmetropolitan and rural districts that have high percentages of Mexican Americans will undoubtedly lag behind because there are insufficient funds to replace worn out or inadequate facilities. California has already succeeded in eliminating many of its older buildings, partly because state laws require earthquake-proof structures. More subtle discrimination, such as teacher placement policies, will probably continue. The elementary school teacher shortage will continue to cause hardship on low-status children. Unless the Mexican American community or the states themselves actively protest such discrimination, it can be predicted to continue.

SUMMARY AND CONCLUSIONS

The processes through which school practices, teachers' attitudes, and irrelevancies and rigidities in the curriculum have contributed to the low educational attainment of Mexican Americans have been touched upon here. These factors act in combination and probably in mutually reinforcing fashion. There is neither a theoretical framework nor empirical evidence that would make it possible to isolate and assess the impact of each of the numerous forces through which the school system contributes to deficient education for Mexican Americans. Hence, the influence of the school's inadequacies might best be seen by observing the results of its work.

One probable result is a negative school experience for the Mexican American child, causing him to reject the institution and, since it is often his first and most intensive encounter with an institution of the larger society, to transfer his rejection to society as a whole. When teachers' behavior or institutional procedures encourage a negative social climate within the school, the learner's general reaction will tend to be negative also. Though a certain degree of negativism toward school is common to all groups or classes of children, segregation and isolation of Mexican Americans tend to aggravate it. Negative attitudes toward school are particularly noticeable in segregated schools or among students assigned to low tracks. The individual child attempting to persevere and retain a positive view toward school finds it extremely difficult to counter the attitude of his relatively homogeneous peer group.

Another consequence of the school's inadequacies is the familiar culture conflict between home and school. Teachers drill minority-group children to accept middle-class norms of achievement, individual responsibility, and good manners in order to gain a good grade or the acceptance of the teacher. It can be argued that what is so "learned" may soon be forgotten, and it is also often the case that culturally different children do not see the symbolic reward of a higher grade as significant incentive. The norms taught may deviate from those at home and derogate the family and the peer group. Children learn one culture (language, values, expectations, and roles) in their home or from their peers, and the school enforces another and different culture. In order to stay in school, the child is required to drop the "bad" culture he has learned at home and at least outwardly manifest the cultural characteristics expected by the school. Many cannot do this and ultimately drop out—mentally in the primary or intermediate grades and then physically as soon as local law or practice permits. Others reject their home culture. Still others cannot cope with the situation at all, and caught between two sets of norms they may be subject to personal disorganization.

To make matters worse, the attempt to convert Mexican American children to "our way of life" inadvertently creates a school environment that does not reflect the reality of American culture. Thus, the school that has a high percentage of Mexican American students usually demands conformity to "super-middle-class" Anglo norms of behavior. Its curriculum tends to be more rigid than that of middle-class institutions in the same locale.

Tracking and other practices that isolate Mexican American children not only discourage equal-status interaction between them and their Anglo peers but also serve to reinforce the stereotypes each group holds of the other. The track system reinforces teachers' stereotypes as well, and affects their work: their expectations are lowered, and they may therefore make less effort, have lax achievement standards, and offer less encouragement.

Thus through innumerable practices and policies, the school inadvertently discourages Mexican American children from succeeding there. There is a crying need for objective institutional self-analysis as a step toward remedying this situation.

CHICANO
CULTURE

Chapter 4: Mexican American Reactions to School and Community

In this examination of the Mexican American experience in Southwestern formal educational institutions, two major considerations have not yet been explored. One of these, the minority group's view or perception of the school and education, is clearly important. It has been argued here that school policies, practices, stereotyping, teachers' attitudes, and so forth encourage low achievement and low levels of participation in school. If these conditions do indeed exist, Mexican Americans as a group might logically be expected to have a negative reaction to school and perhaps to education. Very few researchers have delved into students' perceptions of school. Educators are so imbued with the idea of their own superiority, a perspective almost universally supported by the elite segments of their respective communities, that a sampling of their relatively "inferior" clientele's view is seen as unnecessary, perhaps even threatening. The general orientation of educators is that reasons for the failure in school of a child or group of children are to be uncovered by examining the child or group. There is a problem also in the confusion between what is meant by "school" and by "education." The few studies made of students' views of school rarely separate students' or parents' perceptions of "education," an abstract concept with diverse interpretations, from the social reality of "school." It may be argued that an individual or group may indicate positive attitudes toward education and see school quite negatively.

The other consideration not yet discussed is the relationship between Mexican American children's academic success and perseverance in school on the one hand, and the nature of the community social order on the other. There is no research available specifically examining this relationship, but it is contended here that a connection does exist.

This chapter covers these two points. The lack of hard data is regrettable, and the great importance of both considerations strongly suggests fields for intensive empirical investigation.

PERCEPTIONS OF SCHOOL AND EDUCATION

Reports that the traditional Mexican American culture devalues education or sees it as a prerogative of the aristocracy seem to have little relevance today. Although there is no contemporary, widespread, systematic research that would verify it, there is every indication that as a group Mexican Americans view education positively, adhering generally to the American belief that "getting a good education" is a prerequisite of upward social mobility. While the idea of education in the abstract is well accepted, minority-group views of the school, as an institution, may diverge considerably from those of the middle class. Neither the Coleman report (1966) nor the Los Angeles School Study (Gordon *et al.*, 1968) questioned parents directly about their views of education or perceptions of the school (see Chapter 1 of this book for discussion relevant to these points). However, children's responses shed some light on the perceptions of their parents.

It can be assumed, for example, that parents providing an encyclopedia for their children do so to promote education and encourage success in school. Although the purchase of such reference works may be an economic burden on the family, there seems to be evidence of a willingness to make the necessary sacrifice. The Los Angeles School Study of sixth, ninth, and twelfth graders found that more Anglos had encyclopedias at home for all three grade levels than did Mexican Americans. Yet no fewer than 55 percent and, in some cases, as many as 79 percent of the minority-group homes had encyclopedias (Wenkert, 1966, p. 33). In a more rural agricultural setting in California, about 50 percent of Mexican American eighth graders and 70 percent of Mexican American twelfth graders said they had encyclopedias at home (California State Department of Education, 1965, p. 40). In both studies, the higher the grade level the more the ethnic minority tended to approximate the majority in number of homes that had encyclopedias. This may indicate nothing more than low sales resistance or supersalesmanship, and perhaps it is an inappropriate measure, but it could be argued that it also indicates a willingness on the part of parents to do whatever they can to further their children's education.

Interviews of school personnel during the course of this investigation support the thesis that Mexican Americans think of education positively and have high educational goals for their children. However, many interviewees report that Mexican American parents are quite unrealistic about educational goals and are uninformed about the number of years and the nature of the schooling required to reach given aspirations. The relationship between education as an abstract idea and schooling as the required institutional procedure are quite clearly recognized by middle-class individuals, but low-status Mexican Americans often fail to recognize the all-important difference.

As a general rule, low-status Mexican American parents think of the school as an institutional arm of the dominant American society. They accept it as a necessary and legally instituted entity, but its practices often are not fully understood, nor is the behavior of its staff. Many of the poor lack the skills essential to meet the expectations of the school. Middle-class parents tend to share the school's expectations: what is expected of them by the institution they expect of themselves, and vice versa. Low-status Mexican American parents tend to see the school as staffed by highly trained professionals having the best interests of their children at heart, often failing to recognize that a child's success in school depends greatly on the appropriate participation of his parents. This failing places their children at a serious disadvantage. For example, they may not understand the necessity for attending P.T.A. meetings or making regular inquiries about the progress of their children. The subsequent lack of participation by parents shatters the expectations of school people. Most of those interviewed during this study commented that Mexican American parents rarely participate in school activities and therefore ipso facto are not concerned about their children's schooling or education. It would be wiser to assume that many Mexican Americans don't know how to participate, or don't see the need to. The dearth of real communication and interaction between the school and the Mexican American *barrio* community provides little opportunity for the average poor family to learn the appropriate steps necessary to support its children. Schools rarely modify their P.T.A. or other activities in any real way to encourage meaningful interaction with the community. School-community activities in *barrios* differ only rarely from those in suburbs. While suburbanites expect, accept, and are familiar with such practices, many Mexican Americans are not and regularly shun such meaningless experiences, which they may even find degrading.

The mental withdrawal of many Mexican American children, beginning usually in the intermediate grades, perplexes educators. Numerous explanations have been offered. One holds that the child finds the intermediate grades too difficult, the curriculum too abstract. This notion contributes to the belief that Mexican American children cannot cope with abstractions and that schools should concentrate on the more concrete. Others contend that withdrawal and resulting poor achievement are due to the child's recognition of his own chances in life—what the future offers—and the influence of his socially awakening peers. Undoubtedly there is much truth in this latter point of view. Another theory implies that low-status minority-group parents share the objectives of the school more during the primary grades than in the later years. It is reported that they see the role of the school as twofold: to teach children "to behave" and to teach them basic skills. Because the primary grades concentrate on these two aspects, less disappointment or lack of support exists at the primary level than at higher grades. As the curriculum diverges, or appears to, from these objectives and begins to delve increasingly into areas viewed as more irrelevant and without connection to life, the home may fail to support the school to the degree it previously did.

The curriculum and authority structure of each year of school, from the first grade to the twelfth, become progressively more rigid. Even in the most traditional systems, the primary grades are more flexible than the higher levels. As the set grade-level requirements and the acquisition of information become progressively more rigidly defined and controlled, school may come to seem less relevant. This may be true for all children, but poor children are ill-equipped to cope with the situation. By the time a middle-class child reaches the intermediate grades, a system of support, reinforcement, and reward has been well established by his family and his peers. Many, if not most, middle-class parents carefully prepare their children to expect little intrinsic reward from the academic aspects of school; they firmly establish the idea that the reward of school is future entrance into society at a level they see as acceptable. They tend also to teach that while the academic aspects are essentially hurdles to be jumped, great intrinsic reward is to be found in the social, athletic, or other extracurricular activities. This suggests that middle-class parents teach their children to put up with school by encouraging them to find reward in its nonacademic aspects. As much as school people may not approve of this perspective, it does appear to correspond to the school's expectations and does encourage the idea that schooling guarantees future social success. Poor parents may not generally support the idea that school is a series of steps that must be climbed regardless of the boredom or unpleasantness involved, nor are they able to guarantee their children significant future social rewards for perseverance in and graduation from school. The fact that they lack the funds for higher education, and thus the means for paving the way to higher-status occupations, is particularly important.

Junior high schools, often located quite a distance from the *barrio,* may be viewed by Mexican American parents quite differently from the neighborhood elementary institution. The nature of the two institutions is usually different. The relatively warm, personal, accepting, and flexible elementary school is replaced by the more inflexible, impersonal, and mechanistic secondary school. The self-contained classroom disappears, replaced by subject classes with special teachers. School policies as well as the content of the courses are not well understood by low-status parents. Rarely do they comprehend the tracking system begun at this level or its significance to their children's future. Unfamiliar and uncomfortable with the impersonal secondary school, they either fail to interact or do so in ways that violate the staff's expectations of proper parent participation. They fail to recognize the degree to which they might acceptably influence staff judgments and actions relative to their children (Cicourel and Kitsuse, 1963).

In a recent study of two New Mexico communities, Anderson and Safar (1967) were able to investigate the views held by three ethnic groups (Spanish American, Indian, and Anglo) of the adequacy of local school programs for their children. Their findings do not directly support statements made earlier here, but they are of general interest:

"The Spanish-Americans on the whole feel that the school program is designed more for the Anglo student, while the Anglo community sees little difference in the adequacy of the school program for the three groups of children. Generally, however, all of the community groups perceive relatively little difference in the adequacy of the educational program available to pupils from the three ethnic groups.

"Moreover, the Spanish-American families interviewed in both communities evidenced the highest level of satisfaction with the present educational program despite the fact that their children do poorly in the schools in comparison with their Anglo classmates. In view of previous findings that demonstrate a ubiquitous lack of confidence in the ability of Spanish-American children to achieve the same goals expected of Anglo children it may be that the Spanish-Americans and Indians in the Southwest attribute the failure of their children in the schools to a lack of ability rather than to inadequacies in the schools' programs.

"On the other hand, school administrators and teachers in both communities perceive considerable variance in the adequacy of the school program for students from different backgrounds. For the most part, they perceive the educational program to be most adequate for Anglo pupils, less adequate for Spanish-American pupils, and least adequate for Indian pupils. It seems obvious that members of the school administration and teaching staff have been unable to communicate their discontent with the present educational programs to the community, or in Community A [one of the communities studied], even to the school board."

Thus Anderson and Safar find that Spanish Americans (Mexican Americans) tend to see their school and its programs as adequate. Such findings as these, if representative of the communities studied (the sample was quite small), may indicate a lack of knowledge on the part of the minority group. They may also have another and rather delicate reason behind them: Mexican Americans in many small

Southwestern cities, usually under Anglo political and social domination, might be unwilling to say anything that would rock the boat. Minority groups are becoming quite vocal and militant in larger and more socially open cities such as Los Angeles and Fresno. Even in Texas, murmurings of discontent about schools are being heard. There has been a boycott by Mexican American parents in the village schools in Sierra Blanca and complaints and some student action in the larger cities.

Many have speculated on Mexican American children's perceptions of formal educational institutions, and a few investigators have studied them. Naturally their findings are contradictory: there is no *one* Southwestern school and no *one* Mexican American view of it. The social climate of local institutions and their reputations in the community strongly influence children's perceptions and reactions. Since there is no homogeneous minority-group culture, each area is different; each school is different as is the minority view of it.

In the late 1950s, Demos (1962) administered a questionnaire to 105 Mexican American and 210 Anglo American secondary school students. Although Demos did not say so, it is assumed that these students were in a junior and senior high school in the same Southern California school district. The questionnaire contained 29 items assumed to represent important attitudinal variables; of these, 14 related to students' perceptions of school practices, social climate, and teachers—in other words, to school not to education in the abstract sense. Significant differences between groups were found in 7 of the items. In general, Mexican American students saw teachers as less understanding, the staff as less concerned about students, themselves as less willing to seek counseling, the administration as less helpful, and themselves as having less freedom to disagree with teachers than did the Anglo students. Mexican American students also manifested more desire to drop out, saw "gangs" as more desirable, and saw good school attendance as less important than did Anglos. While differences were found, they were of much smaller magnitude when the two groups were matched according to age, grade, sex, social class, and intelligence (IQ). In most areas, the mean scores of the two groups were not significantly different, but in all but one variable Mexican Americans saw school more negatively than did Anglos. From interviewing during this study, this author would generally concur with Demos' findings but would add that many minority-group youngsters see teachers as prejudiced and discriminatory toward their group.

Another source of information about Mexican Americans' perceptions of school is the so-called "dropout studies." The majority of these fail to delve deeply into perceptions of school, however; most report the expected relationships between social class, IQ, academic achievement, school behavior, and dropping out. Others report only the percentages of loss and the superficial reasons for leaving that are given by students or assumed by school officials.

In 1954, Wilson studied 462 Mexican Americans who were dropouts from six Texas high schools. The questionnaire he used provided a more thorough analysis of students' perceptions of school than do most such studies. Table 12 indicates the percentages and numbers of students participating in this study and their reasons for leaving

TABLE 12: Reasons Given by Dropouts for Leaving Six Texas Schools

Reasons	*Males*	*Females*	*Total*	*Percent*
Family needed financial help	52	34	86	20.4%
Not interested	45	33	78	18.5
To take a job	28	6	34	8.1
To enter armed forces	28	2	30	7.1
Failing	17	12	29	6.9
Moved too often	16	10	26	6.2
Marriage	8	17	25	6.0
Needed money	18	3	21	5.0
Needed at home	5	12	17	4.0
Work too difficult	5	7	12	2.9
Preferred to work	3	8	11	2.6
My illness	3	8	11	2.6
Family thought I should quit	5	4	9	2.1
Others	20	12	32	7.6
TOTAL REASONS	253	168	421	100.0%
No reasons given	22	19	41	
TOTAL OF SAMPLE	275	187	462	

Source: Wilson (1953, Table XXI).

school. Two principal reasons for leaving are evident: one is economic, and the other is lack of interest in school. It is impossible to say what percentage of the sample would have found means to meet their financial problems, would not have joined the Armed Forces or taken a job, if school had been an intrinsically rewarding experience. These same students were asked, "In what manner could the school have aided you more?" Their responses rather clearly indicate that these Mexican American dropouts consider their high school experience to be unpleasant. Forty-nine percent felt that teachers could have helped them either by being friendlier, more understanding, less prejudiced, or by giving them more individual attention. Fourteen percent indicated that being less segregated or having "more democracy" would have helped. Eleven percent would have liked the other students to be friendlier. Eleven percent also felt that the school could have helped them by providing more time for study and more athletics. The remaining 15 percent responded in ways not mentioned by Wilson.

Wilson also reported on the schools' concern for the withdrawal of students. He said that faculties of the schools were aware of the intentions of most of the students to drop out but that in only about one-third of the cases investigated were attempts made by the staff to keep them in school. The fact that nothing was done in two-thirds of the cases suggests a lack of concern. Wilson says, for example, "The attempts to change the pupil's curriculum to encourage him to stay in school were reported in only 2.6 percent of the cases. Apparently such steps were either too difficult or were overlooked." Perhaps the staff concerned wanted the students to drop out. Wilson's study is dated and reports only on conditions in Texas. It is strongly suggested here that much of the Mexican American negative attitude toward school may be a reaction to the negative attitude of the school toward them.

Current research on dropouts tends to corroborate Wilson's study. Wages, Thomas, and Kuvlesky (1969) studied 74 Mexican American dropouts from four school districts in the Rio Grande Valley of Texas—an area included in Wilson's work. While this study involved a smaller number of students and was restricted to one particular area of the state, their findings are similar in spite of some 15 intervening years: (1) School-related factors and financial reasons were subjectively perceived to be most important as reasons for dropping out; girls put slightly more emphasis on the former and boys on the latter. (2) Few respondents indicated the following as important reasons for dropping out: social pressure from inside the school (teacher, principal, or student) or outside (family, friends); and marriage. The research team studied the origin of social pressure to stay in or return to school and found that: (1) Few respondents received encouragement from any source to remain in school, but after leaving most of them experienced social pressures from various sources to return to school. (2) The few experiencing pressure to remain in school usually named parents as the source. However, pressures to return to school came from a wider variety of sources. The school seemed not to take much of an interest in their either remaining in school or returning to it. The authors also studied the educational aspirations of the dropouts, finding that "the majority desired at least high school graduation." A familiar pattern seems to emerge: relatively high educational aspirations, financial problems, little effort on the part of the school toward keeping potential dropouts, and finally withdrawal from the school.

The Coleman study indicates that Mexican Americans manifest more negative attitudes toward school than do their Southwestern Anglo counterparts. Thirty-seven percent of the Mexican Americans studied, contrasted to 47 percent of the Anglos, would "do anything to stay in school." Fifty-nine percent of the Mexican Americans and 69 percent of the Anglos had no willful absences (Coleman *et al.*, p. 25). While these responses do not give any reasons, they do imply differences between the two groups in their perception of school and their desire to stay in it.

In contrast to other research, the Los Angeles School Study staff found that in general a slightly higher proportion of Mexican American than Anglo children say they like school (Wenkert, 1966, p. 63). They found this to be especially true at the twelfth grade, less so at the ninth, probably reflecting a culling out of dissatisfied students in the lower grades. In this same study, in response to the statement "I usually enjoy my classes here at school," some rather startling differences were found between elementary and secondary school students. The percentages of children of both ethnic groups "disagreeing and strongly disagreeing" with the statement increases from sixth to ninth to twelfth grade. This increase may demonstrate, although certainly not clearly, that children of both groups find school more intellectually rewarding in the lower grades and see school becoming progressively less enjoyable. Or it may suggest that the children are learning to consider the authority structure or classroom climate. When the percentages of children answering "strongly agree" and "agree" are combined, the same pattern emerges. It was found that the percentage of Mexican American children who are from "lower blue collar" (unskilled, semiskilled) homes who state they usually enjoy their classes is: 93.1 percent in the sixth grade, 87.2 percent in the ninth grade, and 88.0 percent in the twelfth grade. A similar pattern was found for other occupational categories of both ethnic groups. When it is recognized that the "lower blue collar" Mexican American child is probably most prone to drop out before the twelfth grade, the magnitude of Mexican American disaffection with school is strongly suggested. The Los Angeles School Study group estimated a 50 percent withdrawal rate among Mexican Americans in some of the schools they investigated. This study, like others, strongly suggests that the school culls out lower-class and culturally different children, retaining those whose values, aspirations, conduct, and home life most closely correspond to those of the majority middle class.

There is little doubt that both child and parent approve of education as an abstract goal. Yet too many obviously do not find school a rewarding experience or cannot afford to continue. If the problem is purely monetary, perhaps scholarships or other financial aids will resolve the situation. If not, other factors must be investigated and other remedies found.

INFLUENCE OF THE COMMUNITY

It can be convincingly argued that the school holds little intrinsic reward for many, if not most, children; that even the best of school curriculums are in conflict with the home, that school authority is oppressive, that teachers have negative feelings, and so forth. If the school is seen negatively by so many children, why do the majority of them put up with it, performing academically and behaving in institutionally acceptable ways? One answer to this question is that some schools, because of the institutional conditions and practices discussed previously, are less intrinsically rewarding and more punishing than others, and that while a conflict definitely exists between the real world of living and the school for all groups of children, the degree of difference, and thus conflict, is greater for low-status, especially culturally different children.

However, the crucial factor is not the relationship between home and school, but between the minority group and the local society. Future reward in the form of acceptable occupational and social status keeps children in school. Thus, factors such as whether a community is socially open or closed, castelike or not, discriminatory or not, has restricted or nonrestricted roles and statuses for its minority-group segment, become as important as the nature of the curriculum or other factors in the school itself, or perhaps more important.

Most educators interviewed in the course of this study and the evidence presented by research indicate that middle-class children in general are successful in school. The relationship between school achievement and attendance and social class is well established. The middle-class Mexican American is no exception, although he may have certain problems not common to majority-group children. However, the case is different for low-status Mexican Americans. A few low-status children find a great deal of reward in school; for them, some aspect of continued involvement with the institution is more pleasing than available alternatives. Some find association with their peers as the principal benefit; others find athletics or other extracurricular activities particularly gratifying; a minority find academic excellence or the curricular content intellectually satisfying to the degree necessary to counterbalance the advantages of withdrawing. If the secondary school classrooms observed during this study are representative of other Southwestern schools, it is completely understandable that this latter group is very small in number. The present high school curriculum rarely provides the reward of intellectual stimulation; classes appear to have little intrinsic meaning or relevance. Those low-status minority-group children who find school more rewarding than alternatives learn to conform, at least to a minimum degree, to the expectations of the school by studying, turning in work assignments, taking tests, and behaving acceptably. The child who finds insufficient reward in school will not bother to conform even to the minimum degree.

For the majority of low-status Mexican Americans, no or little such intrinsic reward exists. Nevertheless, if high school graduation realistically guaranteed a future social or economic reward, youngsters would tend to persevere and perform at least up to minimum standards. Most educators stress that high school graduation provides its own reward in the form of preferential treatment on the job market. Indeed, national statistics clearly demonstrate that high school graduates do earn more and generally have higher-status occupations than do those who fail to finish. However, what is true nationally may not be true locally, especially where ethnic minorities are considered separately. Statistics for smaller geographic divisions describe what may be a totally different situation. For many Mexican Americans, high school graduation does not guarantee either economic advantage or social advantage. Low-status Mexican American youngsters gauge the local job market carefully and are likely to come to the valid conclusion that the kinds of occupations available to their ethnic group in their community do not require a high school diploma. They can plainly see that others like themselves who have dropped out are earning as much as they can expect to if they continue in school. They observe that "Mexicans" hold the same kinds of jobs regardless of their level of schooling. Many cases are reported of high school graduates working in the fields alongside dropouts. In some geographic areas, certain skilled or semiskilled occupations require a high school diploma and are "open" to Mexican Americans. However, many of these jobs do not pay substantially higher wages than the unskilled occupations. In many sections of the Southwest, especially Texas, wages are unbelievably low. The educator, in analyzing the reasons for the high dropout rate and low academic achievement of Mexican Americans should examine the local job market and discrimination, as well as the nature of social roles and statuses of the minority group within his community or area. He should recognize that: "The major inducement of educational achievement in our society is the promise of future occupational reward. If, however, it is known in advance that these rewards will be largely withheld from certain socio-economic and racial groups, then it is unlikely that high levels of educational achievement can be sustained in such groups. Thus, academic performance may be devalued because the young of such groups see no relationship between it and the realities of their future" (Cloward and Jones, 1962, p. 2).

Perhaps the greatest single incentive for Mexican Americans' staying in school is the desire to make the military a career. While a high school diploma is not mandatory for enlistment, high school graduates usually do get preferential treatment because they can enter the branch and specialty of their choice. In certain areas, the military as a career may well be the principal socially acceptable and legitimate way up for low-status but ambitious Mexican American youngsters.

The local school, so intrinsically related to the community it serves, inadvertently produces exactly the kind of "Mexicans" demanded by the local economic and social systems. If what is needed is a docile, low-skilled worker, the school provides individuals with these characteristics. The school is a sieve producing the kinds of humans necessary. In rural areas where the population is composed of isolated and parochial groups of Mexican Americans, youngsters are hampered by not being aware of the greater rewards and higher status afforded their ethnic group outside the immediate area; they tend to judge their future on the basis of the restricted local model. Schools appear to be quite unsuccessful in demonstrating opportunities available elsewhere; if local opportunities are restricted, Mexican American children are likely to drop out of school early.

This relationship between open-closed social systems (apparent opportunity) and school participation may provide the best explanation of the extreme variation in median years of schooling among Mexican Americans in different areas of the Southwest (see Table 1 of this book). Two factors seem to be operative. More socially open communities provide more and diverse social roles and occupational slots for Mexican Americans. There is less discrimination and more opportunity. Mexican American youngsters recognize this and "put up with school" albeit of little intrinsic reward, in order to reap the future reward of entrance into society at relatively high levels. The more closed and castelike the community the less future reward graduation provides and the higher the dropout rate. The other factor of importance is that even in the most closed communities some low-status Mexican Americans persist in school because some aspect of continued participation is more attractive than avoidable alternatives, or because they falsely believe high school graduation promises economic or social reward. These individuals may well be those who migrate to more socially open sections of the Southwest.

SUMMARY AND CONCLUSIONS

A multitude of factors, many already mentioned in other chapters, encourage Mexican American children to withdraw from school. Each student weighs the advantages and rewards of staying in school against the benefits of withdrawing. There is no one Mexican American perception of school, but it does appear that their attitude is generally more negative than the attitude of Anglos. It is argued here that in too many cases this negative view is well grounded. It is suggested that Mexican Americans generally maintain positive feelings about "education" in the abstract but tend to view the institution negatively. Educators who want to keep their Mexican American pupils in school should seriously consider the social environment of their school and the kinds of social or economic rewards realistically available to minority-group youngsters in their community if they graduate. Although it may be difficult, if not impossible, for educators to modify local society it is possible for them to make school intrinsically rewarding. However, such change demands strong affirmative action on the part of teachers and administrators.

Chapter 5: Special School Programs for Mexican American Children

The recent availability of federal financial assistance has spurred Southwestern educators to develop special school programs, usually compensatory, geared to aid Mexican American children. In spite of the limited financial resources available locally, some schools in each state had already begun to develop such programs in experimental and limited ways. The McAteer Projects in California, the Hogg Foundation in Texas, and other private and public institutions provided support before the enactment of the federal Elementary and Secondary Education Act and the Economic Opportunity Act.

The implicit purpose of "compensatory education" programs is the remediation, reorientation, and remodeling of certain children in order to make up (compensate) for their "inadequacies" when compared to middle-class children. Acceptance of the idea of cultural disadvantage provides the rationale for action to overcome real or assumed deficiencies. As Gordon and Wilkerson state (1966, p. 159): "It is not inappropriate that the programs of special education for the disadvantaged have been described as compensatory. They are attempts to compensate for, to overcome, the effects of hostile, different, or indifferent backgrounds. Their aim is to bring children from these backgrounds up to a level where they can be reached by *existing* educational practices and it is in terms of this aim that we tend to judge their success or lack of it . . . the unexpressed purpose of most compensatory programs is to make disadvantaged children as much as possible like the kinds of children with whom the school has been successful, and our standard of educational success is how well they approximate middle-class children in school performance. . . We have said to these children, 'We will prepare you for our school system, we will help you to catch up when you fall behind, we will show you the kinds of lives other kinds of children already know about, and if you get discouraged and drop out, we will try our best to get you back.'" Such compensatory and remedial programs are referred to here as the "adjust the child" position—approaches that attempt to "phase in" the "out of phase" child. The overwhelming majority of special programs for Mexican Americans are of this nature.

Programs that involve a conscious desire to modify the school substantially are extremely rare. This "adjust the school to fit the children" approach finds even fewer practitioners than adherents. Although a number of educators argue that the school has failed the Mexican American child, few are able to institute programs that substantially modify the curriculum, teachers' attitudes, the school's social climate, or the relationship between the home and the school. Few implement programs that imply to the child that "We will take you as you are, and ourselves assume the burden of finding educational techniques appropriate to your needs. We have asked of them [the disadvantaged] a degree of change far greater than any that we as educators have been willing to make in our own institutions" (Gordon and Wilkerson, 1966).

Programs to "adjust the child" continue the long- and well-established tradition that requires the school to function as an agent for acculturation, its role being to remake foreigners and the culturally different into full-fledged Americans. There seems to be general suspicion that radical modifications of the curriculum and the function of the school in this regard are somehow un-American. Yet it is interesting to speculate that bicultural schools, drawing their curriculum from both the American and the foreign culture, might be just as successful or more so as agents of acculturation and assimilation than are traditional schools. The argument is difficult to substantiate, since so few schools are attempting to modify their curriculums to make them bicultural.

The school programs examined in this chapter are categorized according to whether they are intended to "adjust the child" or "adjust the school." In some schools, of course, the two categories overlap. Programs in Texas and California are stressed here because data are more readily available from them and because they serve a numerically larger Mexican American population than programs in other states.

REMEDIAL AND CORRECTIVE PROGRAMS

Programs geared to remedy Mexican American academic or assumed psychological deficiencies constitute the overwhelming majority of special school endeavors. These are quite obviously attempts to adjust the child and his family to the expectations of the school. Most rely on traditional approaches and are in a sense efforts to give Mexican Americans an extra dose of what they had previously failed to grasp. This report does not attempt to evaluate the effectiveness of these efforts; however, other researchers' findings are reported.

The state departments of education in California and in Texas reported the percentages of given types of programs for the school year of 1965–66. Table 13 gives the percentages of differing kinds of activities provided in Texas and California under Title I of the Elementary and Secondary Education Act. They are reported in terms of what percent of Title I projects included given activities.The two states reported differently: Texas combined activities rated as primary and secondary objectives to give total percentages of types of given projects; California reported the percentages of projects rated as being primary or secondary objectives. Texas reported some shift from proposed to accomplished activities. The ranked order of the five most prevalent Title I activities in Texas schools in 1965–66 was: (1) providing reading and language arts instruction, (2) providing health and physical education services, (3) extending guidance services, (4) strengthening teachers' inservice training materials relevant to school environment, (5) providing instruction in basic academic subjects (Texas Education Agency, 1966). Activities 1, 2, 5, and possibly 3 were reported to be generally remedial in nature, although extending guidance services usually involved increasing personnel and testing and thus its purpose generally was to improve school facilities and staff. With the possible exception of "guidance and counseling" all of California's listed projects were remedial or compensatory in nature. In all five states the most prevalent Title I activities reported are "adjust the child" projects of one kind or other.

Preschool Programs. Almost all districts that have high concentrations of low-status Mexican Americans are undertaking some variety of preschool education, usually funded by the federal government. In Texas, only a very small percentage of districts provide free kindergartens; in California, all districts provide them. Therefore, in Texas preschool programs usually replace kindergarten and become the child's first school experience.

Preschool programs vary greatly, and their effectiveness is extremely difficult to assess primarily because of the absence of clearly specified objectives and the lack of adequate instruments to measure achieve-

TABLE 13: Types of Activities and Services Provided under Title I of the Elementary and Secondary Education Act, Texas and California, 1965-66 (Stated as Percentages of All Title I Projects)

TEXAS		
Type of project	*Primary and secondary objectives combined*	
Reading instruction	76	
Language arts instruction	46	
Mathematics instruction	21	
Basic academic instruction	41	
English as a Second Language (ESL)	26	
Physical fitness	16	
Guidance services	45	
CALIFORNIA		
Type of project	*Primary objective*	*Secondary objective*
Remediation and correction	47.5	21.4
Guidance and counseling	5.1	9.8
Cultural enrichment	10.3	12.8
Attitude change	1.8	6.4
Prevention of dropout	.04	.3

Source: Texas Education Agency (1966, Table 35); California State Department of Education (1966b, Table 1).

ment in such young children. The great percentage of programs are intended to improve preschool children's reading readiness and to increase their verbal ability in general. Some also desire to familiarize them with school materials or classroom procedures (how to listen to stories, march, and so forth). Many programs are geared to teach English as a second language. In the vast majority of preschool programs the curriculum is drawn from the dominant culture with perhaps just enough of what is assumed to be Mexican American culture to encourage the child to feel comfortable. A few pre-first-grade classes are reported to tend toward having a bicultural program but still emphasize the need to "prepare the child for school"; they draw curriculum from both cultures. The efficiency of either type of program is almost impossible to determine objectively, as is their long-term effect on the school achievement or perseverance in school of the children who attend them.

The necessity of teaching English to monolingual Spanish speakers has long been recognized as a prime objective. Many educators continually emphasize this as the single best way to improve Mexican Americans' achievement in school. They are certainly correct if indeed it is true that the principal reason for Mexican American school failure is inability to speak English. They argue that adjusting the child to the school's demands in this regard must take precedence over other objectives involving more radical changes in the nature of the school. The child is easier to modify than the institution. Preschool programs for Mexican Americans stress English language learning, sometimes as a stated objective and sometimes not. They approach this goal in diverse ways with widely differing degrees of competence.

Preschool English-as-a-Second-Language (ESL) programs have long been advocated, and there have been sporadic attempts to implement them. In the late 1940s, Tireman, after finding Mexican American children in New Mexico to have vocabulary ranges in Spanish equal to English-speaking children's ranges in their native tongue, developed a minimum English vocabulary list and used it in the pre-first-grade section of his experimental schools. Excellent results were reported (Ulibarri, 1959, p. 18). Herr (1944, p. 135), experimenting in nine towns in New Mexico during the same period, found that first and second graders with a year of preschool language instruction achieved much better than the control group that had no such experience. Average IQ scores for the experimental group were raised almost 30 points in one year (from 66.01 to 95.92), while the control group gained only 10 points.

As early as 1922, Los Angeles City schools had preschool English language training programs (Sumners, 1939). McAllen, Texas, was another site of early experimentations, and substantial gains in achievement were reported there in the 1920s. Seventy percent of the experimental group were promoted from the first to the second grade, a situation almost unknown in Texas schools at that time. Apparently the early experience had a sustained effect on achievement. The children in the third and fourth grades who had been in the experimental class, and were promoted the first year that they were in school, made higher grades on an achievement test than did those pupils who had spent two years in the first grade. In the late 1950s a number of Texas districts began experimenting with preschool ESL programs. The LULAC (League of United Latin American Citizens) organization gave significant impetus to such programs, establishing the "Little Schools of 400" (named for the 400-word basic vocabulary taught). In 1960, the state supported additional programs with an allocation of $480,000. By 1963 the state was able to report (Kennedy, 1963, p. 14) that of the 16,532 children participating in the ESL pre-first-grade program in 1961 and 1962, 3,168 or about 19 percent were retained in the first grade for two years. The remaining children were promoted at the end of first grade. Of a control group of 10,817 first graders who did not have the program, 8,870 repeated the first grade. Reports relative to the influence of preschool ESL programs on the classwork of Mexican American children and their promotion from first to second grade were almost universally positive. Whether achievement will be sustained through the third and fourth and upper grades is open to serious question. Whether the basic problem of these children in school is lack of English, with subsequent low achievement and frustration, or a series of other problems as has already been discussed, remains to be seen. The dire need for well-controlled longitudinal studies is certainly obvious.

More general preschool programs suffer the same lack of follow-up and are equally difficult to assess. California reported in general that:

"(1) Pupils developed listening and speaking skills, learned to play and work together, and learned to care for themselves and their possessions in a group setting; (2) the program enhanced, to a significant degree, the pupil's potential for success in the first grade; (3) parents and school staff indicated a satisfaction with the project and recommended its continuation; (4) pre-kindergarten teachers rated the project as high in the development of the child's communication skills, speaking vocabularies, listening vocabulary, interest in books, and other readiness skills; (5) teachers observed changes in students in all rating areas; (6) the program was effective in developing positive adult-child relationships; (7) children in the program exhibited an increase in desirable social traits or group characteristics, and a decrease in undesirable social traits or group characteristics" (California State Department of Education, 1966b).

Pierce-Jones *et al.* (1966, pp. 173–174) concluded, after a most comprehensive evaluation of preschool projects in Texas and the Southwest, that children with experience in Project Head Start: ". . . scored significantly above their first grade compeers [who had no preschool]. Although these non-Head Start children were older than Head Starters when tested, they had had about the same amount of formal schooling, yet the Head Start children consistently excelled them in intellectual performance. [Teachers were asked] to nominate any of the children then in their first grade classes for 'learning proficiency,' intellectual curiosity,' and 'potential educational failure.' These teachers named children *later identified* as Head Starters significantly more often than non-Head Starters for the first two attributes and significantly less often as 'potential educational failures.' [However,] the persistence of the changes apparently wrought in the disadvantaged population of children is at issue. Many factors in a child's home, peer society, school, community, and ethnolingual subculture may work in complicated ways to prejudice, sustain, or promote Head Start initiated changes in childhood."

Johnson and Palomares (1966) undertook an interesting research project to determine what differences existed between parents who sent and did not send their children to Head Start classes in the Coachella Valley of California. Practically no dissimilarities were found between the two groups of parents. The authors suggest that a principal difference was that ". . . non-sender parents were not contacted by the school and were apparently ignorant of the program or were not 'induced' to send their children." The breakdown of school-community communications appeared evident.

It is entirely too early to determine whether special English-as-a-Second-Language programs or more general preschool programs will sustain achievement among Mexican American children through the subsequent years of school.

Language Arts Remediation. Most Southwestern schools are providing some form of remedial program to improve the ability of Mexican American children in the language arts. It is a rare elementary school that does not have remedial reading or special language programs. Secondary schools also have remedial reading classes, but many do little more than place "slow readers" in low ability tracks. The overwhelming majority of reading or language-arts remedial programs for Mexican American children are not substantially different from those for "slow" learners of the general population.

Most remedial reading programs make little attempt to diagnose the individual's reading problems; few teachers have the skills necessary, and most materials are inadequate. Most teachers of special reading classes use substantially the same teaching techniques and materials for Mexican American children as they use for Anglo children. Thus, although Mexican Americans can usually learn to verbalize graphic symbols, they do not comprehend their meaning. The majority of remedial programs observed during this study would be equally appropriate or inappropriate for poor readers who are Spanish-speaking and those who are not.

Most remedial reading classes merely reexpose children to the same approaches and materials that failed them in the past. An extreme example of this method was encountered in one Texas *barrio* elementary school in which phonics was reported to be the only accepted or permitted technique of reading instruction in any grade. One remedial reading teacher in a higher grade indicated that the results she got using phonics were quite good. Whether her reported success was due to the fact that children in her classes had reached a mental age permitting them to learn by this technique, or to the teacher's empathic approach, or to the smaller sized class, or to other reasons is unknown. Other districts do not so rigidly adhere to a given technique. However, few introduce other than standard approaches for their Mexican American poor readers.

A major problem reported at all levels is the inappropriateness of text or other reading materials. Some progress is being made with elementary school materials that incorporate the assumed "background" of students and eliminate the most blatant middle-class content. Secondary school materials geared to the life experiences or cultural background of "deprived children" are rarely found in use in the classrooms. The vast majority of schools at both levels use traditionally acceptable standard materials. The difficulty of preparing reading or other materials relevant to the culture of the subgroup is apparent. The diversity of the group is great, and no one set of materials could be relevant to all Mexican Americans. The children's real life experience, if known, might be perceived as inappropriate in American schools or defined as "bad." All these problems, plus publishers' desire for a mass market, encourage the persistence of irrelevant and perhaps conflict-inducing reading materials.

Three kinds of curriculum materials offer possible solutions to the problem of cultural irrelevancy or conflict or both: "projective" materials, materials constructed by students or teachers, and culturally "fair" or "universal" materials.

Since 1964, Southwestern schools have been experimenting with the Miami Linguistic Readers, often referred to as the "Dade County materials." These materials were originally designed for Spanish-speaking Cuban refugee children. One feature of the series is its cultural neutrality, which is accomplished by the use of cartoon figures of animals acting out more or less universal themes. Numerous classes using these materials were observed during this study. In many cases it was obvious that the children were projecting themselves into the characters and events. Some of the animals are characterized so vaguely that even their sex is not identified; arguments about whether one character was male or female were noted. Projection was particularly obvious in the children's role-playing activities, which are part of the recommended curriculum.

Riverside, California, schools are experimenting with a primer involving stories and characters from a culture unfamiliar to all the children being taught. In Gearing's primer entitled *Big Cat* (1967), the third culture introduced is American Indian. This ethnologically accurate, linguistically based experimental reader and its recommended activities are intended to encourage children to project their life experiences into those of the Indian boy, Big Cat, and his family and to see their own experiences newly through the contrast. Very favorable preliminary results are reported. An analysis and evaluation of Gearing's approach is being financed by the state of California.

Photographs or drawings intended to be neutral or universal in nature are often used to encourage children to interpret a scene individually. Usually they are used to stimulate creative writing, but they also are used to induce children to make up their own primers. The language-experience approach and other similar techniques are used fairly commonly and teachers report good results. In these approaches teachers encourage children to use their own life experiences, elicited through story-telling or other devices, to construct their own reading materials. The children's art work is sometimes used for illustration materials, usually produced through joint efforts involving a whole class. In some classes each child makes his own individual "book." Through such approaches the real group experience (culture) can be incorporated into text materials. These techniques are usually supplemental to the use of standard reading materials and more traditional teaching methods. Teachers report high student interest and good results with these language experience approaches, especially at the primary level.

Content assumed to be culturally universal or "fair" can become the basis of reading readiness and language instruction as in The San Antonio, Texas, Language Research Project. Concepts from science and mathematics form the principal content base of this ongoing experimental project. Horn (1966) states that these ". . . 'culture fair' science materials were materials which [it may be hoped] did not contain elements providing an unfair learning advantage to pupils of either Spanish-American or Anglo cultures." More informal attempts to introduce "culturally fair" content were observed. Almost invariably, these related to numbers or science (nature study).

Objective proof of the success or failure of reading or other remedial language programs is almost impossible to procure. Almost all the well-constructed evaluative studies available are for only one year, and questions remain about the long-range effect of specific programs. California reported that in the 1965-66 school year, 368 districts undertook remedial reading programs as a primary activity of their projects under Title I of the Elementary and Secondary Education Act, and that 47 districts undertook them as a secondary activity (California State Department of Education, 1966b). The results of the year's activities were difficult to quantify because of the diverse measures used, but they did not appear to be overly encouraging, as indicated in Table 14. In a sense, these ratings reported in Table 14 are not so much descriptive of how much children changed, but how adequately the program was evaluated. Very similar "success" was reported for the more general remedial and corrective language arts "communicative skills" programs in California (California State Department of Education, 1966b, p. F2).

Researchers on the staff of the California State Department of Edu-

TABLE 14: Progress in Remedial and Corrective Reading, California School Districts, 1965-66

	*Substantial progress**	*Some progress*	*Little progress*	*Progress not specified*
Prekindergarten	—	—	1	—
Grades 1-3	—	12	11	4
Grades 4-6	4	40	79	12
Grades 7-9	—	—	2	1
Grades 10-12	2	18	18	4
Other categories (not specified by grade)	3	70	59	28
TOTAL	9	140	170	49

Source: California State Department of Education (1966b, p. F2).

*"To obtain a rating of 'substantial progress,' a project had to result in growth or change that was statistically significant. This growth had to be demonstrated by a statistical test at or beyond the .05 level of confidence. . . . In addition, the district had to use a control or comparison group in evaluating growth. To obtain a rating of 'some progress,' positive change had to be demonstrated by some objective method such as test scores, teacher surveys, and attendance records . . . but no statistical tests were conducted on the level of confidence. 'Little progress' was applied to projects which were evaluated only by subjective methods which were funded late in the school year or which could not be fully implemented because of difficulties in hiring staff or delays in delivery of equipment. The 'not specified' rating was applied in cases where no data were supplied or where the project did not get started" (California State Department of Education (1966b, pp. S12-S13).

cation, after examining the wealth of test results, teacher ratings, anecdotal records, and so forth, summarized their findings as follows (California State Department of Education, 1966b, pp. S19–S20).

"Two general conclusions were obtained from evaluation of ESEA Title I reading and language programs:

"1. In the short time that ESEA Title I projects were in operation, students tended to achieve a month's growth for every month of instruction—a substantial increase over the .7 of a month growth for every month of instruction they had been averaging before the program started.

"The month-for-month growth was based on objective test data and was demonstrated in the majority of districts which operated the reading program for at least four months. . . .

"2. School district personnel generally agree that the students improved in attitude, motivation, and interest toward learning. As these are important factors in learning, continued growth may be anticipated. Teachers also reported a positive change in their own attitudes towards these children and in their techniques in working with disadvantaged children.

"It is not appropriate at this early stage to single out any one approach to the improvement of achievement level. However, several generalizations can be made from the evaluation of the first semester's programs:

"1. The growth in achievement was highly and positively related to the length of time the children participated in the activity. . . .

"2. The most significant growth was demonstrated in projects in which:

"a. the students were thoroughly screened and diagnosed to discover the causes of their learning problems;

"b. trained specialists were employed to devote full time to remediation of reading difficulties;

"c. a variety of approaches, including reading laboratories and special textbooks and materials, were used;

"d. remedial reading activities were conducted for a specified period of time each day in facilities other than the regular classroom.

"3. The least significant growth seemed to occur in smaller districts where remedial reading was taught in the regular classroom by the regular teacher in small groups for indefinite periods of time during the school day.

"4. The most success appeared to have been achieved in grades 1–4, with lesser growth demonstrated in the upper grades."

Conditions encouraging "significant growth" as described above are rarely found in rural areas of the Southwest or in smaller cities. Specialists, diagnostic facilities, and reading laboratories are generally more readily available in California than in the other Southwestern states. However, the large metropolitan areas in all five states are fairly comparable. California is reporting on all children involved in remedial language arts, not solely Mexican American children. The differences in "growth" between Mexican American children and Anglo or Negro disadvantaged children can only be speculative.

Correction of Mexican-Spanish accents represents an area of remediation being attempted on a very limited scale in the Southwest. The failure of the child to learn unaccented English is not generally recognized as the problem this author contends it is. Only a very few educators consider this a problem at all; most believe an accent is acceptable if communication between individuals is not impaired. Few seem to recognize that accented speech can be a severe stigma operating to the social and economic detriment of Mexican Americans. It is commonly held that Mexican American children's accents result from interference induced by the differences between Spanish and English. Only a very few educators interviewed believe, as does this author, that Mexican American children's accents result principally from socialization within groups where this brand of English is the only one socially acceptable. Adult Spanish speakers do find correct English pronunciation difficult, because of the differences between the two languages, but it is suggested here that children learn accented speech patterns from their peers. It is further suggested that the school, because it segregates and thus isolates Mexican American children from Anglo teachers and pupils, unintentionally encourages the perpetuation of accented speech. A few educators commented that teachers sometimes encourage accented speech by rewarding youngsters who use it with a smile, a laugh, and so on.

Calderón has long stressed that standard English is essential and possible for Spanish speakers provided teachers recognize the problem and use correct instructional procedures. Linguistic techniques to overcome pronunciation difficulties are well established but rarely employed except in a few ESL programs (Calderón, 1959, p. 26). Approaches toward correcting accented English that recognize that such speech is learned from peers, Mexican American teachers, and other adults were not encountered during this study.

Regardless of the cause, many Mexican American children have strong accents, and little is being done to encourage them to use standard English pronunciation. Only one formal program to remedy accents is known to this author. In El Paso, Texas, a high school class ". . . comprising seniors considered by the school to be potential college material, was conducted in English but [the teacher] often switched to Spanish to point out contrast in pronunciation in both languages. He wrote sentences on the chalkboard, then wrote the phonetic symbols. The students were instructed to repeat after him, then read in chorus. Finally, individuals were asked to read" (National Education Association, 1966, p. 24). High morale and substantial success are reported for these "well-motivated" Mexican American students. What is particularly interesting is that while the techniques to overcome accents are available and easy to use, only one district is known to be using them in a formal manner.

English and Spanish Programs. There is widespread confusion about the objectives, techniques, content, and organization of school programs involving foreign languages. The basic distinction between foreign- or second-language teaching and bilingual school programs is rarely understood by school practitioners.

A foreign- or second-language program involves the introduction of a language new to students into a classroom where it is to be learned essentially for its own sake. In a bilingual program, two languages are used as media of instruction (carriers of curricular content). English as a Second Language (ESL), Foreign Languages in the Elementary Schools (FLES), or any other program to teach a new language to whatever group of children at any level, are second- or foreign-language instruction programs. A school would not be defined as bilingual merely because two languages are taught in it (for example, Spanish to English speakers and English to Spanish speakers). Besides second- (or foreign-) language projects in the Southwest, new projects to teach native Spanish speakers in Spanish are gaining popularity. These projects can be classified according to the nature of the content taught and according to objectives. If those content areas traditionally associated with foreign-language teaching are taught—for example, the language's grammar, pronunciation, spelling, drama, literature, business correspondence, and so forth—it is a "language program." If other content is taught—for example, world history, biology, arithmetic, algebra, and so forth—it is a "bilingual program."

Table 15 is an attempt to depict graphically the status of language programs in Southwestern schools for native speakers of Spanish and of English. All such programs involve two major objectives: (1) competency in listening, speaking, reading, and writing the second language; and (2) knowledge of the culture the language carries (art, literature, history, great men, great events, and so forth). In addition to these two major objectives, given programs state or imply other goals as indicated.

Three "normal" or common types of programs are depicted in Table 15. The types described as "English for English speakers" (C-1) and "English for Spanish speakers" (the regular school program: B-2) are the standard school approaches. In these, both Spanish- and English-speaking children are presented the regular school curriculum carried in the English language. The objective is to make both linguistic and ethnic groups competent in English and carriers of the dominant culture. "Spanish for English speakers" (A-1, 2) is a very common foreign-language program in the Southwest. Its teaching approach varies tremendously from the older grammar emphasis to more modern audiolingual techniques.

The most common special (compensatory) language program is some variant of teaching English as a "new" language to Spanish speakers (B-1). The ESL program represents a departure from regular school efforts. It usually provides more intensive and structured exposure and employs techniques associated with the audiolingual approaches. However, the content changes little regarding United States culture: the objective continues to be bringing the child into American culture.

The use of the ESL approach and the audiolingual technique are still considered by many schoolmen to be unproven and experimental. For example, the Texas Education Agency (1966, p. 124) cites the

Pharr-San Juan-Alamo Independent School District's program as an "innovation project": "Non-English speaking children aged 10-16 were afforded extended instructional oral English, reading and writing, and advanced reading materials. A major aspect of the program was the use of special audio-visual materials, such as filmstrips and other visual aids." California and other states consider what appear to be rather standard ESL programs as innovative. One might think that the audiolingual approach would be well established by this time, but it is still considered experimental by many schoolmen and its use is nowhere near as widespread as would be expected.

The Miami Linguistic Reader, with its recommended activities, is being used apparently quite successfully as a method of teaching Eng-

TABLE 15: English and Spanish Language Programs in Southwestern Schools

PROGRAMS TO TEACH NEW LANGUAGE			
Type	*Program*	*Content*	*Objectives*
A. Spanish for English speakers	**1.** Foreign Languages in the Elementary Schools (FLES)	**1.** Hispanic culture	**1.** Competency Knowledge of Hispanic culture
	2. Traditional Spanish language program	**2.** Hispanic culture	**2.** Competency Knowledge of Hispanic culture
B. English for Spanish speakers	**1.** English as a Second Language (ESL)	**1.** United States culture	**1.** Competency Knowledge of United States culture
	2. Regular school program	**2.** United States culture as represented in standard curriculum	**2.** Acculturation

lish and reading to Spanish monolinguals, and as a regular reader for the general population. The system was well thought of by all interviewees for this study who were actually using it. From observation of classroom situations and interviews of teachers, it appears that: (1) children project themselves into the content and characters, as mentioned earlier; (2) the organization of the small instructional groups encourages children's spontaneity and naturalness; (3) teachers understand and can use the linguistic approach, as exemplified in this series; and (4) teachers seem quite comfortable with the system as explained in the manual.

The Miami series is based on a set of carefully constructed premises. Paramount among these is ". . . that the child must have aural-oral

PROGRAMS TO TEACH NATIVE LANGUAGE

Type	*Program*	*Content*	*Objectives*
C. English for English speakers	**1.** Regular school program	**1.** United States culture as represented in standard curriculum	**1.** Competency Knowledge of native culture Enculturation
D. Spanish for Spanish speakers	**1.** Hispanic culture	**1.** Hispanic culture	**1.** Fluency Knowledge of Hispanic and Mexican culture Pride in antecedents Enhanced self-image
	2. Bridge	**2.** Hispanic culture as bridge to United States culture "Universal" or "fair" culture United States culture	**2.** Fluency Knowledge of both cultures Biculturism Acculturation

control over the material he is expected to read." In other words, the child must know and attach meaning to the English he later reads. Robinett (1966, p. 3) elaborates this point: "The *introductory* (readiness) *unit* preceding the introduction of formal reading, and the oral language activities surrounding the reading, attempt to provide systematic, meaningful oral practice on the basic features of American English. The linguistic content for oral mastery is structured in its presentation, taking into account contrasts within the English language system and contrasts between English and Spanish. In the ordering of the linguistic content, less concern has been shown for the 'logical' sequences and manipulation typical of materials produced under the direction of linguists, and more concern has been shown for the communication aspects of the language experience and the relevance of the language to the content of the pupil's reading materials." Children appear to comprehend and communicate in the words and phrases later encountered in the reader. If this series is successful, as it appears to be, in teaching oral English before written English, it has overcome one of the principal and most common failings of other systems. Most systems reverse the procedure, expecting the child to read and understand a language he does not speak or understand. It is of course possible that the apparent success of this system is merely a placebo effect. Regardless of this possibility, which can be inherent in the introduction of any new curriculum, the series does seem to exemplify what can be accomplished by serious application of theory to educational practice.

Unfortunately, teachers almost invariably report more success than do more objective evaluators. On the basis of district reports, the ESL program in California was judged to be "generally successful": "On the average, students who could speak no English before the program gained a reading and sight vocabulary approximating an average second grade English-speaking child" (California State Department of Education, 1966b, p. 522). These programs lasted about five months. More concrete evidence, based on teachers' ratings, tests, and so forth, indicate that schools undertaking "English for non-English speaking" Title I projects as a primary, secondary, or "other" activity during 1965–66 showed "substantial progress" in 2 percent, "some progress" in 25 percent, and "little progress" in 55 percent of the classes. Approximately 18 percent of the schools did not specify their progress (California State Department of Education, 1966b, pp. F3, F21, F41).

Great variation exists among programs of English as a second language. A few classes observed quite adequately utilized modern audiolingual techniques and so forth, but many relied almost exclusively on traditional grammar approaches. A few districts use sophisticated electronic language laboratories, yet many fail to take advantage of the most rudimentary mechanical or electric teaching aids. The variations in materials are great. In summary: (1) if the audiolingual method is to be used, a massive inservice teacher-training program is essential; (2) few language laboratories observed during this study were being operated to maximum efficiency; and (3) often the teachers observed were poor language models because of their own nonstandard, sometimes accented, speech.

The other infrequently encountered but significant "new" language program is the teaching of Spanish to Spanish speakers. These programs share the two major objectives, language competency and knowledge of culture, common to all language programs. Some are based on the premise that a sound grounding in Spanish will provide a "bridge" to speed the learning of English (Table 15, D-2). According to Guerra (1967, p. 2), one aspect of such programs is: ". . . to establish psychological rapport between teacher and learner in order to begin English instruction using Spanish as the familiar frame of reference; that is, Spanish as a bridge to learn English." All the contemporary language programs to teach Spanish to Spanish speakers are meant to provide a bridge to English, but they differ in their stress on Hispanic culture and their priority of objectives. "Hispanic culture" programs (Table 15, D-1) appear to have as an overriding objective the promotion of the youngster's pride in his "Mexicanness" and Hispanic cultural tradition. The emphasis is intended to remedy the child's assumed negative self-concept and to "develop a positive sense of identity." This strategy is compensatory in the sense that it glorifies a culture in order to enhance the child's ego function and to improve his self-image.

The program in Tucson's Pueblo High School appears to be a good example of this strategy: for the four high school years, ". . . attention is given to the basic skills of speaking, reading and writing [of Spanish].

Equal, if not even greater, emphasis is given to helping the student develop a more positive self-concept through the study of his rich Spanish and Mexican cultural heritage" (National Education Association, 1966, pp. 22–23). Tucson's experimenters are exuberant over the success of their program. How successful such projects will be in facilitating English language learning and in instilling pride in things Hispanic is not known. The principal of a Pueblo, Colorado, elementary school was described as giving the following subjective evaluation of a program to instill pride (National Education Association, 1966, p. 22): "She was delighted with the progress already evident. Student attitudes and behavior had noticeably improved. The Mexican-American children carried themselves a bit more proudly. They got along better together. There was little or none of the name-calling that had been so prevalent before—calling which, though engaged in by Mexican-American children, was anti-Mexican in nature. The parents of these native speakers had reacted with enthusiasm to the new Spanish classes and the new spirit developing at Minnequa School . . . the last PTA function, a sort of Mexican fiesta, had been attended by more parents than ever before and there had been more parental cooperation in its planning and arranging." No objective data were found during this study to support such statements. Much criticism has been directed at such programs on the grounds that they may be divisive, that they idealize Mexican culture and society rather than validly portray them, and that the content is of little relevance to the poverty class of Mexican American children (indeed the program at Pueblo was initiated for academically superior students). A great many questions concerning the objectives of programs like these must be considered.

The "bridge" programs (D-2) for teaching Spanish to Spanish speakers emphasize Spanish as a linguistic bridge to English but neither stress Hispanic cultural heritage nor use it as a vehicle to overcome any assumed negative self concept. This kind of strategy might encourage individuals to find their identity within their own real social context. The Harlandale Independent School District in San Antonio is experimenting with programs that appear to be oriented this way. In one such program, four first grades in different schools were taught reading and writing in Spanish, as well as in English. The control first grades in each school received instruction in English only. A relatively short time, about an hour a day, was devoted to Spanish instruction. The students used reading materials created by specialists especially for them. The children were randomly selected for placement in the control and experimental sections, although there were some exceptions in the selection process. Pryor of Our Lady of the Lake College, who was principal consultant to and evaluator of the project, states (1967, p. 62): "Pre-tests and post-tests were used, as well as personal adjustment rating sheets, personal data sheets, attendance records, reports of observers, and indications of pupil and parental attitudes. The design was to determine to what extent the sections of the first grade were equal or different at the beginning of the school term and how much relative change had taken place at the end of the term. That is, it was the design to determine the relative status or position of the experimental [instructed in Spanish] section of the first grade among all the sections of the first grade in the same school and to determine the extent of change of relative status or position among the groups at the end of school." Pryor reported that in one of the four elementary schools, the first grade that was instructed in Spanish ". . . clearly made more progress in practically every aspect of the measures than the sections which were taught in English only." In the two other schools this was also true, but the degree of difference between the control and experimental classes was not nearly so pronounced. In the fourth school, no evidence to favor Spanish instruction was found. Pryor cautions that a multitude of variables are present that may bias the findings but suggests that enough success was demonstrated to warrant further experimentation. The closing words of Pryor's report are: "The pupils in the bilingual [Spanish] sections of all four schools could speak, read, and write in two languages at the end of the first grade. This in itself might be considered a justification for the program." This final point deserves the serious consideration of educators.

Programs to teach Spanish to Spanish speakers are now enthusiastically advocated by many linguistic scientists, social scientists, educators, and by a large percentage of Mexican American leaders. Bills are before state legislatures to abolish laws prohibiting instruction in languages other than English, federal legislation provides limited funds for experimental programs in non-English instruction, and a widespread movement to teach in children's own vernacular is gaining momentum and influence among educators generally. In spite of the numerous possible benefits of such programs to the child and to the nation, a note of caution must be interjected. Conservative or prejudiced school boards or educators could favor programs to teach Mexican American children in Spanish. Classes in Spanish for Spanish speakers could be used to justify present or future segregation of the group: if it is best to teach such children in Spanish, it could also be argued that it is most efficient to isolate them from those taught in English. "Spanish speaker" suggests Mexican American to most educators, and all children with Spanish surnames or dark faces could be "encouraged" to learn their "native tongue," regardless of the status of the language in their homes or their ability to use it. Given only two polar choices, ethnic segregation with instruction in Spanish or desegregation without it, this author would choose the latter as most beneficial to the child and society. Many will violently disagree.

Historically there have been three types of schools that taught native speakers in Spanish: (1) some elementary schools in Northern New Mexico and Southern Colorado, (2) "Mexican Dame Schools" along the Rio Grande River in Texas, and (3) some Roman Catholic parochial schools, especially those of the Oblate Fathers in the Lower Rio Grande Valley. These schools were fairly common in certain small geographic areas until World War II. The Oblate Fathers are reported to have taught in Spanish in some classes and schools until the middle 1950s. One can consider these schools as institutions contributing to the preservation of ethnic traditions and the Spanish language, but only in the case of the Catholic schools can preservation be assumed to be the explicit objective of the institution. The other types of schools apparently taught in Spanish more out of convenience than design. Some rural public elementary schools in New Mexico and Colorado apparently followed the required state curriculum but taught some or all subjects in Spanish; every teacher handled her particular situation differently. The Oblate Fathers are reported to have stressed Spanish values and tradition but in general to have followed an American curriculum. Except for one or two courses in English, most courses were taught in Spanish. Each program and parochial school differed.

The existence of what may be termed "Mexican Dame Schools" is an interesting and little known fact. There appears to be no reference to them in the literature, but a number of interviewees for this study attended such institutions. From perhaps 1900 until the end of World War II, a number of private "parlor schools" conducted in Spanish operated in the Laredo, Texas, vicinity and perhaps farther east. Most schools included primary grades only, and none are reported to have gone past the seventh grade. Most were one-room, one-teacher establishments, but "La Escuela de los Jornaleros" (the school of the workers) in Laredo is reported to have had an enrollment of over 100 and to have employed four or more *profesoras* in the 1930s. The teacher-owners, almost invariably women, of these schools were usually graduates of *normales* (secondary level teacher-training institutions) in Mexico and were certified to teach in Mexico but unable to teach in Texas. Many of the ladies entered the United States as brides of Mexican Americans and, desiring to supplement their family income, converted their homes to schools.

The Dame Schools generally followed the Mexican curriculum of their day; Spanish was the language of instruction. In some, English was taught as a traditional foreign language, and in others perhaps one subject area was taught in English. The type of instruction varied greatly with the individual teacher. Understandably, these schools were attractive to "better off" or upwardly mobile Mexican Americans. Parents preferred to send their children to such schools because of the anti-Mexican nature and poor quality of the local schools, because Mexican culture and the Spanish language were taught, and, most interestingly, because graduates of such schools were usually ahead of their grade when they entered the public schools. The Mexican curriculum followed was more advanced academically than the American, and content covered in the third grade in Mexico was taught in perhaps the fifth in Texas. Therefore, a child transferring to public school was well grounded academically and might be promoted one or two grades. By the age most children were ready to transfer to public school (10 or 11), they would have had ample time to learn English. Thus, the Dame Schools permitted children of upwardly mobile parents to enter public schools with an advantage rather than a disadvantage. Rather than be retained in the first grade, according to what was and still is a common practice, such children were likely to be accelerated when they entered public school. Numerous educators interviewed during this study in the Laredo area are graduates of such schools, and many of them mentioned other Mexican Americans in business and the professions who were their classmates.

Other Remedial Services. It is not necessary to describe here all the differing types of programs for Mexican Americans. Gordon and Wilkerson's study on compensatory education programs (1966) details the general types; projects for Mexican Americans are not substantially different.

During the interviewing for this study numerous programs were described whose objectives were to add cultural enrichment to the lives of Mexican American children. Projects in these programs run the gamut from trips to the opera to picnics in the country. In California, cultural enrichment included ". . . study trips, speakers, development and acquisition of aesthetic materials, creative expression, outdoor education (camping) and, on a few occasions, summer field trips (California State Department of Education, 1966b, p. S10). Through such activities Mexican American children are exposed to small segments of the kind of middle-class experiences assumed by the school to be important factors in encouraging school success. Almost invariably, these projects assume culture to be "the great works that have survived the ages" and provide the poor with suitable exposure to museums, "good music and art," and so forth. How educators have determined that such "culture" characterizes the typical middle-class home is unknown, but teachers apparently assume that exposure to it will enhance the learning ability or at least "broaden the horizon" of low-status Mexican American children.

The real function of such quick excursions (figuratively or literally) into the world of affluence, "culture," and middle-class life should be investigated. Certain questions must be answered: Do such trips accomplish their objectives? What are these objectives? What meaning does the child ascribe to such experiences? How does he react to this different world? Does such exposure increase or decrease hostility toward the dominant society? It seems futile to include here quotations and reports concerning the success of such cultural enrichment projects, since most are extremely subjective. Suffice it to say that school people generally contended that such programs were of value.

Schools can become cultural centers within their communities, the school functioning as the focal point for a number of social, cultural, economic, and recreational activities. In such all-encompassing projects, the school almost literally becomes a year-long, 24-hour operation encompassing activities far beyond its normal scope. One interviewee in Texas had proposed such a project, but it was given low priority by his district and was not submitted for federal funding. No programs designed to make the school the "cultural center" of a Mexican American community were observed or reported.

Another approach to cultural enrichment is a corollary to "Hispanic culture" language programs for teaching Spanish to native speakers. In this case, the Mexican American child is seen to be highly deficient in knowledge of and pride in his "rich cultural heritage." This condition is assumed to encourage a negative self-view, and to remedy this, the child is exposed to Hispanic culture. Like other programs, such "culture" is assumed to be the "best of the past." Programs of this nature taught separately without the Spanish language component were not found during this study, but numerous interviewees commented that such cultural activities are needed. One California high school reported similar objectives for a previously popular club for Mexican American youngsters. Some schools are collecting materials and establishing "Hispanic cultural corners" in their schools. No courses in Latin American history or Hispanic culture especially designed for Mexican American youngsters were encountered during this study, but they probably exist or are in the planning stage. There is no appropriate text or even collection of materials now available that reflect the history or contributions of Mexican Americans to the nation's development. Unfortunately, much of the text material on the Southwest either slights Mexican Americans or describes them in ways that contribute to the local negative stereotype. History or social studies texts on Latin America often distort the Spanish conquest and colonization. This situation may be remedied in the near future with the publication of materials appropriate for different levels of school. How such new material will be used is unknown: will it be used principally to enhance Mexican Americans' pride in their heritage and perhaps themselves, or will it be used by all ethnic groups to promote better understanding of this nation and its history? Perhaps both objectives can be reached.

Interesting attempts are being made to reeducate Mexican American parents. The school usually sees its role as that of modifying the Mexican Americans, encouraging English speaking, cleanliness, a balanced (American) diet, school attendance, and so forth. Most approaches to change Mexican American behavior are highly traditional, and there has been little effort to evaluate their success. Activities such as using school social workers, nurses, teachers, or the P.T.A. to encourage parents to conform to what the school (the middle class) wants are quite common. A few districts are modifying their P.T.A. by using Spanish in meetings, a change reported to improve Mexican American attendance.

The school-community program of one middle-sized metropolitan Texas district is of particular interest because it appears to be representative of a number of projects. With the assistance of federal funds, the district hired and trained bilingual community-school aides. The prime objective of this program appears to be the reeducation of Mexican American parents. However, encouraging the organization of parents was also desired in order that they might operate "self-help" projects. While the overriding objective was a one-way communication (school to Mexican American), mechanisms for two-way interchange and communication were also established. This approach to school-community relations is not uncommon. According to the director of this particular project, the aides were trained to "listen" to parents as they expressed their needs and to work as liaisons between the school and the ethnic community to solve problems. The director stressed that the aide did not function solely as a referral agent or intermediary between the parent and other social agencies, but rather as a catalyst to stimulate the school and community to resolve problems jointly. However, referrals to agencies were made. The aides and parents discussed "school problems and what parents can do to help the child in school," as well as health and sanitation. "Where we have done these things parents have taken a greater interest in school and attended PTA more regularly." Lectures and films on narcotics, health, child rearing, and so on have been presented at such meetings. The director said: "We set up neighborhood get-together programs, social get-togethers . . . they sang songs that the children sing . . . they did some of the things the children do in school." Other projects are using school-community aides, apparently primarily as tools to reach and change Mexican American parents. Most programs are one-way, but their long-term results may be the organization of low-status Mexican Americans and perhaps their increased participation in school and community affairs.

Encouraging participation in nursery school programs run by the school is another approach to involving Mexican American parents. Only the Colton, California, experiment was observed in this study, but Pico Rivera, California, and other districts are reported to be conducting similar activities. In the Colton project, Mexican American parents, mostly mothers, bring their preschool children to school where a special nursery school program is provided. Mothers participate in two ways: by assisting in the children's program and by taking part in small-group discussions relative to child rearing and family relations. In both ways parents are taught about "proper" child care. The small-group discussions are considered quite productive; in the one session observed, parents appeared to be interested and contributed to discussions. To what degree parents changed their beliefs or modified their child-rearing practices, as a result of exposure to the Anglo way, is unknown. To what degree parents who participated represented the poorest and least acculturated is also unknown. The participants observed by the author appeared to be middle class and *agringado*.

PROGRAMS TO IMPROVE THE SCHOOL

Schools are improving the quality and quantity of their facilities, staffs, and programs for Mexican Americans. These efforts can be viewed as attempts to equalize facilities and to raise the economically poorer districts to the same position as that of richer districts. Efforts to "improve the school" rarely involve more than: (1) the purchasing of more equipment, (2) the hiring of additional staff (often specialized), and (3) the addition of programs considered essential by educational authorities.

Equipment and Facilities. All Southwestern states use federal funds to purchase such diverse equipment as: complete language laboratories, reading diagnostic equipment, language skills centers, books and supplemental teaching materials, phonographs, and all kinds of audiovisual equipment.

Texas ranks "... weaknesses in school environment (largely lack of learning materials)" as the third most important "pupil need" to be met by federal financial assistance. This need to improve the school's facilities is ranked third in even the largest metropolitan districts. Texas enumerates the following school facilities or programs to be improved (percents represent the percent of all Texas school districts undertaking each activity): health and welfare services, 22 percent; health services and examinations, 21 percent; expanding library services, 17 percent; acquiring additional equipment, materials, and facilities, 14 percent; providing modern teaching equipment, materials, and techniques, 31 percent. Rather clearly, the federal government is assisting districts to reach "normalcy" or at least minimum levels of facilities (Texas Education Agency, 1966, pp. 85–87). In California as in Texas: "The third most prevalent primary activities . . . were in the area of supportive and auxiliary services, listed in 9.9 percent of the district reports. . . . Common activities were acquisition of library materials, special counseling techniques, physical education activities and speech therapy" (California State Department of Education, 1966b, p. S10). California and Texas cannot be compared directly in their need to compensate for inadequate facilities or equipment. However, it does appear that California needed to improve material facilities in a smaller percentage of cases than did Texas.

In a sense, the federal outlay of funds to upgrade school facilities implies that the federal government is doing a job that the people of the state are unwilling or unable to do. For example, Texas is a rich state but one that regularly refuses to tax itself adequately to support quality school facilities. Federal funds are then used to do what the state won't do, and in many cases federal taxpayers are helping most the states that won't or can't help themselves.

There is no way to evaluate quantities of equipment objectively. The relationship between given equipment or facilities and achievement is extremely difficult to establish, and neither California nor

Texas attempted to do so. However, California reports that increased or improved libraries produced "little progress" in 20 districts out of 58 reporting, "some progress" in 8, and "substantial progress" in 3; 27 districts did not report. Similar results are reported in 24 other districts that are improving libraries as a secondary objective of their Title I ESEA projects (California State Department of Education, 1966b, pp. F5, F23).

From observations of the use of new equipment and facilities, this author suggests the following: (1) Too much rather sophisticated equipment is not used to full advantage; teachers tend not to understand its full potential. (2) Some equipment (for example, the almost omnipresent overhead projector) is often used to teach in a rote and very traditional way. (3) Books, like other teaching equipment, are often used in traditional and apparently unproductive ways. (4) Some of the simplest equipment (for example tape recorders and filmstrip projectors) seems to be used most advantageously.

A great deal of money is expended on facilities and equipment. Whether they pay the anticipated return depends on their use. Many interviewees commented positively on the benefits of particular facilities or special pieces of equipment, but none were able to demonstrate their benefits conclusively. This holds true for some of the most expensive and complicated setups. Two factors seem obvious: teachers are not being trained to use equipment properly or creatively, and equipment alone causes little or no difference in the amount of children's achievement. It does seem strange that so little is done about teacher retraining, when equipment is being bought on an ever-increasing scale.

Staff. The shortage of trained teachers and other staff is ever present. Some of the more economically depressed areas are those requiring the most additional staff. Teachers tend to flee these areas in search of better salaries and better living or working conditions. The rural areas are particularly hard-pressed to procure adequately trained staff for their special activities, but all areas suffer. This problem is compounded by the federal government's giving very late notice of funding to school districts. Often the normal hiring period has passed before a district can anticipate its personnel needs.

Nonprofessionals are being used and trained for various positions in schools, most commonly as teachers' aides or assistants. Districts vary greatly in what they perceive the assistant's role in the classroom to be. Of the aides observed during this study, about half functioned as clerical assistants, freeing the teacher from the more routine duties. The others served as "teachers," instructing and supervising pupils in many ways. The five states studied showed little difference regarding the use of nonprofessionals, and state policy or law regarding their role seemed to make far less difference than did district or teacher policy. District reports on the availability and success of aides vary greatly. The attitude toward aides recruited from the "indigenous poor" depends on a community's perspective of its poor. Many interviewees stated that they were unable to find qualified (well-enough-educated) Mexican American poor to act as aides and so recruited their aides from the more middle-class Anglo or Mexican American population. Others argued that aides drawn from the lower class worked out very well and were intelligent even though they had little formal schooling. Administrators and teachers were both divided on the usefulness or propriety of using aides; some feared that the encroachment of untrained people on the teaching profession would adversely affect public regard for teachers, others saw nonprofessionals as enhancing both the teacher's performance and his status. There seemed to be consensus on only one point: if teachers' aides are used in classrooms in any role whatever, preservice and inservice training programs must be given for both teachers and aides.

The Mexican American teacher's aide can do much to help Mexican American children feel comfortable in Anglo schools. She can introduce the real Mexican American culture into an otherwise foreign classroom and act as a bridge between the ethnic community and the school. These roles and more are possible, but the jobs performed by aides depend more on the attitudes of the school district than on the ability or willingness of the aide or the Mexican American community.

Surprisingly, no secondary school program to train teachers' aides was encountered during this study. A great shortage of acceptable jobs for Mexican American youth exists in many parts of the Southwest. It would seem that programs to utilize this surplus of youth as teachers' aides would be of benefit to all concerned.

The hiring of nonprofessional school-community aides or workers is also common. As in the case of teachers' aides, opinions vary concerning their appropriate role and effectiveness. The majority of school-community aides are reported to be "one-way" agents, sent into the ethnic community to relate the school's desires and expectations. In fact, in some areas these aides are little more than Spanish-speaking truant officers. "Two-way" aides that act as a bridge between community and school are rarely encountered. Community aides commonly function as referral agents to social welfare agencies. They often help the poor to take advantage of available services and elicit the assistance of the school in behalf of the poor.

Prevocational and Work-Study Programs. Prevocational and work-study projects, not strictly remedial in nature, are becoming increasingly common. These augment the school's regular program and, in the case of work-study projects, somewhat modify its traditional role.

The school has moved into the area of employment counselor and supervisor. Some arrangement to permit youngsters to attend school while earning money is becoming a standard feature of most secondary schools serving large percentages of disadvantaged students. If the principal reason for an individual's withdrawal from school is economic, such programs can go a long way toward keeping him in school. In general, good results for work-study projects are reported, as long as the work is considered by the individual to be meaningful and not degrading. Placing youngsters in nonschool or institutionally related jobs is likewise reported to produce good results. Inasmuch as these programs tend to place youngsters in apprenticelike roles in occupations they themselves choose, the chances for success seem to be greater than in normal work-study projects.

Vocational- and occupational-training programs are common to many high schools in the Southwest, but recently a newer type of program, called "prevocational," has been encouraged and funded. Prevocational programs are quite common in Texas poverty-area secondary schools, although they are not universal by any means. They are geared to poverty youngsters who are predicted to drop out before they finish high school. They are often junior high school programs, though the youngsters enrolled in them (often segregated from other students) average 16 to 17 years of age. Terminal prevocational programs are intended to prepare teenagers to enter semiskilled or low-skilled occupations at the lowest level and to raise to a minimum the academic skills required by that occupation. While the very existence of such programs implies recognition of the failure of the school system, their approach, as a last resort, appears to be realistic. It must be remembered that these are programs to teach the rudimentary skills and knowledge related to groups of occupations and are not vocational programs geared to provide entrance into the crafts or skilled occupations at an apprentice level.

In general, girls in prevocational programs are taught the rudiments of home management, table service, food preparation, and dressmaking. Often such courses are designed to prepare girls to become domestic servants, restaurant helpers ("busboys"), garment workers, or perhaps at best waitresses. Boys are introduced to shop skills, electricity, body and fender work, and mechanics. While the expressed objective is to prepare them to become helpers in a shop, such jobs are often unavailable; usually boys enter agricultural work. It may be hoped that certain kinds of prevocational training will help them to find a permanent job that involves more than regular field work. In certain geographic areas, the wages that boys and girls can expect after prevocational training are only slightly above public welfare assistance. In certain areas of Texas, a Mexican American works in the fields or in a restaurant for as little as $3 a day. If successful, terminal prevocational training may keep individual youngsters off welfare but can hardly be expected to do more.

PROGRAMS TO CHANGE THE SCHOOL

The average special program for Mexican American children does not drastically modify the curriculum or organization of a school, nor do such activities change the role of the school in the community. Nevertheless, a very few schools have made significant changes to relate to their communities more adequately and to teach their charges more efficiently.

Inservice Teacher Education. Almost every educator interviewed during this study commented that some form of special training, either preservice or inservice, was essential for teaching Mexican American children. Yet there was no clear-cut consensus about what these programs should consist of or should stress. As usual, opinions were divided about equally between those arguing that teachers should be taught "effective techniques" for teaching Mexican American children, and those contending that it is essential that teachers learn to "understand" the child and his culture. Those arguing for effective techniques were usually unable to describe any special techniques that do "work better" with Mexican American children. The advocates of "understanding" seemed to feel that a knowledge of the Mexican culture and the child's "adjustment" problems is crucial and will lead to more positive teacher attitudes. Many administrators stated that the attitude of teachers toward Mexican Americans was negative. Programs expressly devised to change this perception were regularly advocated but rarely encountered.

Institutes established under the National Defense Education Act or with other federal assistance are common throughout the Southwest. Most of these work toward both new techniques and better understanding. The following description of an institute at The University of Texas at El Paso in the summer of 1967 is representative (Barber, 1967): "The Institute for Teachers of the Educationally Deprived . . . concentrated on . . . helping teachers to understand the problems of children who are living in poverty, and the development of methods and techniques specifically designed for working with children in this category. Members of the Institute studied the sociology of the economically deprived as well as the Mexican-American culture which is dominant in this area. Activities included the study of reasons for difficulties Mexican-American children have in learning to read, speak, and understand the English language." Numerous other institutes concentrate on the audiolingual approach to second-language teaching. While many institutes and other similar inservice activities stress other objectives, implicit in most is a desire to modify teachers' perceptions of Mexican American children and basic attitudes toward them. The degree and direction of attitudinal shift are rarely assessed objectively. The difficulties in determining such changes are well known. Even assuming a valid individual shift toward a more positive view of Mexican Americans, its permanence is always open to question: how long can the new perspective be maintained after the teacher leaves the supportive environment of the institute?

California financed 12 experimental projects related to teacher education in 1965–66 with state funds for research and development in compensatory and intergroup education. These projects include one experimental preservice program. It is not related especially to Mexican Americans, but it is one of the very few known experimental preservice programs in the Southwest for teachers of the disadvantaged. This project was conducted jointly by San Francisco State College and the Sausalito School District. Its approach appears to be based on "the development of basic experience through the seminar-tutorial" and the use of a great deal of practice teaching in the field. Reference to the California State Department of Education's report on these projects (1966a) might provide guidelines for action, although none of the projects deals specifically with Mexican Americans.

A number of schools observed during this study seemed to be successful in changing teachers' perceptions, or at least behavior, toward Mexican American children. No single approach was evident. Elementary schools in Laredo, Texas; Albuquerque, New Mexico; and Carlsbad, Azusa, Oasis, and Escondido, California, seemed to exemplify what can be accomplished in modifying teachers' outlooks and the general school social climate. While all schools were different, they appeared to share most of the following characteristics: (1) The district administration permitted each institution a great deal of freedom to experiment. (2) The local administrator presented no pat solutions to the problems of Mexican Americans; problems were approached jointly by teachers, administrators, and sometimes the community. (3) Teachers were given a free hand to experiment, try new approaches, develop materials, and so forth, and were supported in their efforts. (4) Parents were asked to help and advise, not asked to conform or to change their life patterns. Parents were allowed to make decisions whenever possible. *Barrio* parents were hired as teachers or other school aides. (5) Older children were given increased responsibility; often they were permitted to help teach younger children. (6) Some method to encourage frank interchange of ideas among staff and to evaluate the program constantly was established (for example, "open" or nondirective teachers' meetings).

In other schools observed teachers had become enthusiastic about a given technique. In these schools also, teachers tended to change their behavior toward Mexican American students and thus perhaps to generate student enthusiasm and academic learning. The effect of both the "panacea" and "problem-solving" approaches can be similar, but the latter approach seems to generate more enthusiasm, and since no limit of "solutions" is possible, may function to encourage teachers' involvement and thus a more positive school social climate. Enthusiasm and cooperation are likely to be maintained if the participants feel they are involved in the decision making. The "panacea" approach while having short-term benefits may lead to teachers' discouragement and pessimism if faith in the panacea wanes.

Desegregation. As mentioned earlier in this book, only a very few school districts are moving to end de facto segregation. Yet some educators argue that desegregation would be the single most effective measure to improve Mexican American achievement and participation, as well as to encourage the group's assimilation and acculturation. Close and sustained equal-status interaction between Mexican Americans and Anglos in mixed schools could contribute to the eventual destruction of mutual stereotyping. Regardless of the social, ethical, and educational arguments favoring desegregation, little is being done to accomplish it. This failure of the schools to act in the apparent best interests of children can only be interpreted as a reflection of community views or attitudes. Few educators are willing or able to counter the views of a board of education or the vocal and powerful elements in a community. As reported earlier, the state of California is attempting to end ethnic imbalance in schools. Title I funds are being used to aid districts to prepare for and implement desegregation. California cites two innovative projects for the mixing of Negro and other children. One was the temporary combining of ethnic and racial groups; two districts cooperated in this effort. The other was true desegregation (California State Department of Education, 1966b, pp. 130, 131). Both these projects involved Negroes, but other California cities desegregating their Mexican American schools receive aid from either the state or federal government. No Texas district is reported to be implementing real desegregation. Even in California only a very few districts have ended de facto segregation. It will be many years before this attempt to adjust the school radically to serve children becomes general in the Southwest. It is clear that the principal reason for the slowness is the bias and prejudice of the local population.

School-Community Relationships. Formal experiments to effect twofold modifications of school have been undertaken in the past. These were attempts to convert existing institutions into "community schools" by: (1) radically modifying the curriculum to eliminate irrelevancy and conflict, and (2) making the school the focal point of community development. Only the formal experiments have been recorded; undoubtedly other educators worked toward similar objectives. No formal attempts in the present-day Southwest to change a school's role in the community from that of "culture imposer" to "culture stimulator" have been reported or were observed during this study, although certain schools may be changing from traditional roles as a result of other activities.

The so-called Taos and Nambe projects are the two best-known and best-documented school-community development projects. Both were rural experiments in Northern New Mexico. The Taos County Project was organized and administered by the University of New Mexico with financial assistance from the Carnegie Corporation and private individuals. The project was begun in 1940 and terminated formal activities in 1943. Its objectives were twofold: (1) to involve the rural people in the solution of their own problems, and (2) to revitalize the school in order to serve all elements of the population. The community cooperated in numerous ways: the adults built libraries, canned food for use in school cafeterias, arranged for educational movies, raised money for books, and, in a multitude of other ways, worked cooperatively with the school and other institutions for their own social and economic betterment. No decisions were made without consulting the people of the community. Through cooperative efforts between the community and school and other agencies, the people were able to accomplish a number of improvements. Needless to say, the project had its share of failures and setbacks. The Taos Project was more nondirective and less school-oriented than the more well-known Nambe Project (see Reid, 1946).

The Nambe Project was also organized around concepts of community development, and the school was used as the primary structure through which change was to be stimulated and effected. The project represents a significant attempt to develop a curriculum fitted to the life patterns of the Spanish-American and Indian population. While this program had considerably more central direction than did the Taos Project, it too relied heavily on getting the people interested and involved in the solution of their own problems. The program was organized in 1938 by a prominent Nambe family who requested the University of New Mexico to revise the work of the village school. With the permission and cooperation of the county school board, the Nambe school was declared experimental and placed under the authority of the University of New Mexico. The county continued to pay the school's normal operating expenses; funds to meet the school's additional requirements were donated.

The principal objectives of the project were to discover community problems and endeavor to solve them; to construct a school curriculum drawn from the local culture; to discover and utilize the resources of the community; to develop a craft program suitable for young children; to develop a health program; to make known to the people the services available through various governmental agencies and to teach them how to procure these services.

There was an attempt made to relate the curricular content of the school to the life of the Nambe people. The school emphasized the study of natural science through the study of local plants and animals; the school's grounds were used as a soil and agricultural experiment laboratory. The program was very flexible as can be seen in the fact that the study of arithmetic was eliminated in the pre-first, first, and second grades. It seemed to the staff that the time could be more profitably utilized in the learning of oral English and reading. As the children progressed, the curriculum was changed so that it became increasingly more related to the world outside Nambe. Some attempts were made to direct the population toward more modern agricultural, health, and nutritional practices. Tireman and Watson (1943, p. 117) reported on the success of the school aspects of the project: "One of the outstanding accomplishments was the increased interest in education on the part of both parents and children. Fathers could see the value of a program that taught the boys how to improve their farms. They ceased to keep the boys out [of school] for trivial jobs. Sometimes they hired help. At other times, arrangements were made to excuse boys early in the afternoon. The children liked to come to school and 'playing hooky' was unusual. This interest was instrumental in changing the attitude of some parents toward attendance. Perhaps the percent of attendance each year is the most amazing fact. . . . The percentage of attendance varies from 90–93 percent . . . a very high figure for a rural school. In New Mexico as a whole, the percent of attendance among rural children for the school year of 1936–37 was 76."

No present-day counterparts of the Nambe or Taos projects were encountered during this study. Although the specifics of these programs may not be applicable in urbanized environments, the general approach might well be used to advantage.

Quite prevalent in the past, and still common today, is the practice of placing strong but sympathetic principals in *barrio* elementary schools. This practice may encourage the development of a *patrón-peón* relationship between the principal and the Mexican American community. The principal firmly establishes himself as the mediator between the Mexican American *barrio* and the dominant society and its institutions. The community, in turn, relies heavily on the principal for all manner of assistance, advice, and intercession. The school administrator becomes a "father figure" to his flock; he has shepherded many generations of them through elementary school, supported them in secondary school, and ultimately helped them adjust to adult life. Such a principal's role is multifaceted; he is father confessor, bail-bondsman, ombudsman, employment agency, community leader, family counselor, and much else.

School and community relationships of the *patrón* type appear to be disappearing; many *patrón* principals are at the point of retirement. However, some younger men just beginning their careers appear to be consciously or unconsciously establishing themselves as *patróns*. This kind of relationship is seen by many as advantageous to Mexican Americans, since a *patrón* provides the necessary buffer from Anglos, support of many kinds, and a type of relationship perhaps familiar to the older generation. For each argument favoring the relationship, there is an opposing position. Rodriguez (1966, p. 11) sees the *patrón* as impeding ethnic progress and questions his incentives: "I wonder what motives possess those who profess a desire for an advancement of the Mexican-American socially, educationally, economically, yet will fight against the main key to the elimination of these problems [desegregation and the closing of *barrio* schools]. The part that is so pitiful is that too often it is the educator who has led the opposition. Usually it is an administrator who has taken the role of the community *patrón*. . . . Because the school is accepted by the Mexican-American community as an authority not to be questioned, his word [the principal's] then becomes a fact and the children are relegated to an education that will not prepare them for life."

All too often these relationships are well-established and difficult to sever, and the elimination of the *patrón* principal must await his retirement. This type of school-community relationship may well serve a stable and castelike social order but must be reexamined in light of present-day society and the awakening desires of the Mexican American community. The *patrón-peón* relationship is not the rule; the vast majority of principals do not develop it. In most cases there is little attempt to develop more than the traditional, somewhat aloof, relationship between school and *barrio*.

Bilingual Schools. The shift from the traditional school organization, based on a standard curriculum taught in English, to bilingual organization represents an extreme modification of the institution. There are some experimental schools in San Antonio and Laredo, Texas, and elsewhere in the Southwest that are classified as bilingual. They adhere to the definition by teaching diverse subjects in two languages. The primary objectives of these schools are not the teaching of a second language per se, or the use of the children's vernacular as a bridge to facilitate the learning of English, although these can be secondary objectives.

Gaarder (1966, p. 110) suggests there are two distinct types of bilingual programs and two sets of reasons for implementing them. The reasons "for adding the mother tongue as a teaching medium" (for example, Spanish for Spanish speakers) are: "a. to avoid or lessen scholastic retardation in children whose mother tongue is not the principal school language; b. to strengthen the bonds between home and school; c. to avoid the alienation from family and linguistic community that is commonly the price of rejection of one's mother tongue and of complete assimilation into the dominant linguistic group; and d. to develop strong literacy in the mother tongue in order to make it a strong asset in the adult's life." The reasons for adding a second tongue as a teaching medium (for example, Spanish or French for English speakers) are: "a. to engage the child's capacity for natural, unconscious language learning; b. to avoid the problems of method, aptitude, etc., which beset the usual teaching of second languages; c. to make the second language a means to an end rather than an end in itself; and d. to increase second language experience without crowding the curriculum."

Both sets of reasons apply in the case of the United Consolidated School District of Laredo. The first applies to the school's Spanish speakers, and the second applies to its English speakers. San Antonio experimental bilingual schools most closely follow the thinking of the first position, but the view that Spanish is a "bridge" to English is strongly influential.

Gaarder differentiates between "one-way" and "two-way" bilingual schools. The former are schools in which one group of children (for example, Spanish speakers) learn in two languages, either the national language plus their mother tongue, or the national language plus a second language. The San Antonio experimental project is a one-way school offering instruction in the mother tongue (Spanish). Examples of one-way schools offering instruction in a second language include a school in Virginia using Spanish and French to teach world history to advanced foreign language students; a school in Utah using German to teach biology; an experimental elementary school in Illinois using Spanish to teach nontraditional language arts and other subjects (Stubing, 1966, pp. 20, 22).

A two-way school instructs children from two linguistic communities (for example, Spanish speakers and English speakers) in both languages, so that children from each community learn both their own and the other group's language. Children are either segregated by linguistic group or mixed. The experimental Coral Way Elementary School in Miami, Florida, segregates Cuban and Anglo children through the third grade. (Basic experimentation in this bilingual project, originally funded by the Ford Foundation, produced the Miami Linguistic Readers previously mentioned. See also Gaarder, 1967.) In the Laredo experiment, both Mexican American and Anglo children are mixed in all academic and play activities at all ages.

The San Antonio and Laredo programs mentioned above are well-known examples of bilingual school organization in the Southwest. Less well-known and more informal efforts are reported. Houston, Texas, is reported to be experimenting with a one-way program (national language plus mother tongue) to teach Mexican Americans Spanish-language arts, music, and social studies in their vernacular (Stubing, 1966, p. 22). Del Rio, Texas, is experimenting with Spanish instruction for Anglo and Mexican American children mixed together. This author observed one Head Start two-way (mixed) bilingual project in California in which the two groups were mixed. Other informal efforts toward bilingual organization of preschool classes are reported (Stubing, 1966, p. 111).

There is some disagreement concerning the categorizing of programs. The Southwest Council of Foreign Language Teachers considers some programs for teaching Spanish to Spanish speakers to be one-way bilingual programs (the "national" language plus the mother tongue). Such differences are due to failure to agree on definitions. For the purposes of this book, the nature of the content taught in Spanish, and the objectives implied, determine a program's classification. Many educators consider the terms "bilingual" and "bicultural" to be synonymous, but an important distinction should be made. In a bilingual school two languages are used for instruction, and in a bicultural school two languages and two cultures are used. The curriculum in many bilingual schools is drawn almost exclusively from the dominant Anglo culture and merely translated into another language. In a bicultural school, the content, method, and sequence of instruction are drawn from two cultures. No truly bicultural schools serving Mexican Americans in the Southwest have been reported or were observed during this study. However, the Laredo experiment is attempting to incorporate and draw from Mexican American culture as it exists locally.

The San Antonio, Texas, Language Research Project, directed by Thomas D. Horn of The University of Texas, is probably the best known of the Southwestern experiments. This program must be classified as bilingual; science and mathematics are taught in Spanish, and hence it is not an ESL program or a program for teaching Spanish to Spanish speakers. Since 1964, nine San Antonio Independent School District

Elementary Schools have been involved in the experiment. Almost 100 percent of the children in these schools are Mexican American, the vast majority are from slum or "near-slum" environments. Nick E. Garza, at the time principal of the largest elementary school in the project, described the project in an unpublished and undated paper:

"The San Antonio, Texas, Language Research Project was an outgrowth of experimental approaches to teaching oral language and reading to disadvantaged children of Mexican-American background. The Language Research Project . . . was the first organized research on language development and reading wholly concerned with educationally disadvantaged Spanish-speaking children in Texas. The progress of these children was previously slow. This fact is evident from reports . . . which clearly show an alarming number of failures among first grade children with non-English-speaking background. The Texas Education Agency estimates that between 40 and 60 percent of these children drop out of school before completing the elementary grades. Simply stated, curriculum materials and methods now being used may be appropriate for middle-class Anglo children, but are not suitable for disadvantaged youngsters with a language barrier. Their use has caused feelings of frustration and failure. This has been a major cause of children leaving school much too early in their educational endeavors.

"The primary purpose of this project study was to develop oral language and to use it to promote the teaching of English as a second language. 735 children from 28 first grade sections from nine elementary schools in the San Antonio Independent School District were the participants. These children were assigned to one of three different [experimental and control] groups, OAE (Oral-Aural-English), OAS (Oral-Aural-Spanish) and NOA (no Oral-Aural technique used). These classes were taught thirty minutes in the morning and thirty minutes in the afternoon. . . . Lesson plans were formulated by the Consulting staff based upon science and self-concept content and forwarded to each of the project teachers.

"Teaching was performed in English and Spanish through the Audio-Lingual approach. Children learned from what they could see and hear. Basic sentence structures were modeled, then practiced orally by individuals, small groups, and then by the entire group. The teacher served as a model for the purpose of correct structure and accurate oral speech usage.

"The Audio-Lingual technique then was used to develop fluency in both the English and the Spanish patterns being introduced, although not taught at the same time nor to the same group of children. One class was instructed for one hour per day in Spanish, the other a like amount of time in English. One hypothesis to be tested was that learning and achieving competency, maturity, and oral and written fluency in one language could be transferred in the actual development of promoting English as a second language. This was not difficult for the majority of the children, and it was only a short time before they began to establish relationship of concepts to language."

Early attempts to evaluate the project's numerous components produced inconclusive findings. At present, the project staff is continuing the research aspects of the project. However, the staff was able to draw some rather significant implications from formal and informal observations of the children. Horn (1966, pp. 9–10) reported that the children observed tended to suffer from "disadvantagedness." They did not possess ". . . basic abilities and knowledge or experiential background associated with beginning academic/school learning and reading, e.g. auditory visual discrimination, simple classifying [and lacked] information about objects and events supposedly familiar to children. The second fact [of disadvantagedness] related to a critical intangible, namely, the development of a sense of personal identity or a concept of self. The style of responding reflected by these children toward the school environment could be characterized as generally apathetic, fearful, bewildered, and/or just passive. Most of these children revealed a marked lack of self-concept in handling various kinds of seemingly simple tasks, e.g. cutting with scissors, copying figures, feeling gross differences among objects. One of the most striking characteristics among these children was their general insensitivity to the world around them. The kinds of observations noted in these categories presented a discouraging setting in which a child might acquire positive feelings of self-esteem and a continuing sense of personal identity. The science based program and its techniques appeared to be making a direct assault upon the category of language and the first above noted aspects of disadvantagedness, namely, the abilities and knowledge specifically needed for academic learning and reading. However, only indirectly did this program assault the second facet of disadvantagement, namely, the concept of self." In order to remedy the assumed lack of a sense of identity and negative self-concept, as interpreted from staff observations, special activities were added to the experimental oral language project. Garza described the approach to enhance self-esteem: "The self-concept approach is built upon simple facts known about an individual, e.g. the child's name, street address, physical description, and progresses to more complex relationships—e.g. roles in various settings such as the home and the school. The basic and most fundamental idea was to develop in each child an awareness of himself, of his importance, of his value to society, his inherent capabilities. Simply then, the child was helped to feel that he was an individual and important, and with these attributes, he may well take his place in society." In teaching "self-concept" to Mexican Americans, the teacher used either English or Spanish questions and drills characteristic of the audiolingual approach. An individual child or the class might be asked such questions as: Which of the children is tallest? Who is Maria? Is Mary taller than John? What is your name? The child or children referred to in the questions might stand in front of a mirror.

Analyses of the strengths and weaknesses, success and failure of this project must await further objective evaluation. However, it seemed to this author that regardless of the merits of the new curriculum the participating teachers and the children were enthusiastic. Both seemed overjoyed to perform and appeared to like their classroom activities. Participating teachers and principals interviewed for this study seemed to consider the program "an answer to a prayer" and had high expectations that it would substantially raise Mexican Americans' academic achievement as well as improve their self-concept. Such enthusiasm, if it persists, can be of great benefit to the social environment of a school and a *barrio*. (For additional information see Ott, 1967; MacMillan, 1966; McDowell, 1966; Jameson, 1967.)

The United Consolidated Independent School District of Laredo, Texas, is conducting bilingual classes up to and including the fourth grade. In this author's opinion, United Consolidated has made the most radical modifications in its schools of any district of any size in the Southwest. No other district has attempted more or anywhere near as much. Full explanation of the program is difficult.

Two districts serve the Laredo area: one serves the large metropolitan area, and United Consolidated serves the suburban and agricultural areas surrounding the city. Although United's enrollment is relatively small, its boundaries encompass 2,440 square miles (an area larger than Rhode Island). Three elementary schools and one junior-senior high school serve the student population. The student population of these schools is about 30 percent Anglo and 70 percent children of Mexican descent. Perhaps 10-20 percent of the latter are from middle-class families, and the rest are children of farm and ranch hands. The middle-class Mexican American children tend to speak both English and Spanish upon school entrance. Most of the Anglo children are middle class although there are a few at both extremes of the socioeconomic ladder. Many are children of United States Air Force personnel stationed at the local base, and as is typical of many military families are highly mobile. The children have been exposed to numerous sociocultural environments and many of them have attended school in foreign countries. Thus, the student population of United is somewhat different from that of the Laredo Independent School District, which serves the more metropolitan area. The larger district has a larger percentage of Mexican Americans, the vast majority of them from homes of very low socioeconomic status. The percentage of mobile and perhaps more "cosmopolitan" Anglo families is probably also lower in the city. The city of Laredo is reported to be one of the most economically depressed areas in the Southwest.

United Consolidated, under the guidance of Superintendent Harold C. Brantley, has advanced on a number of fronts to reverse the high attrition rate among its Mexican American students. Some of these advances were formally planned activities, such as bilingual instruction, and others were informal outgrowths of planned activities. A two-phase program was established to solve the problem of the high Mexican American mental and physical withdrawal rate. "Phase I" is a series of attempts to salvage the overage and low-achieving Mexican Americans already in the upper elementary and secondary grades. "Phase II" is a bilingual experiment to promote normal achievement and eliminate the problems that necessitate Phase I. In other words, much of Phase I is remedial, meant to overcome the problems traditional schooling has created, and Phase II is intended to accomplish radical adjustment of the curriculum and organization of the school. Activities toward these two objectives have been in operation since 1964. These formal attempts have produced some interesting side effects. It is unknown whether these are directly attributable to the two-phase program, to the nature, personality, and organization of the staff, or to some combination of these or other factors. But it does seem obvious that teacher and staff morale is very high, that the school social climate is positive, that student morale is high, and that the staff is oriented toward the students.

Phase I, the "salvation" of the older students, includes instruction geared to keep the child in school while remedying his academic deficiencies, training him for a useful and satisfying occupation or role in life, and maintaining or raising his self-respect. School must be made intrinsically rewarding. According to Brantley, "We feel we have to get immediate help to these Mexican American youngsters and that is in the form of furnishing them some means of achieving so they can retain their self-respect." In order to facilitate student achievement, a number of strong programs have been developed. Activities in the field of art and music are reported to give youngsters a sense of personal achievement and to make school rewarding. "We find that in these programs, whether the child paints a picture in Spanish or in English, or whether he blows a horn in English or Spanish, it usually comes out about the same. . . ." Achievement is thus encouraged and apparently realized in the areas that are not dependent on English language ability. In addition to such programs geared to keep students in school, United provides "about three periods a day in a language laboratory with a completely bilingual teacher who is able to reinforce [the student's] ability to operate in the English language and American culture." United's philosophy appears to be that such programs are not going to get these children into college but will substantially aid them to live and function in American society. To function adequately they must be prepared to earn a living. The high school provides what appears to be an excellent building-trades vocational program; it is not a prevocational activity but is geared to prepare students to enter certain crafts at least at the apprentice level. Girls are given homemaking and business training. Some become bilingual secretaries, but the majority marry and establish homes.

None of the Phase I programs in themselves are exceptional, but some unknown combination of factors appears to produce excellent results. The combined efforts and enthusiasm of the school board, administration, and staff apparently encourage the kind of school social climate essential for the success of lower-class children. This author has nowhere else observed so many pupils really participating in so many different kinds of school activities. The physical plants are new, rather distinctive, and well-maintained, which may also contribute to the happy situation.

The Phase II bilingual program in the first through sixth grades is based on the idea that "it is a crime to let any child grow up monolingual" in areas where two languages are used. The personnel at United would undoubtedly concur with the following set of objectives stated by Michel (in Stubing, 1966, p. 39): "Perhaps the most important objective of the bilingual program is to enable all children to operate comfortably in two cultures. The non-English-speaking child who is suddenly taken from his home and introduced into the strange environment of the school experiences embarrassment and confusion. But if he is greeted in his own language by a teacher who is obviously a member of his own language community and finds that his language is used freely in the classroom and throughout the school, his situation is made less traumatic. If, in addition, he finds that as a member of a non-English-speaking group he is not treated as a second-class human being, the boost to his self-esteem is likely to result in all sorts of psychological and social benefits. . . ." However, the staff would add that the English monolingual would benefit equally by knowing two languages and being exposed to sustained and equal-status interaction with the Mexican American segment of his community. In addition to the objectives mentioned above, others of the "experimental biliteracy program" in Laredo include (1) "to provide all pupils with a better understanding of the nature of language"; (2) "to cultivate in each pupil a pride in his mother tongue and the culture it represents . . . as well as a respect for the other language and culture"; and (3) "to achieve a more complete liberal education" (National Education Association, 1966, p. 16).

In order to accomplish these objectives bilingual instruction was begun in all the district first-grade classes in 1964. In general, Nye Elementary School serves as the model for the other two district elementary schools. The "biliteracy" program there is organized in the following manner. (1) English and Spanish are used equally and receive approximately equal treatment in the first grade. It is hoped that eventually all grade levels will equally stress the "two vernaculars." However, lack of bilingual teachers results in some unequal attention given to English in the other grades. (2) All teachers of the first grade are bilinguals; in the other grades English monolinguals teach in English and bilinguals teach in Spanish and English. (3) All subjects are taught in both languages at the first grade. Spanish and English are used interchangeably but never mixed. No predetermined content is taught in one language; the teacher uses both for all kinds of content and in all manner of classroom situations. In the higher grades certain subjects, depending on the teacher's language and subject skills, may be taught in Spanish. (4) Listening, speaking, reading, and writing in both languages is stressed. Children learn to read in both languages. Reading is taught in the first grade. None of these rather different approaches creates any particular problems. (5) Most of the commercially prepared materials in Spanish are from Mexico (see Cruz-Aedo, 1966, pp. 33–37). Many, if not most, of the supplemental materials and some of the text materials are prepared by the staff.

The program at United has not been formally evaluated. However, the staff is convinced that it is superior to older and more traditional approaches. Victor Cruz-Aedo, the District's Director of Elementary Education at the time of the study, is reported to have drawn the following conclusions (Yarborough, 1967): "The Spanish-speaking pupil who formerly withdrew from the group due to his inability to understand or to be understood is now part of the class. . . . English-speaking children have also benefited, not only in learning a second language, but in grasping sounder English reading habits. Many of the English-speaking students are far advanced in their reading levels and the Spanish-speaking students have improved comprehension in their reading."

Cruz-Aedo and this author collected achievement and IQ data on each child who began the program in 1964 and was still enrolled in the winter of 1967. Only 41 such children were found, which attests to the high mobility rate of some of the population. The children were divided into three groups according to their language ability when they entered first grade: Spanish monolinguals, English monolinguals, and bilinguals. The Spanish monolinguals were almost exclusively from lower socioeconomic backgrounds (children of agricultural workers); the bilinguals were generally from middle-class homes, and all were of Mexican descent; the English monolinguals were almost all of middle-class backgrounds. After analysis of the children's achievement and IQ scores, and observation in class, the following *very tentative* conclusions were reached: (1) Only children who were bilinguals at school entrance retained any noticeable accent in English. The two other groups speak unaccented standard English and Spanish. (2) Total reading achievement (mean and median taken from the California Achievement Test) for the Spanish monolinguals was slightly above normal at the first grade and slightly below grade-level norm at the second grade. Both English monolinguals and bilinguals were substantially above grade-level norms for both years. English monolinguals achieved better than bilinguals. (3) Median "total IQ" (from the California Test of Mental Maturity) rose from the second grade to the third for all groups. Percentage increase was not great for any group. Bilinguals showed the largest percentage increase.

The sample described above was entirely too small and the analysis too crude to make any firm conclusions possible. A longitudinal study should be made of students who continue in the program, as should a year-by-year analysis of achievement and participation for the three groups.

Whether the esprit de corps and high enthusiasm so obvious at United is the result of the program or vice versa is immaterial. Undoubtedly the program and the high morale are interrelated. Some unusual and interesting comments were made by Cruz-Aedo concerning the high morale. He suggested that factors that contribute much to the teachers' (and thus perhaps the students') enthusiasm are the frankness of the administration in dealing with problems, and the fact that teachers are given a free hand at innovating (making, experimenting with, and evaluating new materials and approaches). "Solutions" are not handed down by the administration but are jointly conceived.

Cruz-Aedo stated also that the "lack of research in this area [bilingualism] is an asset. . . . I can't go into a book and see what they did in a situation like ours . . . that's a blessing in disguise." While recognizing the necessity for research, he implied that the creation of new programs designed to serve particular situations can be discouraged by too much objective analysis, and that the act of creating may itself provide a kind of built-in guarantee of positive results.

Additional information about the United Consolidated program appears in "Texas Magazine," *Houston Chronicle,* August 9, 1964; or can be obtained from Harold C. Brantley, Superintendent, United Consolidated Independent School District, P.O. Box 826, Del Mar Hills, Laredo, Texas 78041.

SUMMARY AND CONCLUSIONS

The overwhelming majority of special programs for low-status Mexican Americans are little or no different from those for other "disadvantaged" children. Few special programs significantly modify the school; most are intended rather to change (improve or remodel) the child. To what degree such attempts to equalize the educational chances of children by giving them additional dosages of English, reading, or "culture" will be successful is unknown. Whether the causes of Mexican American children's failure in school are in the children themselves, and therefore amenable to remediation, or whether the causes lie within the school and society, is the unanswered but provocative question.

Compensatory education programs for Mexican Americans are not substantially different from regular school programs. Usually programs for minority-group children are merely "more of the same," often administered to smaller-sized classes. However, some significant "new" and "different" programs exist—for example, English-as-a-Second-Language classes (ESL) in which native speakers of Spanish are taught English; and, rarest and most different, bilingual school curriculums. Excluding these and a few other specific efforts mentioned in this chapter, the special programs for Mexican Americans can be summarized as: (1) Highly traditional—that is, based on remedial reading, smaller class size, more books, visual aids, cultural enrichment, and so forth. (2) Successful in the eyes of many educators. However, such success is almost invariably unsupported by objective evidence, or the program evaluated is of such short term as to make reported "success" of questionable value in the long run. Hard data clearly demonstrating a program's long-range influence on Mexican American behavior, academic performance, attitudes toward school, attendance, or any other aspect of school and education, were not found. (3) Particularly beneficial to the children if the teacher becomes enthusiastic about a given program, project, or technique. Such enthusiasm may cause the teacher to raise her expectations for the Mexican American child. Some special programs clearly do excite teachers. How long such excitement and concomitant dedication persist depends on factors too numerous to enumerate.

The availability of federal and state funds for special programs for the disadvantaged Mexican American has brought forth few truly innovative projects and done little to modify institutional climate. Compensatory and remedial education projects will probably continue for the foreseeable future but will probably be lost as they become accepted as part and parcel of normal institutional procedures. When this "institutional digestion" occurs, teachers' enthusiasm for, or dedication to, specific programs probably also will wane. Whatever value accrues from the newness and the experimental nature of a program will probably lessen as time progresses and the program becomes a standard feature of the school.

Federal funding of special programs has and does serve numerous functions; many are by-products of the projects themselves, including: (1) A gradually increasing awareness that the traditional Southwestern school does not provide the Mexican American, or perhaps any child, with the optimum opportunities to achieve and a very slight recognition of the need to modify curriculum and organization. (2) An understanding on the part of educators that the allocation of federal funds to the public schools does not entail undue federal control of local educational institutions. Conversely, schoolmen are learning that federal bureaucracy is demanding of their time, energy, and patience. Unless some of the more blatant governmental inefficiencies are overcome, it can be anticipated that some school systems will drop out of the Elementary and Secondary Education Act programs.

Unfortunately, the existence of functioning special programs for Mexican American children can make a bad situation even worse. If programs exist, regardless of their quality or effectiveness, the school perceives itself as making a supreme effort to aid Mexican American children. Any subsequent failure of the child is then seen as even more the responsibility or fault of the home environment. It could be argued that after all the school is expending x number of dollars in the kinds of special programs advocated by educational authorities, that it is doing its best, and that now it's up to the parents and children. Special programs must not be allowed to act to the detriment of Mexican American children by encouraging self-satisfaction on the part of institutions and discouraging their further self-analysis and modification.

Chapter 6: Where to from Here?

The socioeconomically disadvantaged and subordinate status of Mexican Americans has been recognized by Southwesterners for many years. Concomitant with this recognition was the belief that such a situation was the "natural order" and that "Mexicans" were somehow doomed by their genetic or cultural inheritance to second-class citizenship. Racists explained the minority group's position as being a result of its generally inferior intelligence. The less biased among the Anglos rationalized it in terms of the widely accepted stereotype of the lazy, apathetic, and noncompetitive "Mexican." Unfortunately, many social scientists inadvertently contributed to this stereotype by their repeated stress on the concept of a "folk" or traditional culture. Their research findings were overgeneralized, extended, and misinterpreted by laymen and educators. (For a strong indictment of social scientists see Romano V., 1968.) Although the concept of the ethnic or racial inferiority of the minority was and is erroneous, Anglo society was correct in one sense: the Southwestern social system (the "natural order") did function best with a pool of cheap and unskilled labor and a subordinate "caste." The low-skilled, poorly schooled "Mexican" fitted admirably into the rather distinctive social and economic systems of the region and helped to sustain them. Although it is a gross overgeneralization to assume that the five-state Southwestern region had one common social system, it is fair to say that certain elements were held in common.

SCHOOL AND SOCIETY

Most Mexican immigrants, as well as those of Spanish ancestry resident in the Southwest for generations, were well-integrated cogs in the social system. Most possessed the skills, experience, and perhaps temperament demanded to mesh into the rural agricultural economy. The economy was, and still is in certain areas, based on a *hacienda* and a dual "caste" system, reminiscent of the social arrangements of the plantation of the South. With the continuing disappearance of the *hacienda,* a new system emerged, agricultural industry. This newer system is socially not unlike the *hacienda,* except that the paternalism of the *patrón* is not continued by modern management. Mexican Americans who had not entered the agricultural system in earlier periods meshed equally well. They had the skills and knowledge essential for the closed social systems spawned by mining and railroading interests. In a sense, the Mexican immigrant never left home: the social, economic, and perhaps political arrangements on both sides of the Rio Grande were very much alike.

Society and its schools produced an adult Mexican American population prepared for participation in the agricultural economy of the traditional Southwest. The school was, and in many geographic areas still is, "successful" in equipping most Mexican Americans with the knowledge and skills appropriate to low status: minimum English language ability, rudimentary reading and figuring skills, and the values necessary to a law-abiding, although nonparticipating and essentially disenfranchised, citizen. The fact that the school failed to Americanize or to raise the group status of so many Mexican Americans was evidence of its success. Local society functioned well with an easily controlled, politically impotent, and subordinate ethnic caste. School practices evolved that functioned to perpetuate the social and economic system by unconsciously encouraging the minority group to fail academically, drop out early, and enter society at the low status traditional for Mexican Americans, thus producing the human types necessary to perpetuate the local society. Mexican American failure to achieve well in school contributed to the Anglos' belief that they had innately inferior intelligence, that they were lazy, passive, fatalistic, and lacked initiative. This self-reinforcing circle of circumstances became well established in the Southwest and persists to the present.

Social changes are occurring rapidly today, but the school is rarely able to keep up by modifying its practices or policies, or its teaching staff and their attitudes and perceptions. Too often school conditions "appropriate" to past social circumstances persevere into the present with devastating influence on minority-group children as well as on society in general. Some areas of the Southwest continue to follow the earlier ranch and small-town social patterns, even though most of the area has undergone rapid and profound change.

Since the beginning of World War II, the Southwest has: (1) become predominantly urban; (2) rapidly industrialized; (3) in the rural areas, replaced earlier occupational and socioeconomic arrangements with agricultural industry; and (4) placed much less emphasis on mining and railroading activities. The majority of Mexican Americans, like their Anglo counterparts, now live in metropolitan areas, and most compete in the urban industrial job market. Far too many Mexican Americans find it difficult or impossible to compete with other groups because of the substandard schooling they previously received. The stability of the older social system is disappearing. Radical and rapid demographic, economic, and social changes contribute to grievous personal, social, and economic maladaptations and malfunctions.

Leaders in the Southwest now recognize that maintaining a rapidly increasing Mexican American population with low status as a group and poor education represents a serious threat to societal stability. While such a population may have served the old rural Southwest well, presenting no threat to the social equilibrium, its persistence at present contributes to many undesirable and unsettling conditions. Even the more politically and socially conservative Anglo groups see these conditions as alarming and are exerting pressure on the schools to eliminate overt manifestations of the Mexican American's low social status. Society is directing the school to "raise the group" by insuring that the young achieve academically and persevere in school. With improved school achievement and increased years of schooling, higher group status is anticipated and the subsequent elimination of unemployment, unemployability, underemployment, dependency on welfare, juvenile delinquency, and adult crime. Pressures from within society are forcing action to resolve grave problems, problems partially created by the fact that schools inadvertently functioned to maintain the minority in a subordinate position. It must be acknowledged, regretfully, that it is not educators' altruism that is coming to the fore. Rather, it is the controlling political groups who see that societal peace and balance are threatened and encourage or demand whatever school action is evident. Society is slowly becoming concerned and is beginning to direct its institutional arms, especially the schools, to solve the problems created by radical changes in the Southwest. A low-status Mexican American is no longer functional; the "natural order" has changed.

The community and its formal educational institutions are inexorably interrelated. It is impossible to separate institutions from the society they serve; each functions for and contributes to the maintenance and continuity of society. The school reflects the sociocultural totality, incorporating the professed values as well as the mores, the good and the bad, the static and the kinetic, and the progressive and the conservative. The dependency of the American school on local society for direction as well as economic support almost guarantees that little initiative will be forthcoming from educators. While this local control is deemed essential in America's democratic society, it nonetheless discourages attempts by schoolmen to use their institutions as agents of directed, or even nondirected, social change. Educational leaders are all too often members of the conservative establishment or are dominated by them, impotent to counter their wishes. If these controlling elements manifest little interest or concern about the status of minority groups and see the situation as "natural," and if the minority groups remain mute and powerless, little initiative will be forthcoming from the educational establishment. If no group or problem is rocking the boat, the school comfortably assumes it is performing adequately. These conditions characterized the Southwest in the recent past—the few who raised their voices to advocate school reform found they had an unresponsive, though polite, audience.

Educators' concern about the low socioeconomic and educational status of Mexican Americans and pressure to raise the minority group's position are related to forces within society to a much greater degree than they are to the forces within the institution. Southwestern society has and does determine educational practices; as this society changes, slow but perhaps steady changes can be anticipated in the school. Many of the school's practices so perfectly mirror the local society's mores that any substantial modification must await changes in the community. Legal intervention to force local school mores (practices) into alignment with national values or mores are usually countervened, subverted, or evaded by local schools, as is exemplified by attempts at enforced desegregation. Other school practices are not so closely aligned with the mores but are nonetheless exceedingly difficult to modify because of "institutional habit" and the inability of the highly bureaucratized school to modify itself. For many reasons, educators and schools resist change, whether the force for change emanates from within or without institutional walls.

THE SCHOOL'S POSITION

There is no one explanation of why Juanito can't read, is "poorly motivated," and flees the school early to assume the low status traditional for his group. Searching for the reasons for the low school achievement and years of schooling of the Mexican American minority has resulted in the isolation of three complex and interrelated sets of factors: (1) the nature of the diverse Mexican American subcultures and the socialization afforded Mexican American children, (2) the kind and quality of formal education available to Mexican Americans, and (3) the nature of the local and regional social systems and the equal or unequal opportunity they afford the minority group. Unfortunately, most educators fail to recognize the latter two points and stress only the first, that the minority group's low status, lack of assimilation and acculturation, and failure in school are due to the group's distinctive Mexican culture. The widespread, if not almost universal, acceptance of this "theory" is easily understood, since it exonerates society and school from complicity in the situation. The low status and continued "foreignness" of minority groups are situations caused by innumerable social and economic factors within the dominant society as well as cultural characteristics of the minority. However, Americans generally tend to blame the minority for its own low status and for being the cause of its own "problem."

In rejecting this simplistic argument of "cultural distinctiveness," there may be a strong tendency to overreact and fail to understand the interrelationships between the three major factors involved. The nature of the minority subcultures or subsocieties is influenced in untold ways by local society and institutions, and vice versa. The complex whole is not amenable to facile separation or clear definition; a total social situation *causes* the Mexican American tendency to achieve poorly in school and drop out early.

One not-so-startling conclusion can be drawn from analysis of the kind of children who succeed in schools: those who do so tend to be children who are culturally and personally similar to what the school expects. They are almost invariably the "normal" children from "normal" homes, average middle-class American youngsters. The "different" child, whether he be Anglo, Negro, lower class, or whatever, rarely measures up at school entrance or exit to the normal or "standard" child. It is easy to conclude that the cultural, social-class, or personality differences of "different" children, faced with an undifferentiated or standard middle-class-oriented school, cause them to fail in school. Most educators, with the support of the vocal elements within the middle class, assume that the school is adequate and validly represents the core values and content of American culture. Therefore, it is not difficult to understand why school people, when given a choice between seeing Mexican Americans' poor school performance as attributable to either their home or the nature of the school, readily opt to blame the "deficient" home.

In order to support this position, educators have developed elaborate and detailed descriptions of the life-styles and personalities of Mexican Americans and their children, setting forth the assumed differences in world view and life-style that account for the minority-group child's lack of school and social success. Unfortunately, the common beliefs of educators about Mexican American children have these common failings: (1) they are based on little, if any, current objective evidence; (2) they are derived from older, though perhaps valid, descriptions of rural "folk culture"; (3) they demonstrate little insight into the nature of culture, society, or language; (4) they describe one monolithic Mexican American culture, whereas in reality great diversity exists; (5) they picture a static minority culture changing little over time; and (6) they correspond beautifully with the common

Anglo stereotype of "Mexicans" in general. Armed with this formidable arsenal of false or exaggerated beliefs, schoolmen find the reasons for Mexican Americans' school problems and in so doing put the burden on the minority—who unfortunately may sometimes believe that the educators' reasons are correct.

Having identified the Mexican American home and culture as the source of school problems, school personnel proceed to remedy the situation in the only way their logic allows: the school must eliminate cultural difference or "deprivation" and thereby insure institutional and social success. This position is fortified by the widespread belief among educators that the school was a principal agency in the acculturation of other "foreign" groups. Most educators argue that a prime function of the school is the rapid, perhaps ruthless, Americanization of children of foreign backgrounds. In this regard, the school supports the general American concept that members of minority groups are acceptable as soon as they cease to be culturally distinct and become indistinguishable from everyone else. Compensatory education and remedial programs to "meet the needs" of "deprived" Mexican American children (to reorient, reconstruct, retool, or remodel them) are undertaken and generally supported by most educators and civic leaders. Such programs and projects result from the combination of three prevalent assumptions: that the home culture is the cause of school failure, that the school is satisfactory as it is, and that a principal function of the school is to Americanize foreign peoples by eliminating their alien language and cultural orientation. This author contends that school programs based exclusively on these three highly questionable assumptions are doomed to failure and that there is little or no objective evidence indicating otherwise.

In spite of the dearth of evidence of success, vast sums of federal and local money have been and are being spent in efforts to reorient or modify the lowest social classes and "foreign" groups into what the middle-class school sees as desirable. In a sense, federal funds contribute to the highly questionable assumption that children of such groups are intellectually inferior or culturally deprived or both. Federal efforts also implicitly support the proposition that if the minority-group child is successfully remodeled into an "acceptable American," society will willingly embrace him and offer him equal opportunity.

Federal financial assistance has only rarely resulted in substantial school reform or modification and instead tends to reinforce the local educational status quo.

There are two major factors that impede the Mexican American's ability to use the school to raise his socioeconomic status. The nature of the school discourages academic achievement and attainment; and discrimination and the limited number of statuses open to his group in much of the Southwest discourage his aspirations (which are usually high). Local society often does not reward Mexican Americans for their efforts upward. The school is now charged with raising the school achievement and years of schooling of the group in order to insure their incorporation into the rapidly changing society, but in many areas, the present society provides only limited social or occupational slots, thus eliminating the future reward so crucial to school perseverance, achievement, and motivation. In a sense, the school must produce Mexican Americans able to occupy statuses that are not now available locally and to learn roles that are not appropriate in many locales. This indeed is a big order. Few educators contend that the school can change the social system; it is too closely controlled by its parent society and interrelated with it. The school cannot provide the open statuses necessary to encourage postponement of reward; only changes in the socioeconomic order can do so. Nevertheless, the school could make school participation so intrinsically rewarding that it would encourage Mexican Americans to persevere in preference to withdrawing early. Attending school could be personally gratifying. Unfortunately schools are usually unable to change radically. It is difficult to modify conditions and practices, since many reflect local mores and attitudes. Not only are the attitudes of educators themselves conservative, but the practices and curriculums of the schools are also, reflecting the older and controlling generation's beliefs. Schools thus continue practices that tend to lower achievement and perseverance, encourage early mental and physical withdrawal, and in general cause school participation to be of little intrinsic reward.

Unfortunately, the school has reached or is reaching a stage that makes substantial modification most difficult. A contributory factor encouraging the maintenance of the institutional status quo is the fact that the practices that inhibit Mexican Americans in school tend to be supported as essential by the powerful conservative elements controlling schools. These groups usually demand the continuance of instruction in English only, strong reliance on IQ test scores, rigid tracking, de facto segregation, the inculcation of middle-class values, and strong authoritarianism within schools—practices that have become almost "core values" in the local educational scene. The aggregate of these and other practices creates the negative school social environment that is seen as a crucial factor in the failure of Mexican Americans in school. Although exceptions exist, the majority of Southwestern educators are unable either to analyze their schools objectively or to make the modifications necessary to encourage minority-group success. The majority of institutions seem static: "The structure has become too intricate, or too rigid, or the idea of function has faded from the minds of the functionaries" (Waller, 1961, p. 442). The functionaries of the school appear to be overly concerned with the maintenance of their own positions, which is guaranteed by the continuance of the institutional status quo. The professed objectives of American education (equal opportunity, reaching of maximum potential, and so forth) are increasingly voiced by educators, but all too often they seem little more than shallow utterances. The means by which such ends are to be attained are likely to function to impede their realization. School practices, curriculums, overreliance on testing, and rigid ability grouping can inhibit the reaching of such exemplary goals. These conditions are difficult to modify, especially since they are often the very foundations of an individual functionary's power, prestige, and income. Schools seem to be guided quite commonly by the need for self-preservation and self-justification.

A difficult situation exists, but the modification or elimination of certain practices or conditions and subsequent affirmative action could bring about improvement in the performance of Mexican Americans in school. Theoretically, educational leadership has three possible avenues toward accomplishing this improvement: attempting to change the children themselves, attempting to change the school, and attempting to change society.

CHANGING THE CHILD

In spite of the clamor for equality of educational opportunity and more efficient schools and programs for minority-group children, one is hard pressed to demonstrate that any of the almost universally recommended and used compensatory or remedial programs are producing the long-term results desired. While limited evidence suggests that some Mexican American children are reaching short-term goals of reading readiness, English language ability, and so forth, no proof is available to demonstrate that such readiness and ability result in sustained higher achievement, fewer school dropouts, or exit from school into higher-status positions than those held by their parents. There is little doubt that the school will continue its attempts to remodel children into facsimiles of middle-class Anglos. Although this author believes that compensatory or remedial education will not substantially improve the school success of Mexican Americans, there is as little hard evidence to support this position as there is to support the argument that it will.

Certain recommendations can be made about the collection of evidence bearing on this problem. It is essential to know exactly what kinds of programs reach both their short- and long-term objectives. Agencies financing such projects should make continued funding contingent on detailed study of a program's effectiveness. Guidelines for such programs must be reset to insure adequate objective data collection and analysis. Compliance must be insured. In order to overcome the widely divergent methods of evaluation now used, agencies should develop, or sponsor others to develop, standardized master proposal forms and data-collection and evaluation procedures. The standardization of forms and procedures should present little difficulty, since most compensatory and remedial programs for the disadvantaged are quite similar (almost identical) throughout the nation. These standard forms should require the delegate agency (usually the school) to describe clearly the short-term and long-term objectives of the program proposed, the methods (techniques) assumed to reach them, staff characteristics, the number and kinds of students involved, and the outcomes.

Every program has both short- and long-term objectives. For example, English-as-a-Second-Language programs have as their principal short-term objective competence in English, and their long-term or major goal is success in school. Both objectives are measurable, the short-term more easily than the long. To measure the short-term goal, federal guidelines and the standard form could demand measurement of children's English competency both before and after they have gone through the program. A standardized test for this purpose must be found or developed. All districts could employ the mandatory test(s) or substitute others that are agreed upon as comparable. Whether students reach or do not reach the long-term objective of success in school is much more difficult to measure, but it is nonetheless the crucial consideration. This is the obligation of the funding agency. Provision should be made for a continuing (longitudinal) appraisal of students' academic performance, school behavior, participation, and status after leaving school. Either the agency must provide funds for a term longer than the usual fiscal year, or future district projects must be required to put aside money for continuing research on students from prior years. With the data assembled and reduced for computer processing, the agency involved can make its analysis of program effectiveness. Without these or similar measures there will doubtless be a continuation of inadequate evaluation and inadequate decisions based solely on subjective rather than objective analysis. Evidence must be generated to show what works, when it works, with whom it works, and ultimately how it works. Such evidence *might* encourage educators to cut down the present waste of money and effort and perhaps curtail practices that are detrimental to minority-group children, but it must be recognized that information alone cannot be expected to change present school efforts. For example, assuming that traditional compensatory programs will indeed be demonstrated to accomplish little, it does not necessarily follow that schools will curtail or modify them. Such programs become institutionalized and as resistant to change as other school practices.

Concomitant with schoolmen's desire to "phase in" the out-of-phase Mexican American child is the less often expressed, but equally cherished, desire to change the child's parents. Common examples of this desire are schools' efforts to encourage English speaking at home, American or "modern" child-rearing practices, and changes in diet.

The child is often used as the vehicle to encourage the rapid acculturation of his "foreign" parents. If the goal is to change cultural aspects of the home (and many authorities feel that it should not be), certain steps can be suggested. As with efforts to modify the child, present attempts to modify the home must be seriously evaluated. The conditions under which distinct groups of Mexican Americans will accept and incorporate cultural items transmitted to them from the school must be determined. This author questions the feasibility (and morality) of using the school in this way, but most schoolmen do not. They need to know what works. Careful objective studies of the school as a cultural innovator must be undertaken, but it is doubtful that most educators have the skills or insights necessary to carry them out. For this reason anthropologists or other social scientists should be commissioned to study the school in regard to this function; an objective analysis of the influence of the school on minority culture is essential.

The crucial question here is not one of approach but of ethics: should the school "change foreigners" or should it incorporate distinct cultures into the school and its curriculum? Objective information should help educators to improve the quality of not only their pragmatic but ethical decisions such as this.

CHANGING THE SCHOOL

Radical modification of the school to eliminate factors discouraging the success of minority-group children, or to incorporate factors assumed to encourage it, is rare. School conditions contributing to the success or failure of these children are not clearly spelled out, and much discussion of them is conjecture. How successful would bilingual schools be? No one really knows. Would the elimination of rigid tracking encourage higher academic achievement, discourage mutual stereotyping, and enhance the minority-group's self-concept, as suggested? Again no one knows for sure. One can continue in this vein, each question receiving essentially the same reply. In order to come to at least a partial resolution two steps are necessary: (1) schools must make substantial changes in their staffs, curriculums, and organization; and (2) schools that do so must be studied carefully, objectively, and over long periods of time. In other words, procedures must be implemented to encourage and support large-scale experiments, and these must be carefully and critically evaluated.

It is recommended here that outside funds be withheld from districts that fail to comply with standardized evaluation procedures or fail to modify conditions assumed or found to be detrimental to Mexican Americans. This might be a particularly valuable technique of governmental intervention, as many districts have come to rely very heavily on federal financial assistance. However, such intervention should be considered a last resort, as it is in the case of desegregation. It must be remembered that such action would be most likely to hurt the Mexican American children more than the Anglo children or the district as a whole. Perhaps reward would work better than punishment. Money could be used as a catalyst. Large amounts could be made available to districts or schools willing to undertake radical modifications and subsequent study of outcomes. One important outgrowth of relatively widespread experimentation would be objective information concerning the causes of change itself. It would be very useful to know what causes substantial institutional change and under what conditions certain approaches or interventions could be expected to result in less rigidity, more flexibility, and the minority group's greater success in school.

One approach to changing the school that is commonly advocated is attempting to prepare teachers more adequately. Certainly no one would argue against this, but it must be remembered that teachers are only one component of the institution. Without other institutional changes it is doubtful that even the best teachers could encourage the amount of minority-group improvement needed. In any case, improved teaching staff is a step in the right direction. Inservice reeducation of teachers could, if handled creatively, provide avenues leading to the overall improvement of the school. Whether attempts to improve teachers focus on the college or the school (preservice or inservice), a number of factors must be considered: (1) What are the weaknesses of teachers that need to be overcome? (2) What programs will best overcome these weaknesses? (3) How is it possible to convince or force the college or school to implement these programs? In many ways it may be easier to modify inservice than preservice programs. The teacher-education "establishment" may well be more resistant to change, more rigid and formalized, than lower-level institutions. In any case, means to change teachers need to be found; if colleges of education are unwilling or unable to change their approaches, other institutions must be established to perform the needed functions.

Any program of preservice or inservice teacher preparation should include three essential components (Carter, 1969). First, the formal content of instruction must be relevant to the school problems of Mexican American children and to cross-cultural education. It must include such slighted disciplines as anthropology, sociology, psycholinguistics, and the psychology of cultural marginality. A second component crucial to any successful program is vastly increased student involvement with Mexican Americans. Students must be encouraged to interact with the real world within the school, the Mexican American community, and in activities that bridge the two. The third and perhaps most important of the components is small group seminars, modeled after T-group or sensitivity sessions. These seminars are catalysts; without adding any new ingredient, they should hasten the process of interaction, force a reconciliation, or at least a constructive encounter, between content taught by more formal methods and content learned through experience.

Regardless of the program, present or future teachers must: (1) recognize the overwhelming influence of culture on personality and behavior; (2) have a thorough knowledge of Mexican American culture; and (3) understand the function of the school *vis à vis* culturally different peoples. To accomplish these objectives, some rather personal things must happen to teachers. Basic assumptions about themselves, the world they live in, and their explanations of both must be subjected to reappraisal. "Folk myth" explanations of such phenomena as race, achievement, social class, intelligence, and more have to be destroyed; too often such unsound explanations deter teachers' ability to cope with the very real problems associated with them. Sensitivity sessions may provide the framework from which teachers can gain the essential support as they reconstruct themselves and their beliefs. (For more information on this approach see Landes, 1965.) It is not possible to propose specific arrangements of content, seminars, and field exposure, since each situation is distinct. However, it is strongly suggested that each of these three components is equally important in any teacher education or reeducation program.

In the cases of schools that have extremely rigid practices, treat their students unequally, or show very poor results from their special programs, federal agencies could demand what might be referred to as "total" inservice reeducation. The total staff of a particular school, including everyone from principal to secretary, would study, evaluate, and remodel their school and themselves. To accomplish this reeducation, special teams of well-prepared "counterparts" would work with the staff of an individual school for a protracted length of time. Counterpart teams would probably be made up of specially prepared interdisciplinary university and public school personnel. These teams would work toward the three goals mentioned in the above paragraph. Changes in teaching techniques, school organization, curriculum, and teachers' behavior toward the Mexican Americans would be undertaken with the counterpart teams acting as guides to self-analysis. Theories would be exposed to local reality; rational adjustments of school to the local situation would be the objective.

Drastic approaches are probably essential in order to achieve the institutional self-analysis and change so crucial to the school success of Mexican American children. Ideally, the institution will accomplish these things without undo outside intervention. Realistically, however, increased minority-group pressure and governmental intervention will probably not only occur but be necessary. Educators need help to understand such pressure and to react constructively to it. Universities, under contract to government, might be of help. State governments could do more in this area, following the examples set by Colorado and California. However, if only token measures are taken to help educators understand the situation, it should be anticipated that schoolmen will fail to capitalize on the positive aspects of Mexican American pressure and desire for involvement. Educators can be predicted either to do nothing or to overreact if no help is forthcoming. All elements must work to insure constructive reactions to the impending confrontation.

Teachers and schools must change. It may be hoped that those in authority will implement the modifications themselves, but their progress to date has been far less than spectacular. Drastic measures are demanded; perhaps the time has come for taking the action one prominent educator suggests (Sullivan, 1968): "Maybe we should close down our schools for a while and retrain our teachers . . . even if the children were on the streets they'd be learning more than from some of our teachers."

CHANGING SOCIETY

The extreme difficulty of legislating mores is readily evident to the careful analyst of school and society. The subterfuges, counterventions, and delaying tactics employed to circumvent desegregation are cases in point. While efforts to enforce the law should not be curtailed, it must be recognized that many laws run counter to local mores and that much resistance will be encountered. This is as true with desegregation of schools as it is with fair employment, equal opportunity, and other aspects of civil rights. However, the federal government can take advantage of an interesting situation: higher-level occupations appear more open to minority groups than do lower-level occupations. In fact society appears to be rapidly eliminating many of the manual and semiskilled occupations while creating more at the managerial or professional levels. At present, minority-group members face less opposition from the majority at those levels requiring higher education. As the lower-skilled occupations or economic slots become more restricted in number and kind as a result of mechanization, it can be expected that those holding them will more jealously guard their positions, and it seems logical to assume that discrimination against the Mexican Americans filling these lower-level jobs will increase (see Hill, 1966). While competition between ethnic groups for lower-level agricultural slots has been slight, it probably will be greater for industrial positions. A number of peculiar situations exist in the Southwest: (1) Mexican Americans face slight prejudice if they enter high-level (those requiring college education) occupations. (2) Competition for the disappearing low-skilled industrial occupations exists (with much variation throughout the five states) and may increase as it has in the South for Negroes. With competition increased, discrimination may result. (3) Discrimination is more prevalent in the castelike and rural areas than in the more socially open urban areas. (4) There seems to be less discrimination against Mexican Americans in areas where their percentage in the population is low, especially outside the five Southwestern states. Certain steps could be taken to capitalize on these situations to the benefit of the minority group and society in general.

Mexican Americans must be brought to the schooling level required of higher-status and more open occupations. They must also be encouraged to leave the geographic areas of severe discrimination and move to other parts of the region or the nation. To accomplish these two objectives, government might: (1) Establish a "GI Bill" for the poor, guaranteeing the financial assistance necessary to complete the schooling required to enter higher-status occupations. Combined with the following steps (2) and (3), this would promote the motivation necessary to stay in school. (2) Provide information for Mexican Americans about the nature of opportunities open to them in other geographic areas; many know only their local community. (3) Provide financial and other assistance necessary to allow the relocation of individuals and families.

These steps would not change the societies where Mexican Americans are now concentrated (and where discrimination is most intense), but they would at least permit Mexican Americans to capitalize on the present situation.

CLOSING THOUGHTS

This summary chapter is intended to bring together the major themes of this book and to suggest possible action to remedy the low academic achievement of Mexican Americans and to keep them in school. Since there is no single cause of the low socioeconomic and educational status of Mexican Americans, there can be no single "solution" to the situation.

Mexican Americans' poor record of success in school can be attributed to three main factors: the nature of the subculture, of the school, and of the local society. These three have been isolated here for discussion, but they must be treated as a whole, not as independent factors but as mutually interdependent agents. Each factor varies in its influence according to the local situation. Indeed the exact way that the three factors impinge on an individual's school performance is another complex question. But whether attempting to understand group or individual school performance, all three factors must be considered.

With recognition of the extreme complexity of the social and educational situation, specific recommendations for action become very difficult. In the last three sections of this chapter, more study and evaluation have been advocated, and this will be disturbing to people who demand and truly desire remedies, if not panaceas. The thought that sound information is needed about the relationships among specific programs, curriculums, school organizations, practices, and Mexican American school success may well be naive. In recommending the collection of objective data perhaps the author falls into the trap of his own optimism. But the nagging question remains: if educators knew what to do, would they or could they do it? One certainly hopes so.

While more hard data and more experimentation are certainly essential, some factors seem obvious. Some appropriate affirmative action is now possible. It has been suggested here that school offers both intrinsic and extrinsic reward. Individuals and groups persevere within the school and tend to behave acceptably if their perseverance is personally rewarding or can be demonstrated to guarantee a desired future reward. In other words, success in school will be encouraged if school is intrinsically or extrinsically rewarding. In the case of low-status Mexican American children it follows that to encourage success the school must become for them a relevant, exciting, pleasant, and truly significant experience. To be able to offer this kind of experience entails the elimination of conditions assumed to work against it: rote teaching, rigid curriculums, biased teachers, the overstressing of middle-class norms, and the numerous other points mentioned in Chapter 3. Increased extrinsic rewards for school perseverance entail changes in society that are not usually possible for the school to accomplish. It is far easier to make school rewarding and relevant than it is to guarantee to the minority-group child that completing school will provide the higher social status he desires. Both the nature of the socialization provided minority-group children at home and the nature of the dominant society are exceedingly difficult to modify. However, institutions can be changed, and this avenue toward aiding Mexican Americans represents the most feasible approach.

Mexican Americans suffer in American society from innumerable inequities and injustices. One of these is the failure of the school to provide them with the skills, knowledge, and credentials essential for entrance into the higher levels of society. Optimistically, it can be predicted that Mexican Americans will make it on their own in spite of the school and social conditions. Pessimistically, it can be predicted that the school and society will react negatively to the increasing pressures for change. If this happens, the very practices that can be assumed to deter Mexican Americans' success in school will probably be strengthened, and if so the schools will contribute to, rather than ameliorate, the grievous social problems that confront the national society. The school can help, but it must change. Thoughtful people must encourage it to do so.

Bibliography

Allinsmith, Wesley, and Goethals, George W., "Cultural Factors in Mental Health: An anthropological Perspective." *Review of Educational Research,* Vol. XXVI, No. 4, Oct. 1956.

Allport, Gordon W., *The Nature of Prejudice.* Reading, Mass.: Addison-Wesley Publishing Co., 1954.

Anderson, James G., and Safar, Dwight, "The Influence of Differential Community Perceptions on the Provision of Equal Educational Opportunities." *Sociology of Education,* Vol. 40, No. 3, Summer 1967, p. 228.

Arizona State University, College of Education, *Investigation of Mental Retardation and Pseudo Mental Retardation in Relation to Bilingual and Sub-Cultural Factors.* Financed under contract with the U.S. Department of Health, Education, and Welfare. Tempe, Ariz.: 1960.

Barber, William G., *Evaluation, Institute for Teachers of Educationally Deprived Children.* El Paso, Texas: The University of Texas at El Paso, 1967, Mimeographed.

Bernstein, B., "Linguistic Codes, Hesitation Phenomena and Intelligence." *Language and Speech,* Vol. 5, Part I, Oct.–Dec. 1962, pp. 31–46.

Bernstein, B., "Social Class and Linguistic Development: A Theory of Social Learning," pp. 288–314 in Halsey, A. H., Floud, Jean and Anderson, C. Arnold, eds., *Education, Economy, and Society.* Glencoe, Ill.: The Free Press, 1961.

Blackman, Robert, *The Language Handicap of Spanish-American Children.* Unpublished Master's Thesis, University of Arizona, 1939.

Bloom, Benjamin; Davis, Allison; and Hess, Robert, *Compensatory Education for Cultural Deprivation.* New York: Holt, Rinehart & Winston, Inc., 1965.

Bogardus, Emory, "Second Generation Mexicans." *Sociology and Social Research,* Vol. 13, 1928–29, pp. 276–283.

Boules, Samuel, and Levin, Henry M., "The Determinants of Scholastic Achievement: An Appraisal of Recent Evidence." *The Journal of Human Resources,* Vol. III, No. 1 (Winter 1968). See also James S. Coleman's rejoinder, Spring 1968.

Brogan, D. W., *The American Character.* New York: Alfred A. Knopf, 1950.

Brookover, Wilbur B., and Gottlieb, David, *A Sociology of Education.* 2nd edition. New York: American Book Co., 1964.

Brownsville Consolidated Independent School District, *Educational Statistical Report.* Brownsville, Texas: 1967. Mimeographed.

Burma, John H., "Spanish-Speaking Children," in Ginsberg, Eli, ed., *Nations' Children.* New York: Columbia University Press, 1960.

Burma, John H., *Spanish-Speaking Groups in the United States.* Durham, N.C.: Duke University Press, 1954.

Calderón, Carlos C., *The Education of Spanish-Speaking Children in Edcouch-Elsa, Texas.* Unpublished Master's Thesis, The University of Texas, 1950.

Calderón, Carlos C., "Put Accents on Speech Errors." *The Texas Outlook,* Feb. 1959, p. 26.

California School Boards Association, *A Survey of Problems and Practices Regarding Ethnic Imbalance in California Schools.* Vallejo, Calif.: Vallejo Unified School District, June 1965.

California State Department of Education, *Coachella Valley McAteer Project, 1963–64.* Sacramento, Calif.: 1965.

California State Department of Education, *Orange County Conference on the Education of Spanish-Speaking Children and Youth.* Garden Grove, California, Feb. 14–15, 1964. Sacramento, Calif.: 1964.

California State Department of Education, *Racial and Ethnic Survey of California Public Schools, Part One: Distribution of Pupils, Fall 1966.* Sacramento, Calif.: 1967a.

California State Department of Education, *Racial and Ethnic Survey of California Public Schools, Part Two: Distribution of Employees, Fall 1966.* Sacramento, Calif.: 1967b.

California State Department of Education, *A Report on Research and Teacher Education Projects for Disadvantaged Children; Project Description and Status 1965–66.* Sacramento, Calif.: 1966a. Mimeographed.

California State Department of Education, *Teacher's Guide to the Education of Spanish-Speaking Children.* Sacramento, Calif.: 1952.

California State Department of Education, *Types and Percentages of ESEA Title I Activities, Annual Report, 1965–66, Evaluation of ESEA Title I Projects of California Schools.* Sacramento, Calif.: 1966b.

Campa, Arthur L., *Culture Patterns of the Spanish-Speaking Community.* Denver, Colo.: University of Denver, 1962. Mimeographed.

Carpenter, Charles, *A Study of Segregation versus Non-Segregation of Mexican Children.* Unpublished Master's Thesis, University of Southern California, 1935.

Carter, Thomas P., "The Negative Self-Concept of Mexican-American Students." *School and Society,* Vol. 96, No. 2306, March 30, 1968, p. 218.

Carter, Thomas P., *Preparing Teachers for Mexican American Children.* Las Cruces, New Mexico: ERIC-CRESS, Feb. 1969. Monograph prepared for the Conference on Teacher Education for Mexican Americans, New Mexico State University.

Ceja, Manuel, *Method of Orientation of Spanish-Speaking Children to an American School.* Unpublished Master's Thesis, University of Southern California, 1957.

Chambers, R. L., "The New Mexico Pattern." *Common Ground,* Vol. X, Summer 1949, pp. 20–27.

Christian, Jane McNab, and Christian, Chester C. Jr., "Spanish Language and Culture in the Southwest," in Fishman, Joshua A. *et al.*, eds., *Language Loyalty in the United States.* The Hague: Mouton and Co., 1966.

Cicourel, Aaron V., and Kitsuse, John I., *The Education Decision-Makers, An Advanced Study in Sociology.* Indianapolis, Ind.: The Bobbs-Merrill Co., Inc., 1963.

Clark, Burton C., "Sociology of Education," in Faris, Robert E. L., ed., *Handbook of Modern Sociology.* Chicago: Rand McNally and Co., 1964.

Clark, Kenneth B., *Dark Ghetto, Dilemmas of Social Power.* New York: Harper & Row, Publishers, 1965.

Clark, M., *Health in the Mexican-American Culture: A Community Study.* Berkeley, Calif.: University of California Press, 1959.

Clinchy, Everett, *Equality of Opportunity for Latin Americans in Texas: A Study of the Economic, Social, and Educational Discrimination against Latin Americans in Texas, and of Efforts of the State Government on Their Behalf.* Unpublished Ph.D. Thesis, Columbia University, 1954.

Cline, Marion Jr., *Achievement of Bilinguals in the Seventh Grade by Socioeconomic Levels.* Unpublished Doctoral Thesis, University of Southern California, 1961a.

Cline, Marion Jr., *Improving Language Arts of Bilinguals through Audio-Visual Means: Bridging the Gap between the Speaking, Listening, Reading, and Writing Vocabularies of Spanish-English Speaking Children in New Mexico. . . .* Washington, D.C.: U.S. Office of Education, Grant No. 198, New Mexico Highlands University, 1961b.

Cloward, Richard A., and Jones, James A., *Social Class: Educational Attitudes and Participation*. Report prepared for the Conference on Curriculum in Depressed Urban Areas, Teachers College, Columbia University. Washington, D.C.: ERIC Document Reproduction Service, July 1962. Mimeographed.

Coleman, James S. *et al., Equality of Educational Opportunity*. Washington, D.C.: U.S. Department of Health, Education, and Welfare, Office of Education, 1966.

Colorado Commission on Spanish Surnamed Citizens, "The Status of Spanish-Surnamed Citizens in Colorado." Report to the Colorado General Assembly, Greeley, Colorado, Jan. 1966.

Colorado State Department of Education, "The Public Schools and Spanish-Speaking Children." *A Research Contribution for Education in Colorado*. Vol. III, No. 3, Jan. 1967.

Colorado State Department of Education, "A Study of Anglo-American and Spanish-American Culture Value Concepts and Their Significance in Secondary Education." *A Research Contribution for Education in Colorado,* Vol. III, No. 2, Sept. 1966.

Common Ground, "Federal Judge Outlaws Segregation in Public Schools." Vol. 7, Winter 1947, pp. 102–103.

Condit, Elinor, *An Appraisal of Certain Methods of Treating Bilingualism in the Claremont Elementary School*. Unpublished Master's Thesis, University of Southern California, 1946.

Cooke, Henry W., "The Segregation of Mexican-American School Children in Southern California." *School and Society,* Vol. 67, June 1948, pp. 417–421.

Cornelius, John S., *The Effects of Certain Changes of Curriculum and Methods on the School Achievement of Mexican Children in a Segregated School*. Unpublished Master's Thesis, University of Southern California, 1941.

Corona, Bert C., *A Study of Adjustment and Interpersonal Relations of Adolescents of Mexican Descent*. Unpublished Ph.D. Thesis, University of California, Berkeley, 1955.

Cruz-Aedo, Victor, "Preliminary List of Materials," pp. 33–37 in Stubing, Charles, ed., *Reports: Bilingualism*. Third Annual Conference of Southwest Council of Foreign Language Teachers, Nov. 4–5, 1966.

Daustin, H., "Bettering Inter-American Relations in One Small Elementary School." *California Journal of Elementary Education,* Vol. 12, Nov. 1943.

DeLeon, Marcos, "Wanted: A New Educational Philosophy for the Mexican-Americans." *California Journal of Secondary Education,* Vol. 34, Nov. 1959, p. 399.

Demos, George D., "Attitudes of Mexican-American and Anglo-American Groups toward Education." *Journal of Social Psychology,* Vol. 52, Aug. 1962, pp. 254–255.

Faltis, J., "Understanding Our Student of Mexican Extraction." *California Teachers Association Journal,* Vol. 47, Feb. 1951.

Fishman, J. A. *et al.,* "Guidelines for Testing Minority Group Children." *Journal of Social Issues,* Vol. 20, No. 2, 1964.

Fogel, Walter, *Education and Income of Mexican-Americans in the Southwest.* Mexican-American Study Project, Advance Report No. 1. Los Angeles, Calif.: University of California at Los Angeles, Graduate School of Business Administration, Division of Research, 1965.

Friedenberg, Edgar Z., *Coming of Age in America: Growth and Acquiescence.* New York: Vintage Books, 1967.

Gaarder, A. Bruce, "Organization of the Bilingual School." *Journal of Social Issues,* Vol. XXIII, No. 2, April 1967, p. 110.

Garretson, O. K., "A Study of the Causes of Retardation among Mexican Children in a Small School System in Arizona." *Journal of Educational Psychology,* Vol. 19, Jan. 1928.

Garth, Thomas R., and Candor, Ethel, "Musical Talent of Mexicans." *American Journal of Psychology,* Vol. XLIX, No. 2, May 1937.

Garza, Nick E., *Teaching English as a Second Language: Some Innovations.* Unpublished paper, undated. Mimeographed.

Gearing, Fred, *Big Cat.* Series of six books. 2nd edition. Riverside, Calif.: University of California, Riverside School Study, 1967. Multilithed.

Goldberg, Miriam L.; Passow, Harry A.; and Justman, Joseph, *The Effects of Ability Grouping.* New York: Teachers College Press, Teachers College, Columbia University, 1966.

Gordon, C. Wayne *et al., Educational Achievement and Aspirations of Mexican-American Youth in a Metropolitan Context.* Mexican-American Study Project, Educational Sub-Study, Center for the Evaluation of Instructional Programs. A partial report of the Los Angeles School Study. Los Angeles: University of California at Los Angeles, March 1968. Mimeographed.

Gordon, Edmund W., and Wilkerson, Doxey A., *Compensatory Education for the Disadvantaged. Programs and Practices: Preschool through College.* New York: College Entrance Examination Board, 1966.

Gould, Betty, *Methods of Teaching Mexicans*. Unpublished Master's Thesis, University of Southern California, 1932.

Governor's Committee on Public School Education in Texas, *The Challenge and the Chance*. Austin, Texas: Aug. 31, 1968.

Graeber, Lillian, *A Study of Attendance at Thomas Jefferson High School, Los Angeles, California*. Unpublished Master's Thesis, University of Southern California, 1938.

Grebler, Leo, *The Schooling Gap: Signs of Progress*. Mexican-American Study Project, Advance Report No. 7. Los Angeles, Calif.: University of California at Los Angeles, Graduate School of Business Administration, Division of Research, 1967.

Grebler, Leo; Moore, Joan W.; and Guzman, Ralph C. *et al.*, *The Mexican American People: The Nation's Second Largest Minority*. New York: The Free Press, The MacMillan Co., in press.

Guerra, Manuel N., *Language Instruction of Inter-Group Relations: An Analysis of Language Instruction (Spanish and English) to Spanish-Speaking Learners in California Public Schools, in Relation to the Search for Better Inter-Group Relations*. Sacramento, Calif.: California State Department of Education, June 1967. Mimeographed.

Hayden, Jessie, *The La Habra Experiment in Mexican Social Education*. Unpublished Master's Thesis, Claremont Graduate School, 1934.

Hayden, Robert G., "Spanish Americans in the Southwest, Life-Style Patterns and Their Implications." *Welfare and Review*, April 1966, p. 20.

Heller, C., *Mexican-American Youth*. New York: Random House, 1966.

Henry, Jules, "A Cross Cultural Outline of Education." *Current Anthropology*, Vol. I, July 1960, pp. 267–305.

Hernandez, Luis, "The Culturally Disadvantaged Mexican-American Student." Part I and Part II. *Journal of Secondary Education*, Vol. 42, Feb. 1967 (Part I) and March 1967 (Part II).

Herr, Selma, *The Effects of Pre-First Grade Training upon Reading Readiness and Reading Achievement among Spanish-American Children in New Mexico*. Unpublished Ph.D. Thesis, The University of Texas, 1944.

Herskovits, Melville J., *Man and His Work. New York:* Alfred A. Knopf, 1957.

Hickerson, Nathaniel, *Participation by Negroes and Non-Negroes in the Formal and Informal Activities of a California High School*. Unpublished Doctoral Thesis, University of California, Berkeley, 1962.

Hill, Herbert, "Racial Inequality in Employment: The Patterns of Discrimination," in Murphy, R. J., and Elinsow, H., eds., *Problems and Prospects of the Negro Movement*. Belmont, Calif.: Wadsworth Publishing Co., 1966.

Holliday, Jay, *A Study of Non-Attendance in the Miguel Hidalgo School of Brawley, California*. Unpublished Master's Thesis, University of Southern California, 1935.

Horn, Thomas D., *A Study of the Effects of Oral-Aural English Language Instruction, Oral-Aural Spanish Language Instruction, and Non-Oral-Aural Instruction of Reading Readiness in Grade One*. Unpublished article, May 1966. Mimeographed.

Industrial Union Department, AFL-CIO, "We're Supposed to Believe We're Inferior." *I.U.D. Agenda*, Vol. 2, No. 7, July 1966.

Jameson, Gloria R., *The Development of a Phonemic Analysis for an Oral English Proficiency Test for Spanish-Speaking School Beginners*. Unpublished Doctoral Thesis, The University of Texas, 1967.

Jensen, Arthur R., "Learning Abilities in Mexican-American and Anglo-American Children." *Calif. Journal of Education Research*, Vol. 2, Sept. 1961.

Johnson, Henry S., and Palomares, Uvaldo H., *Coachella Valley Operation Head Start Special Community Evaluation Survey*. Report for the Office of Economic Opportunity, Project Head Start, Contract No. OEO534. 1966. Mimeographed.

Johnson, Kenneth R., *Teaching the Culturally Disadvantaged Pupils*. Chicago: Science Research Associates, Inc., Oct. 1, 1966, Units One-Eight.

Jones, W. R., "A Critical Study of Bilingualism and Non-Verbal Intelligence." *British Journal of Educational Psychology*, Vol. 30, 1960, pp. 71–77.

Judge Skelly Wright, Julian W. Hobson Individually and on the behalf of Jean Marie Hobson and Julius W. Hobson Jr. et al. Plaintiffs vs. Carl F. Hanson, Superintendent of Schools, the District of Columbia, and the Board of Education of the District of Columbia, et al. Defendants civil action No. 82–66, p. 177 (no date).

Kaderli, A. T., *The Education Problem in the Americanization of the Spanish-Speaking Pupils of Sugar Land, Texas*. Unpublished Master's Thesis, The University of Texas, 1940.

Kennedy, B. J., Address delivered at Mexican-American Seminar, 1963, Texas Education Agency. Mimeographed.

Kibbee, Pauline R., *Latin-Americans in Texas*. Albuquerque, N. Mex.: University of New Mexico Press, 1946.

Knowlton, Clark S., "Bilingualism, A Problem or Asset." Address delivered to the meeting of staff and faculty of Anthony School District, Dec. 8, 1965, Anthony, N. Mex. Mimeographed.

Landes, Ruth, *Culture in American Education*. New York: John Wiley & Sons, Inc., 1965.

Leacock, S., "Comment." *Human Organization Monogr. 2*, 1960, pp. 30–32.

Lehman, Victor B., *A Study of the Social Adjustment of the Mexican Americans in Chino and a Proposed Program of Community Action under School Leadership*. Unpublished Master's Thesis, Claremont Graduate School, 1947.

Leis, Ward W., *The Status of Education for Mexican Children in Four Border States*. Unpublished Master's Thesis, University of Southern California, 1931.

Leonard, Olen, and Loomis, C. P., *Culture of a Contemporary Rural Community: El Cerrito, New Mexico*. Rural Life Studies No. 1. Washington, D.C.: U.S. Department of Agriculture, Bureau of Agricultural Economics, Nov. 1941.

Little, Wilson, *Spanish-Speaking Children in Texas*. Austin, Texas: The University of Texas Press, 1944.

Loomis, Charles P., "Ethnic Cleavages in the Southwest as Reflected in Two High Schools." *Sociometry*, Vol. 6, No. 1, Feb. 1943, p. 25.

Lopez, Leo, Address to the Conference, in *Proceedings of the First Annual Conference on the Education of Spanish-Speaking Youth*. Los Angeles: University of California Extension Service, U.C.L.A., May 1964, p. 16.

MacMillan, Robert W., *A Study of the Effect of Socioeconomic Factors on the School Achievement of Spanish-Speaking School Beginners*. Unpublished Doctoral Thesis, The University of Texas, 1966.

MacNamara, John, ed., "Problems of Bilingualism," *Journal of Social Issues*, Vol. XXIII, No. 2, June 1941, pp. 350–353.

Madsen, W., *The Mexican-Americans of South Texas*. New York: Holt, Rinehart & Winston, Inc., 1964.

Madsen, W., "Value Conflicts in Cultural Transfer," in Worchel, P., and Byrne, D., eds., *Personality Change*. New York: John Wiley & Sons, 1964.

Mahakian, Charles, "Measuring Intelligence and Reading Capacity of Spanish-Speaking Children." *The Elementary School Journal*, Vol. 39, June 1939.

Manuel, Herschel T., *The Education of Mexican and Spanish-Speaking Children in Texas*. Austin, Texas: The University of Texas Press, 1930.

Manuel, Herschel T., *The Spanish-Speaking Children of the Southwest—Their Education and the Public Welfare*. Austin, Texas: The University of Texas Press, 1965.

Marcoux, Fred, *Handicaps of Bilingual Mexican Children*. Unpublished Master's Thesis, University of Southern California, 1961.

Mayeske, George W., "Educational Achievement among Mexican-Americans: A Special Report from the Educational Opportunities Survey." An unofficial analysis of Coleman *et al.*, 1966. Washington, D.C.: National Center for Educational Statistics, U.S. Office of Education, Technical Note 22, Jan. 9, 1967.

McDonagh, Edward C., "Social Levels of Mexicans." *Sociology and Social Research,* Vol. 43, July–Aug. 1949, pp. 449–459.

McDowell, Neil Allen, *A Status Study of the Academic Capabilities and Achievements of Three Ethnic Groups: Anglo, Negro, and Spanish Surname, in San Antonio, Texas.* Unpublished Ph.D. Thesis, The University of Texas, 1966.

McEwen, William W., *A Survey of the Mexican in Los Angeles.* Unpublished Master's Thesis, University of Southern California, 1914.

McGarry, Sister Francesca, *A Study of the Variations of Cultural Patterns among Three Generations of Mexicans in San Antonio, Texas.* Unpublished Master's Thesis, Our Lady of the Lake College, Worden School of Social Service, 1957.

Mendez et al. vs. Westminster School District et al., 161 Federal Reporter (Second Series).

Mequire, Katherine, *Educating the Mexican Children in the Elementary School.* Unpublished Master's Thesis, University of Southern California, 1938.

Mercer, Jane R. (Research Specialist, Department of Mental Hygiene, State of California), Letter to Thomas P. Carter, July 26, 1967. Data supplied in part by Socio-Behavorial Study Center in Mental Retardation, Pacific State Hospital, Pomona, Calif. Public Health Service Research Grant No. MH-08667.

Moore, Joan W., and Mettelbach, Frank G., *Residential Segregation in the Urban Southwest.* Mexican-American Study Project, Advance Report No. 4. Los Angeles, Calif.: University of California at Los Angeles, Graduate School of Business Administration, Division of Research, 1966.

Murphy, L. F., "Experiments in Americanization." *Texas Outlook,* Vol. 23, Nov. 1939.

National Education Association, Department of Rural Education, *The Invisible Minority . . . Pero No Vencibles.* Report of the NEA-Tucson Survey on the teaching of Spanish to the Spanish-Speaking. Washington, D.C.: 1966.

National Education Association, Division of Research, *Rankings of the States, 1967.* Washington, D.C.: 1967.

Ott, Elizabeth H., *A Study of Levels of Fluency and Proficiency in Oral English of Spanish-Speaking School Beginners.* Unpublished Doctoral Thesis, The University of Texas, 1967.

Palomares, Uvaldo Hill, and Johnson, Laverne C., "Evaluation of Mexican American Pupils for Educable Mentally Retarded Classes." *California Education,* Vol. 3, No. 8, April 1966, pp. 27–29.

Parsons, Theodore W. Jr., *Ethnic Cleavage in a California School.* Unpublished Ph.D. Thesis, Stanford University, Aug. 1965.

Peal, Elizabeth, and Lambert, Wallace E., "The Relation of Bilingualism to Intelligence." *Psychological Monographs: General and Applied,* Vol. 76, No. 27, 1962, p. 1.

Pierce-Jones, John *et al., Outcomes of Individual and Programmatic Variations among Project Head Start Centers.* Summer 1965. Final Report Submitted to the Office of Economic Opportunity, Project Head Start, for Contract No. OEO508, Sept. 30, 1966. Mimeographed.

Pryor, Guy C., *Evaluation of the Bilingual Project of Harlandale Independent School District, San Antonio, Texas.* Project in first grades of four elementary schools during 1966–67 school year. San Antonio, Texas: Harlandale Independent School District, June 1967. Mimeographed.

Ramirez, A. R., Unpublished survey of elementary teachers in the Lower Rio Grande Valley, 1966. Mimeographed.

Ramirez III, Manuel, *Identity Crisis in Mexican-American Adolescents.* Sacramento, Calif.: California State Department of Education, Aug. 1967a. Mimeographed.

Ramirez III, Manuel, "Value Conflicts Experienced by Mexican-American Students." Article based on research now in progress by M. Ramirez and C. Taylor on "Sex Role Determinants in Attitudes toward Education among Mexican-American Adolescents." Project supported by a grant from the U.S. Office of Education. Sacramento, Calif.: California State Department of Education, 1967b. Mimeographed.

Reid, Jesse Taylor, *It Happened in Taos.* Albuquerque, N. Mex.: The University of New Mexico Press, 1946.

Riessman, Frank, *The Culturally Deprived Child.* New York: Harper & Row, Publishers, 1962.

Robinett, Ralph R., *A "Linguistic" Approach to Beginning Reading for Bilingual Children.* Boston: D. C. Heath and Co., 1966. Reprinted from *Perspectives in Reading,* No. 5, First Grade Reading Program, International Reading Association.

Robles, Ernest Z., *An Analytical Description of Peer Group Pressures on Mobility-Oriented Mexican-American Junior High School Students.* Unpublished Master's Thesis, University of Redlands, 1964.

Rodriguez, Armando M., *Why Higher Education?* Sacramento, Calif.: California State Department of Education, 1966. Mimeographed.

Romano V., Octavio Ignacio, "The Anthropology and Sociology of the Mexican-Americans: The Distortion of Mexican-American History." *El Grito,* Vol. II, Fall 1968, pp. 13–16.

Romero, Fred E., *A Study of Anglo-American and Spanish-American Culture Value Concepts and Their Significance in Secondary Education*. Unpublished Doctoral Thesis, University of Denver, Feb. 1966.

Rosenthal, Robert, and Jacobson, Lenore, *Pygmalion in the Classroom: Teacher Expectations and Pupils' Intellectual Development*. New York: Holt, Rinehart & Winston, Inc., 1968.

Rubel, Arthur J., *Across the Tracks: Mexican-Americans in a Texas City*. Published for the Hogg Foundation for Mental Health. Austin, Texas: The University of Texas Press, 1966.

Samora, Julian, "The Education of the Spanish-Speaking People in the Southwest—An Analysis of the 1960 Data," in *Summary of the Mexican-American Seminar Presented by Careers for Youth and the Mexican-American Community of Phoenix, Jan. 1, 1963*. Phoenix, Ariz.: 1963.

Samora, Julian, "Educational Status of a Minority." *Theory and Practice*, Vol. 2, June 1963.

Sánchez, George I., *Concerning Segregation of Spanish-Speaking Children in the Public Schools. Inter-American Education Occasional Papers*, No. 9. Austin, Texas: The University of Texas Press, Dec. 1951.

Sánchez, George I., ed., *First Regional Conference on the Education of Spanish-Speaking People in the Southwest. Inter-American Education Occasional Papers*, No. 1. Austin, Texas: The University of Texas Press, March 1946.

Sánchez, George I., *Forgotten People*. Albuquerque, N. Mex.: The University of New Mexico Press, 1940.

Sánchez, George I., "History, Culture, and Education," Chapter 1 in Samora, Julian, ed., *La Raza: Forgotten Americans*. South Bend, Ind.: University of Notre Dame Press, 1966.

Sánchez, George I., "Scores of Spanish-Speaking Children on Repeated Tests." *Journal of Genetic Psychology*, Vol. 40, March 1932.

Sheldon, Paul M., and Hunter, E. Farley, *Mexican-Americans in Urban Public High Schools*. Los Angeles, Calif.: Occidental College, 1964. Mimeographed.

Sheldon, W. H., "The Intelligence of Mexican Children." *School and Society*, Vol. 19, Feb. 1924.

Simmons, Ozzie G., "Anglo-Americans and Mexican-Americans in South Texas: A Study of Dominant-Submissive Group Relations." Unpublished Ph.D. Thesis, Harvard University, 1952.

Simmons, Ozzie G., "The Mutual Images and Expectations of Anglo-Americans and Mexican Americans." *Daedalus*, Vol. 90, 1961.

Singer, Harry, and Hendrick, Irving, "Total School Integration: An Experiment in Social Reconstruction." *Phi Delta Kappan,* Vol. XLIX, No. 3, Nov. 1967, pp. 143–147.

Sister Mary Immaculate, *Mexican Cultural Patterns.* A paper presented to the Workshop on Low Socio-Economic and Spanish Cultural Patterns, Denver, Colorado, April 1959. San Antonio, Texas: Our Lady of the Lake College.

Southwest Texas State Teachers College, *Art Activities for Latin American Children in Elementary Grades.* San Marcos, Texas: 1944a.

Southwest Texas State Teachers College, *Music Activities for Latin American Children in Elementary Grades.* San Marcos, Texas: 1944b.

Spindler, George D., ed., *Education and Culture-Anthropological Approaches.* New York: Holt, Rinehart & Winston, Inc., 1963.

Strickland, V. C., and Sánchez, G. I., "Spanish Name Spells Discrimination." *Nation's Schools,* Vol. 41, Jan. 1948.

Stubing, Charles, ed., *Reports: Bilingualism.* Third Annual Conference of Southwest Council of Foreign Language Teachers, El Paso, Texas, Nov. 4–5, 1966.

Sullivan, Neil V., Statement given in discussion reported in "Ghetto Education." *The Center Magazine,* Vol. 1, No. 7, Nov. 1968, p. 57.

Sumners, Helen, *An Evaluation of Certain Procedures in the Teaching of Non-English Speaking Mexican Children.* Unpublished Master's Thesis, University of California at Los Angeles, 1939.

Tanner, George, "Inter-American Relations Education." *Texas Outlook,* Vol. 28, Jan. 1944.

Taylor, Paul, *An American-Mexican Frontier.* Chapel Hill, N.C.: University of North Carolina Press, 1934.

Texas Education Agency, Division of Compensatory Education, *Activities and Services Stated in Project Proposals, Annual Evaluation Report, Special Programs for Educationally Deprived Children under Title I of ESEA, 1965–66.* Vol. I. Austin, Texas: 1966.

Texas Education Agency, Division of Research, *Report of Pupils in Texas Public Schools Having Spanish Surnames, 1955–56.* Austin, Texas: 1957.

Tireman, L. S., "Bilingual Children." *Review of Educational Research,* Vol. II, June 1941, pp. 350–353.

Tireman, L. S., and Watson, Mary, *La Comunidad: Report of the Nambe Community School 1937–1942.* Albuquerque, N. Mex.: University of New Mexico Press, 1943.

Treff, Simon, *The Education of Mexican Children in Orange County.* Unpublished Master's Thesis, University of Southern California, 1934.

Trillingham, C. C., and Hughes, Marie, "A Good Neighbor Policy for Los Angeles County." *California Journal of Secondary Education,* Vol. 18, Oct. 1943.

Ulibarri, Horacio, *The Effect of Cultural Difference in the Education of Spanish-Americans.* Albuquerque, N. Mex.: University of New Mexico Research Study, College of Education, 1958. Mimeographed.

Ulibarri, Horacio, *Teacher Awareness of Socio-Cultural Differences in Multi-Cultural Classrooms.* Unpublished Ph.D. Thesis, University of New Mexico, 1959.

Valdez, Bernard, *Contrasts between Spanish Folk and Anglo Urban Cultural Values.* Denver, Colo.: Colorado Department of Institutions, 1962.

Valdez, Bernard, *Implications of Spanish-American Culture on Family Life.* Denver, Colo.: Colorado Department of Institutions, June 1961.

Wages, Sherry; Thomas, Katheryn; Kuvlesky, William P., *Mexican-American Teen-Age School Dropouts: Reasons for Leaving School and Orientations toward Subsequent Educational Attainment.* Paper presented at the Southwestern Sociological Association Meeting, Houston, Texas, April 1969. Mimeographed.

Waller, Willard, *The Sociology of Teaching.* New York: Russell and Russell, 1961; copyright 1932.

Wax, Murray L.; Wax, Rosalie H.; and Dumont, Robert V., *Formal Education in an American Indian Community.* Society for the Study of Social Problems Monograph, Spring 1964, 126 pp.

Wenkert, Robert, *A Comparative Description of School Youth.* Preliminary Report of the Los Angeles School Study. Los Angeles: University of California at Los Angeles, Department of Education, Dec. 1966. Mimeographed.

Wilson, Joe H., *Secondary School Dropouts, with Special Reference to Spanish-Speaking Youth in Texas.* Unpublished Doctoral Thesis, The University of Texas, 1953.

Wolman, Marianne, "Cultural Factors and Creativity." *Journal of Secondary Education,* Vol. 37, No. 8, Dec. 1962, pp. 454–455.

Yarborough, Ralph, U.S. Senator from Texas, Statement made on January 23, 1967. *Congressional Record,* Vol. 113, p. 8677.

Zintz, Miles V., *Education across Cultures.* Dubuque, Iowa: William C. Brown Book Co., 1963.

This book was designed by Bert Waggott. It was set in linotype Optima at Finn Typographic Service, Inc., Stamford, Connecticut; printed at Connecticut Printers, Inc., Hartford, Connecticut; and bound at Russell-Rutter Co., New York. The photographs on pages xii and 64 and third from the left on the title page are by B. J. Brown, Southwest Educational Development Laboratory. All other photographs are by George Ballis.